CRISIS IN THE INDUSTRIAL HEARTLAND:

A Study of the West Midlands

KEN SPENCER, ANDY TAYLOR,
BARBARA SMITH, JOHN MAWSON,
NORMAN FLYNN *and* RICHARD BATLEY

CLARENDON PRESS · OXFORD
1986

Oxford University Press, Walton Street, Oxford OX2 6DP

Oxford New York Toronto
Delhi Bombay Calcutta Madras Karachi
Kuala Lumpur Singapore Hong Kong Tokyo
Nairobi Dar es Salaam Cape Town
Melbourne Auckland
and associated companies in
Beirut Berlin Ibadan Nicosia

Oxford is a trade mark of Oxford University Press

Published in the United States
by Oxford University Press, New York

British Library Cataloguing in Publication Data
Spencer, Ken
Crisis in the industrial heartland: a
study of the West Midlands—(ESRC
research programme. Inner city in
context)
1. Midlands (England)—Economic
conditions
I. Title II. Series
330.9424'9'085 HC257.W/
ISBN 0–19–823269–1

Library of Congress Cataloging in Publication Data
Main entry under title:
Crisis in the industrial heartland.
Bibliography: p. Includes index.
1. West Midlands (England)—Economic conditions
2. West Midlands (England)—Economic policy.
I. Spencer, Kenneth.
HC257.W46C75 1986 330.9424'0858 85–32048
ISBN 0–19–823–269–1 (pbk.)

Set by Promenade Graphics Ltd.
Printed in Great Britain
at the University Printing House, Oxford
by David Stanford
Printer to the University

FOREWORD

In 1982 the Environment and Planning Committee of the Economic and Social Research Council (SSRC at the time) initiated a three year comparative research programme to examine inner city problems within the broad context of major structural and spatial changes occurring in Great Britain. The programme was developed by the then SSRC Inner Cities Working Party, chaired by Professor Peter Hall, and subsequently the Executive Panel on the Inner Cities, chaired by Professor Gordon Cameron. The proposal for the research was originally described in 'A Research Agenda' (chapter 8) of *The Inner City in Context* (ed. Peter Hall, Heinemann, 1981). The purpose of the programme was to examine the processes of urban change, the effects on urban socio-economic welfare, and the prospects, constraints, and requirements for more successful urban adjustment to structural change. The programme arose from concerns with the urban problems of economic decline, labour market imbalances, social distress, and the effectiveness of public policies in addressing these problems. It was hoped that the programme's findings would be useful for the improvement of public policies to strengthen urban economies (that is, foster growth, employment, and competitiveness), alleviate the distress caused by change and improve the conditions of distressed inner city areas and deprived urban residents.

In practice, the overall programme focused on the economic aspects of urban change. Specifically, the programme sought to identify the key factors affecting urban economic change and to describe and explain the processes of local economic change. Secondly, it aimed to describe the consequences of change for the urban economy and the employment of its residents. Finally, the programme attempted to assess the effects of public policies on the process of change.

The programme was based on the idea that there is diversity in the economic performance of different urban and inner city areas in the UK and in their adjustment to external forces of change; for example, changes in business competition, technology, and residential patterns. A comparative examination of the nature, processes, and effects of economic change on different urban centres should help to clarify and explain the differences in the experiences of economic change among and within urban areas and to identify those factors (including public policies) which impede or facilitate urban and inner city adjustment to change: that is, economic growth, increased business competitiveness, employment generation, employment for the disadvantaged in urban labour markets, and the effectiveness of urban economic policies. The ESRC programme utilized a general framework of topics to assist individual urban studies and the comparative examination of urban economic change. The topics were: the changing nature of urban economic problems; the nature and causes of imbalances in urban labour markets; the unintended effects of central and local government policies on urban economic change, and the effectiveness of national and local urban economic policies; and the capabilities of local authorities to design and implement more effective economic development policies.

The Inner Cities Research Programme addressed these concerns through two avenues of work. The core of the programme was independent studies of four major urban centres of Great Britain which were selected by the SSRC as examples of the diversity of urban economic adjustment experiences: Glasgow and the Clydeside conurbation as an example of 'persistent economic decline'; Birmingham and the West Midlands conurbation as one of 'faltering growth'; the Bristol region as one of 'successful adaptation'; and two areas in London, one (Greenwich, Southwark, and Lewisham) exhibiting 'severe problems', the other (Brent, Ealing, and Hounslow) exemplifying more 'successful adaptation'. These were largely secondary research studies using existing data and analysing existing research. The studies were conducted by independent research teams with distinctive approaches and concerns, but linked by the overall programme's objectives and general framework of topical concerns, dialogue, information exchange, and some common data and analysis. The different research teams decided on the particular approach, subjects, and hypotheses which they considered most relevant to an understanding of economic change in their study areas; and critically examined the characterizations of those areas.

To these four initial studies a fifth study of the Newcastle metropolitan region was added, funded by the Department of the Environment, in order to broaden the sample of urban areas and focus particularly on an assessment of the relationship, impacts, and effectiveness of central and local government urban and regional economic development policies on an economically distressed city region that was a long-term recipient of government assistance.

In addition to these five core studies a number of smaller 'cross-cutting' studies were conducted by various researchers in order to provide a national statistical framework for the five city studies and uniform comparative data on the five city study areas, to examine in greater detail important aspects of urban economic change in a broader sample of urban areas, to explore the effects on change of important public policies, to provide a comparative international perspective, and to increase the general relevance of a case-study-based research programme. A list of the publications and their authors, resulting from all of these elements of the programme, appears at the beginning of this book.

In order to enhance the relevance of the research programme to public policy issues and communication with central government policy-makers, discussions were held with officials of three government agencies: the Department of the Environment, the Department of Trade and Industry, and the Manpower Services Commission. These agencies also assisted the programme through the provision of data, special analyses, and the co-operation of their regional offices. The individual city and cross-cutting studies involved extensive local contacts with government officials, representatives of business, labour and voluntary organizations, and other researchers and analysts.

The five city studies were conducted by members of research teams at the following institutions: the Department of Social and Economic Research at the University of Glasgow; the Institute of Local Government Studies and the Centre for Urban and Regional Studies at the University of Birmingham; the School for Advanced Urban Studies and the Department of Geography at the University of Bristol; the Policy Studies Institute in London and the Urban and Regional Studies Unit at the University of Kent; and the Centre for Urban and Regional Development Studies at the University of Newcastle upon Tyne.

Professor Brian Robson, chairman of the ESRC Environment and Planning Committee, and Professor Noel Boaden and Paul McQuail, both members of the Committee, advised on the implementation of the programme. They were assisted by Dr Angela Williams, Senior Scientific Officer to the Committee. Members of the former SSRC Executive Panel discussed, reviewed papers, and advised on the research during the course of the programme. The programme also benefited from the advice and comments of other urban analysts.

London 1985   VICTOR A. HAUSNER
                          Director, ESRC Inner Cities Research Programme

PREFACE

Following the objectives of the Economic and Social Research Council (ESRC) in launching the Inner Cities Research Programme, the West Midlands was selected as one of four urban environments suitable for initial case-study. The others were Clydeside, Bristol, and parts of London. (Newcastle upon Tyne was added later with funding from the D.o.E.). The West Midlands was selected as representative of an area that had traditionally been seen as prosperous but had recently suffered a rapid decline in industrial prosperity. This decline particularly affected the manufacturing base of the industrial heartland. The area's strong but poorly diversified industrial base, upon which progress and prosperity was built, itself contained the seeds of decline, particularly with the recession of 1979 and subsequently. The symptoms of that decline were already evident earlier.

Our study has concentrated upon the area covered by the West Midlands County Council (WMCC), but has extended to a greater or lesser part of the West Midlands Region as appropriate. Within the framework of the ESRC programme, we have pursued certain objectives and concentrated on a number of key areas. The former can be identified as follows:

(a) to examine the nature of changes in the West Midlands economy, especially since 1960, to relate such changes to local, national, and international economic environments, and to attempt explanations of such changes

(b) to appraise the role of public policy in terms of its action in and impact on the West Midlands.

The latter are as follows:

(a) given the very heavy independence of the economy on the large manufacturing firms operating in the West Midlands, their roles have been of particular significance; hence we have concentrated on the twenty-six largest such firms in the local economy

(b) we have focused upon the inner city in context rather than upon the inner city *per se*, as it is this wider context which is responsible for the present situation in the inner-city areas of the West Midlands.

This book can be viewed as presenting four distinct but linked elements. Chapters 1, 2, and 3 cover the background to the West Midlands and its economy. Chapters 4, 5, and part of 6 are concerned with explanations for the changes which we have identified. Part of Chapter 6 and Chapters 7 and 8 are concerned with policy outcomes. Chapter 9 provides a look to the future.

The research, which began in November 1982, was undertaken by a team drawing on staff from the Centre for Urban and Regional Studies (CURS) and the Institute of Local Government Studies (ILGS), both at the University of Birmingham. Team members were all part-time contributors to the research, with the exception of Andy Taylor who was a full-time research associate. The other team members were Ken Spencer (project co-ordinator), John Mawson, Barbara Smith, Norman Flynn, Richard Batley, and Valerie Karn (until Easter 1984).

We are indebted to a number of former students and other colleagues who helped to prepare our series of nineteen project working papers and six working notes. They are Gillian Bentley, David Naylor, David Miller, and John Gibney. In addition we were joined by Peter Wilde, who was on sabbatical from the University of Tasmania during the latter part of 1984, and who undertook work on Urban Development Grants. To all these colleagues we are most grateful.

Much of our research was based upon the collation of secondary materials, but we also undertook a series of interviews with those concerned with the local economy. To all those individuals and groups we express our thanks for their support, their willingness to meet us to discuss their views on the changing local economy and for providing us with relevant documentation. They include regional senior officials of the Manpower Services Commission, Department of Trade and Industry, and D.o.E. Local-government officials from the WMCC and all the district councils in the county (Birmingham, Coventry, Dudley, Sandwell, Solihull, Walsall, and Wolverhampton) willingly gave time to be interviewed, as did a number of local councillors from these authorities. We talked to regional officials of the Confederation of British Industry (CBI) and the Chamber of Commerce. As part of our research programme we assisted with a CBI survey of future prospects for industry in the West Midlands through a series of interviews with firms. We were provided with the annual reports and accounts of major companies over the last decade or so. We discussed issues as perceived by a number of voluntary organizations operating within the West Midlands. To all these local people, and others, we express our thanks. All had a common concern for issues arising from a deteriorating local economy.

Our book is aimed at a wide audience of those interested in, and concerned about, the local economy of the West Midlands and its future prospects. It draws together work that has already been undertaken and adds to it our own perspectives relevant to an understanding of changes in the local economy and their social consequences and an appreciation of the role of public policy to date.

Finally, we thank the various secretaries who have assisted with project work and typing over the life of the project: Joan Morgan, Florence Denton, Dot Woolley, Kate Wilde, Elaine Gallagher, and Joan Jones.

July 1985   Ken Spencer
                                                        University of Birmingham

CONTENTS

LIST OF FIGURES

LIST OF TABLES

ABBREVIATIONS

AEI	Associated Electrical Industries
AEU	Amalgamated Engineering Union
BCIC	Birmingham Chamber of Industry and Commerce
BICP	Birmingham Inner City Partnership
BL	British Leyland, BL
BMC	British Motor Corporation
BMH	British Motor Holdings
BSA	Birmingham Small Arms Company
BSC	British Steel Corporation
BSR	British Sound Reproducers
CAB	Citizens Advice Bureau
CBI	Confederation of British Industry
CURS	Centre for Urban and Regional Studies
DE	Department of Employment
DI	Department of Industry
DTI	Department of Trade and Industry
EDC	Economic Development Committee (of WMCC)
EDU	Economic Development Unit (of WMCC)
EFTA	European Free Trade Association
ERDF	European Regional Development Fund
ESF	European Social Fund
ESRC	Economic and Social Research Council
GDP	gross domestic product
GEC	General Electric Company
GKN	Guest, Keen & Nettlefolds
ICFC	Industrial and Commercial Finance Corporation
IDC	Industrial Development Certificate
ILGS	Institute of Local Government Studies
IMF	International Monetary Fund
IMI	Imperial Metal Industries
JCRULGS	Joint Centre for Regional, Urban, and Local Government Studies
LQ	location quotient

MLH	Minimum List Heading
MSC	Manpower Services Commission
NUVB	National Union of Vehicle Builders
OECD	Organization for Economic Co-operation and Development
SIC	Standard Industrial Classification
TGWU	Transport and General Workers Union
TI	Tube Investments
TTWA	Travel to Work Area
UDAP	Unit for the Development of Alternative Products
UDG	Urban Development Grant
WMCC	West Midlands County Council
WMEB	West Midlands Enterprise Board
WMEPC	West Midlands Economic Planning Council
WMFCC	West Midlands Forum of County Councils
WMPAC	West Midlands Planning Authorities Conference
YOP	Youth Opportunities Programme
YTS	Youth Training Scheme
YWS	Youth Workers Scheme

SPATIAL UNITS

The West Midlands Region, or the region: the region containing the counties of Hereford and Worcester, Warwickshire, Staffordshire, Shropshire, and the West Midlands before the latter's abolition in April 1986

The West Midlands County, or the county: the former county containing the metropolitan district council areas of Birmingham, Solihull, Dudley, Sandwell, Wolverhampton, Walsall, and Coventry

The West Midlands conurbation, or the conurbation: the term used in official statistics before the creation of the WMCC in 1974 to cover the county boroughs of Birmingham, Solihull, Warley, West Bromwich, Wolverhampton, Walsall, and Dudley; the municipal boroughs of Halesowen, Stourbridge, and Sutton Coldfield; and the urban district of Aldridge-Brownhills

West Midlands County Travel to Work Areas, or the county TTWA: the area containing the five Department of Employment Travel to Work Areas—Birmingham–Solihull, Sandwell–Dudley, Walsall, Wolverhampton, and Coventry—which covered and overlapped the boundary of the county in 1985

The shire counties: the non-metropolitan counties of the West Midlands Region, i.e., all the counties in the region excluding the area covered by the West Midlands County before 1986

1

A History of Economic Development in the West Midlands County

Introduction

Between 1948 and 1966 unemployment in the West Midlands County rarely exceeded 1 per cent; in 1985 it reached 17 per cent. This book is about the causes and consequences of that change. The mid-1960s saw the turning-point, expressed most clearly in the beginning of a decline in manufacturing employment. This chapter examines the history of the county up to that point. It is not a history for its own sake but an attempt to identify some of the main characteristics of the area as it stood on the brink of rapid change in the 1960s and to indicate the trends and forces which had given rise to those characteristics. The capacity of the county to respond to present-day change will be conditioned, as Briggs (1952, p. 328) wrote about Birmingham, 'by its past, by the nature of its inheritance, as much as by hope in the future'.

Since we are referring to the past in order to help explain the present, this chapter is not a chronological history of the West Midlands County but an examination of the relationship between factors which are of key importance to the later chapters of this book—that is, the historical relation between, on the one hand, changes in business organization and activity and, on the other hand, employment and labour organization. Under each of these main headings we try to establish some major conclusions of interest to this work. These conclusions may amount to arguments which apply to the whole county, or may differentiate between the main areas within it. They will as far as possible be simply and even baldly stated before they are elaborated, supported, and qualified with more detailed data. This is a broad attempt to distil some generalizations and contrasts from the long history of a very varied county.

The area which we describe here as the West Midlands County (or 'the county') is that covered between 1974 and 1986 by the WMCC (Figure 1.1). This contains several historically quite separate towns, such as Dudley, Smethwick, Wolverhampton, Walsall, Stourbridge, West Bromwich, and Oldbury, in the Black Country; Birmingham with its satellite towns of Solihull and Sutton Coldfield; and Coventry. The rough division which we will often use between three main areas—the Black Country, Birmingham, and Coventry—ignores the very varied history of the separate towns. In general terms the distinctions between them have probably declined as each has been increasingly exposed to the same national and international economic processes, improved communications, central-government intervention, and,

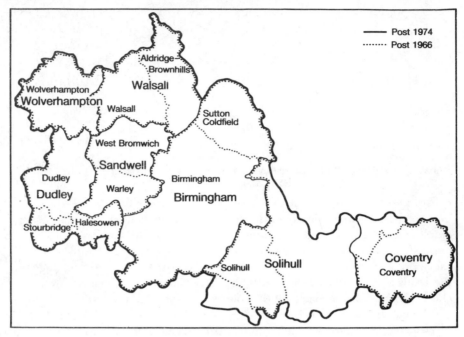

Fig. 1.1. The West Midlands County administrative patterns, 1974, showing the post-1966 county-borough boundaries.
Source: Joyce (1977, p. 18).

between 1974 and 1986, the same higher tier of local government, the WMCC. On the other hand, the economic unity of the county has probably declined as local interlinkages have given way to economic integration on a wider, national and international scale.

Business Change

The establishment of the manufacturing base

The economy of the West Midlands conurbation is peculiarly dependent on manufacturing. Since the seventeenth and eighteenth centuries, this industrial base has developed mainly through participation in different stages of metal-working moving towards more highly manufactured commodities. This culminated in the shift to light engineering and mainly vehicle-related manufacture which gave the Midlands a leading role in national industrial development after the First World War. The industrial restructuring did not take place evenly throughout the area; an unequal interdependence persisted in which the Black Country firms remained committed to more basic industrial processes and eventually to the supply of component parts to the more finished manufactures of Birmingham and Coventry.

The industrialization of Birmingham and the Black Country was a longer and more accretive process than the rapid transformation and expansion of the Lancashire textile industry which is associated with the industrial revolution (Hobsbawm 1968, p. 157). Rich and easily accessible deposits of coal, ironstone, and limestone in south Staffordshire, Warwickshire, and Shropshire meant that small-scale mines and metal crafts had been part of the local rural economy at least since medieval times. Among the factors which led to a growth and diversification of this activity, beginning in the last quarter of the eighteenth century, were:

(a) the increased productive capacity which resulted from technical innovations—initially, the application of coal to the smelting and firing of iron and, later, the application of the steam-engine to mining and metal-working

(b) the expansion of demand for coal, iron, and metal products which followed the development of industrial processes in other parts of the country and the new consumer demands of a growing and more prosperous population

(c) the development of a system of canals and, from the mid-nineteenth century, railways linking the Midlands to wider markets. Mines and ironworks grew in numbers and increased their scale of operation, by 1860 attracting investment capital from outside the region: local manufactures expanded and sub-divided in response to new demands for specialist metal products; trades migrated into the Black Country to take advantage of its materials and skilled labour.

By 1860 the area of Birmingham and the Black Country was the UK's centre of hardware production and also produced about a ninth of its pig-iron (Allen 1929, p. 433). Iron production in the Black Country increased 160-fold in the first half of the nineteenth century to reach its maximum of 743 000 tons in 1854 during the Crimean War (Raybould 1973, p. 11). In spite of this massive increase in output, what emerged, especially in the Black Country, was an industrialization of the countryside or of small towns rather than any great urban–industrial concentration. A pattern of spatially fragmented development occurred which remains characteristic of the Black Country. There were pits and ironworks employing several hundred men, but these were located, according to the availability of materials, in scattered mining villages and townships. The finished-metal trades were conducted by craftsmen working mainly in very small establishments and often in their own homes. These craft works were spread throughout the settlements of the area, grouped together only in the sense that there were particular local specialisms in addition to the most common and widespread trade of nail-making. Hollow-ware was made at West Bromwich and Wolverhampton; glass at Stourbridge; locks at Willenhall; harness and saddlers' ironmongery at Walsall; springs and bayonets at

West Bromwich; chains at Cradley; tinplate, japanned ware, and papier mâché at Wolverhampton.

What appeared to be industrial and geographical fragmentation in fact constituted a high division of labour within an interdependent local productive system which allowed the West Midlands to respond to a rapidly increasing scale and diversity of demand. For most trades a unified factory system began to develop only at the end of the nineteenth century, but there were various earlier forms of co-ordination between craftsmen and between settlements. The finishing trades were clearly strongly dependent on their proximity to producers of materials. Specialist producers and settlements were able to link together to contribute to composite products in response to new and more complex demands. Craftsmen with the same skills could collaborate to increase the scale of production. The human agents of this productive integration in the nineteenth century were, above all, the factors who took a co-ordinating role in finding orders, organizing and financing the work of independent craftsmen, and marketing their goods. There were also larger-scale manufacturers who might subcontract to outworkers, and workshop owners who would bring together semi-independent craftsmen into one work-place by hiring out the use of common facilities such as steam-power, work-space, and tools (Allen 1929, ch. 7).

As part of this interdependence, Birmingham's manufacturers depended throughout most of the nineteenth century on the products of the Black Country. A persistent relationship had been established in which the Black Country produced basic materials and cruder manufactures while Birmingham was developing increasingly highly finished metal goods, often using the basic parts made in the smaller towns. Birmingham's distinction lay not only in the degree of finishing but also in the variety of its products. Its major trades were brass, jewellery, guns, and buttons; other distinctive products were pens, bedsteads, and wire goods; in addition it produced many of the goods made also in the Black Country towns. Wolverhampton was the only other town with anything approaching this variety. Without entering deeply into the question why it was Birmingham which became the dominant town of the region, we can identify some likely important factors: the proximity of the Black Country's coal and iron deposits, the absence of local deposits which would allow Birmingham itself to be drawn into a dependence on simple extraction and basic products, the fragmented specialisms of the surrounding towns, and the variety and relative complexity of Birmingham's own products. The fact that Coventry, historically the more important town, did not take the leading role has been attributed to the more regulated life of the ancient guild towns (Allen 1929, p. 27).

Coventry was not a part of the rather introverted metal-based economy of Birmingham and the Black Country. It had its own traditional industries, particularly the ribbon- and watch-making trades, which pre-dated and, to some extent, went on regardless of the industrial revolution. Such trades increased their production in response to the rising consumer demands of the nineteenth century and with the use of steam power, which was incorporated within the cottage-industry system. New industrial neighbourhoods, such as Hillfields, Earlsdon, and Chapelfields, were built during the first half of the century. But there were constraints on industrial expansion and diversification, notably restrictions on entry into traditional trades and on the availability of land, much of which was designated as common for the use of freemen of the town. Moreover, the ribbon industry quickly succumbed to foreign competition with the abandonment of protection in 1860. This weak industrial development had the long-term virtue that it left Coventry with a relatively clean slate for new investment and large-scale factory development in the new phase of industrialization which began in the 1890s—there was land available, a lack of industrial sprawl and old premises, and little inheritance of outdated craft industries. Nevertheless, it was the declining watch-making trade which provided a bridge to the new vehicle industries in which Coventry really prospered.

During the last decades of the nineteenth century, several interrelated factors precipitated a transformation of the local economy, affecting not only the nature of local products but also working methods and the relation between Birmingham and the Black Country. The great depression of 1875–86 affected most industrial sectors and brought about the permanent collapse of many older and less competitive industries. Protective tariffs were raised in Europe and the USA against many of Birmingham's products; increased Belgian, German, and US competition in domestic and overseas markets exposed the old technologies, plant, and working methods of many of the area's small metal businesses. Birmingham became the centre for agitation for tariff reform and protection. The most far-reaching technological change was the introduction of new processes which allowed the manufacture of cheap steel and the displacement of iron in both the local light metal-working trades and the nation's heavy industries such as ship-building. The Black Country's small ironmasters could not easily invest in the massive plant which was necessary for Bessemer steel production. Moreover, the Black Country's reserves of coking coal and ore were approaching exhaustion and were becoming increasingly expensive to work. Its share of British output of pig-iron fell from 12.3 per cent in 1860 to 3.9 per cent in 1887 (Allen 1929, p. 233).

The transformations in West Midlands industry which these broader changes brought about took place over the period until the First World War and set the pattern for the local economy's future growth. The basic Black Country industries of coal extraction and iron production went into rapid decline; new steel plant and heavy metal industries set up instead in coastal areas and some firms even moved from the Black Country to do so; some local ironmasters switched into the rolling and processing of imported steel but were generally too small to emulate the Earl of Dudley's massive

investment in the Round Oak iron and steel works (Raybould 1973). Many
of the old hardware trades based on iron, such as hollow-ware, bedsteads,
and wrought nails, also went into rapid decline. The old metal industries
which survived and prospered were those producing more highly finished
goods whose value had less direct dependence on the local production of
basic materials—such as tools, brassware, bolts, and screws. But the most
important rising industries were light and medium engineering, above all the
manufacture of cycles, motor cars, and electrical apparatus. These new
industries could exploit the advance of mechanical methods allowed by the
introduction of cheap steel, and also take advantage of the local availability
of skilled labour and component-part industries. Through the demands they
made on other producers, the new industries thus had a wide impact—'the
effect was to modify the whole industrial structure of the area and to render it
a centre, not so much of small metal articles, but of finished products of a
highly composite character' (Allen 1929, p. 313).

Besides the development of new, more composite products, some other
associated changes were taking place. The most clearly associated one was
the spread of the factory system as a form of productive organization; many
crafts gave way to machines capable of integrating several tasks and producing more standardized output; factory development and the rise of larger
firms were in turn associated with the search for new and more spacious
premises outside the old town centres. Secondly, the experience of depression
and competition from other industrializing countries led some of the surviv-
ing older concerns to shift attention away from old export markets in Europe
and the USA to service the rising industries on which Midlands exports now
came to depend; moreover the focus of exports was shifting to the protected
colonial markets (Allen 1929, p. 403). Indeed some new non-metal growth
industries benefited from the new opportunities for raw-material imports
which Empire gave—Cadbury's cocoa and Dunlop's rubber, for example. At
the turn of the century, Birmingham's business interests were at the centre
not only of the call for protection but of the call for protection within the
Empire (Briggs 1952, pp. 34–7). Thirdly, the collapse of the old raw-material
industries and the rise of the more complex engineered manufactures meant
a withdrawal by Birmingham of its dependence on Black Country resources
and, at the same time, an enhancement of the traditional relationship in
which 'Birmingham tended to remain the main centre for finished manufactures of all types . . . while the Black Country concerned itself chiefly with
the making of component parts for the finishing processes and with the
manufacture of cruder products which demanded less labour skill' (Briggs
1952, p. 47).

Besides Birmingham, two other towns made the leap into highly composite
engineering products. Wolverhampton's industry, which in the mid-
nineteenth century was already more diversified than that of the smaller Black
Country towns, was sufficiently flexible to have begun by the end of the cen-

tury to produce switch gear, generators, batteries, cars, cycles, and motor-cycles (Jones 1969, p. 21). It was, however, Coventry-based firms which led the region's move into mass vehicle production on the basis of precision and gearing technologies developed in the watch-making and sewing-maching industries. The first bicycles were made in 1869 by the Coventry Machinists Company, which had transferred from sewing machines, but it was in the 1880s, with the invention of the safety bicycle, gear systems, and pneumatic tyres, that this became a large-scale industry with considerable exports. Coventry cycle companies, such as Singer, Rover, and Triumph, then led the way into car production in the first decade of the twentieth century. Both products had a rapid spread effect, in the sense that they stimulated supplies of components (springs, tubes, tyres, saddles, wheels) from elsewhere in the West Midlands and in the sense that they gave rise to competitor firms in Coventry and Birmingham. Their highly composite nature and initially small and experimental scale allowed a continuous process of sub-division and formation of new firms often by ex-employees. Coventry's new vehicle and machine-tools industries bound the town much more than ever before into the metal-processing tradition of Birmingham and the Black Country. Its other new early-twentieth-century growth industry, synthetic fibres, was not regionally linked in this way.

The restructuring of the West Midlands economy at the turn of the century was not a product of any State planning. It was, however, partly conse-quent on State action designed to have other effects—enclosure acts and canal acts created the conditions which allowed the development of large-scale mining and the opening up of the Midlands; the policy of Free Trade from 1846 to 1931 and the absence of fiscal protection exposed industries to the need to adjust to competition from the rising industrial powers; the for-mal declaration of colonies and 'spheres of influence' in the imperialist move-ment from the 1880s offered alternative, protected markets for some of the old trades and the rising vehicle industries; war contracts affected both the demand for products and the scale and methods of production. The Crimean and Franco-Prussian wars lifted Black Country pig-iron production in 1854–6 and 1871, and even the First World War allowed a temporary resur-gence. Birmingham's early role as a manufacturer had been stimulated by government orders for guns, swords, buttons, and saddlery. The First World War brought orders to Birmingham, Coventry, and Wolverhampton for munitions, tanks, vehicles and spare parts, transforming the scale of produc-tion and speeding up the adoption of mechanized and standardized factory processes (Allen 1929, p. 373; Briggs 1952, pp. 200–26; Richardson 1972, p. 37; Jones 1969, p. 27). The abrupt termination of war-time orders, how-ever, also contributed to slump conditions and the sudden exposure of uncompetitive industries and firms.

The success of Birmingham's and Coventry's transition into light and medium engineering in particular was disguised by the inter-war recession and the continuing decline of the basic materials and hardware trades of the Black Country.

The consolidation of a leading place in the national economy

The inter-war recession and expansion after the Second World War confirmed the leading role of the West Midlands's newer industries. However, the conditions which made Birmingham and Coventry especially successful through this period—protection and a strong dependence on these newly emerging industrial sectors—also made them highly vulnerable to change in the 1960s.

The importance of the West Midlands in the British economy greatly increased in the inter-war years. The international collapse in industrial production immediately after the First World War and in the 1929–33 slump, the associated collapse of demand from the primary producer countries to which the UK sold its products, and the growth of protectionism, undermined the old, strongly export-oriented industries such as textiles, shipbuilding and heavy engineering. Local economies, such as that of Glasgow, with a heavy dependence on a few dominant industries could not make the shift into new sectors (Checkland 1981). Even the West Midlands, with its greater variety of manufactures, was badly hit during the 1914–18 war by the shift away from demand for consumer goods, and immediately after the war by the withdrawal of military demands for munitions, vehicles, iron, steel, and metal parts. However, the centres of light engineering made a rapid recovery between 1923 and 1927. Birmingham's and Coventry's unemployment levels fell to around 6 per cent, with particularly large increases in employment in the electrical-apparatus, car, food, and synthetic-fibres industries (Allen 1929, pp. 399–403). The effects of this resurgence had only begun to extend to increased demand for the component parts of the Black Country when the main force of the 1930's depression struck.

The depression had a very variable impact on the conurbation. Birmingham (with Smethwick) and Coventry suffered less than the national average of unemployment, whereas in the peak year of 1931 the Black Country towns, including Wolverhampton, reached levels which were as bad as that reached in Scotland (27 per cent), and in the case of Dudley, Cradley, and Wednesbury worse than that reached in Wales (33.5 per cent). The variation was accounted for by the continued dependence of the Black Country on iron and steel and the basic metal-components industries which suffered severe unemployment throughout the country (West Midlands Group 1948, p. 125). (See Figure 1.2).

After 1931 unemployment in the West Midlands declined more rapidly than in the country as a whole until by 1936 all employment exchanges in the conurbation showed unemployment rates below the national level of 13.9 per cent. At that time unemployment levels in Coventry, Birmingham, Smeth-

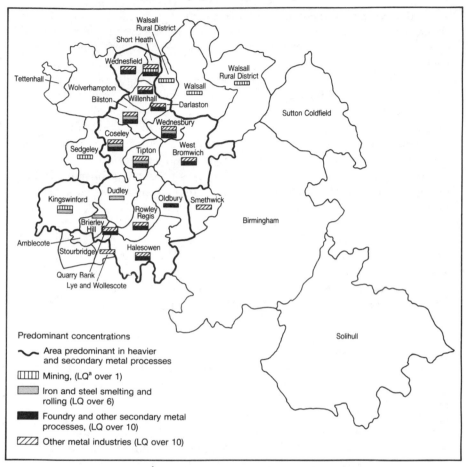

Fig. 1.2. The Localization of miners and workers in earlier metal processes within the West Midlands conurbation,[b] 1931.

Notes: *a* The location quotient (LQ) measures the extent of localization of an industry in the conurbation. It is obtained by using the formula

$$\frac{\% \text{ employed in an industry in the conurbation}}{\% \text{ employed in that industry in England and Wales}} \times 100.$$

b The conurbation here referred to excludes Coventry.
Source: West Midlands Group (1948, p. 114).

wick, and Oldbury were at or below 5 per cent. The West Midlands and the south-east of England led the recovery in national employment and output levels (West Midland Group 1948; p. 118).

To account for the relatively rapid emergence of the West Midlands from the 1930s depression, several factors can be suggested. Firstly, the county contained a high proportion of the industries (particularly cars and electrical equipment) which were growing nationally and very few of those which were in decline. Wensley and Florence (in West Midlands Group 1948, p. 119) show that of the conurbation's main industries only two, iron and steel (blast-furnaces, smelting, and rolling) and jewellery, were losing employment between 1923 and 1937. In other words, West Midlands industry was well structured to benefit from national recovery. Secondly, by comparison with the heavy industrial areas, the West Midlands contained a relatively high proportion of industries which could benefit quickly from a revival of consumer demand and which had suffered less in the recession—vehicles, cocoa, and confectionery, electrical engineering. Thirdly, many of the industries which were characteristic of the Midlands and South-east benefited from the introversion of the economy which followed increased protectionism and the decline in international trade. The mass-production consumer industries flourished in the protected home and colonial markets—more than 85 per cent of UK car exports went to the Empire between 1925 and 1937 (Briggs 1952, p. 288); the aircraft industry and electrical engineering relied heavily on government demand, which gave preference to UK manufacturers; machine-tool firms benefited from other industries' competitive attempts to cut the costs of production. Fourthly, in the nature of the West Midlands engineering industries, their composite character and interdependence on local components manufacturers quite quickly diffused the recovery throughout the area.

There was a negative twist to this local interdependence which became more apparent in the post-war years. There were signs that it was becoming a matter of narrowly focused dependence rather than a loose interrelation between a wide array of industries and firms. It seems likely that the experience of depression and recovery tied smaller firms and specialized industries even more closely as components suppliers to a dependence on dominant manufacturers in the leading industrial sectors (above all, motor vehicles). The importance of the leading sectors had grown; within them, through competition and combination, the number of manufacturers was being reduced; firms without links with these leading sectors were less able to survive the depression. Geographically, too, there was a process of concentration as leading firms eliminated or absorbed competitors and leading sectors squeezed out others—Wolverhampton lost its car-manufacturing companies (Sunbeam, Star, Clyno) before the Second World War (Jones, 1969, p. 21); Coventry's textile industry went into decline, unable to pay the higher wages available in the vehicles industry (Richardson 1972, p. 43). The growing narrowing of focus of the local economy (see Figure 1.3) was not an obvious problem as long as the leading firms and sectors were themselves protected, prosperous, and closely linked to other local producers.

The Second World War destroyed a large amount of industrial plant, especially in Coventry where it is said that 75 per cent of industry suffered war damage (Richardson, 1972, p. 84), but its impact was not wholly destructive. The war effectively maintained the protection from foreign competition which most of West Midlands industry had enjoyed since 1931 and

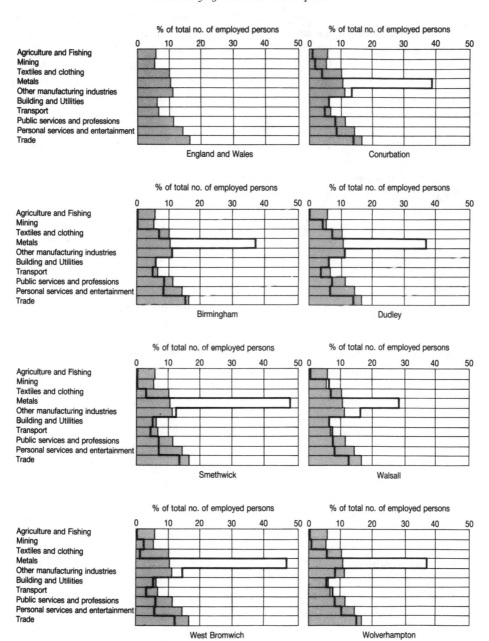

Fig. 1.3. The industrial structure of the West Midlands conurbation[a] and its six county boroughs compared with that of England and Wales, 1931

Note: *a* The conurbation here referred to excludes Coventry.
Source: West Midlands Group (1948, p. 104), based on data from 1931 census.

motor manufacturing had enjoyed since the early 1920s. It also generated government demand for munitions, tanks, aircraft, and telephone equipment. Birmingham's labour force increased by 65 per cent between 1939 and 1942 (Sutcliffe and Smith 1974, p. 43). On the other hand, the war stimulated two processes which in the longer term proved damaging to the diversity and interdependence of the local economy. First, by focusing both government orders and permission for access to scarce raw materials (such as steel) on certain large-scale firms and essential sectors of production, it enhanced the concentration of the economy. Second, through government policy and the direct effects of war damage, it promoted the dispersal of factories to the peripheries of the major cities and beyond. This showed 'many firms that they could operate successfully with widely separated production units and they were consequently more willing to expand outside the city after the war' (Sutcliffe and Smith 1974, p. 54).

West Midlands industry was well placed to benefit from the post-war boom resulting both from national reconstruction and the growth of international trade. The county was the national centre of production in the motor-vehicle and electrical-equipment industries which, with chemicals, were the major growth sectors of UK industry (Hobsbawm 1968, p. 216). Protection from Japanese and European competitors was effectively extended by their war damage and by imperial or Commonwealth trading preference. At this time, until 1960, the UK was the second-biggest national producer of cars and lorries after the USA (Hobsbawm 1968, p. 220). The West Midlands led the nation into the boom; Birmingham and Coventry were second and third only to London in the growth of new jobs between 1951 and 1961. Until the late 1960s, in terms of employment, 'when the country as a whole was doing well, the West Midlands Region was doing even better, and when the national economy was at a low level, the West Midlands Region's economy was less seriously affected' (Liggins 1977, p. 83). The West Midlands electrical engineering, and vehicle industries, which until the Second World War had been strongly oriented to the domestic market, in the post-war period became the basis of a major expansion of UK exports, impelled initially by the policy of suppressing domestic consumer demand (Hobsbawm 1968, p. 219). Even after the initial advantage of low levels of foreign competition had been lost, the West Midlands industries, contributing up to 40 per cent by value of UK exports,[1] were well placed to take advantage of the expansion of international trade, at about 10 per cent per annum, through the 1950s and 1960s (Liggins 1977a, p. 92).

The post-war period until the mid 1960s could be described as consolidating the industrial base which had emerged in the 1890s and developed through the first half of the twentieth century. The West Midlands was the centre of the UK's participation in what Mandel (1975) calls the second technological revolution which produced two phases of international expansion (before the First World War and after the Second World War) and which allowed relatively quick recovery from the inter-war recession. However, there were signs that the county's industrial structure was flawed. Firstly, it remained heavily dependent on engineering and metal manufacture, above all on the motor industry. Secondly, even in its key industries it was facing increasing competition.

The reliance of the county on its leading sectors and firms increased through the 1930s depression and the war and into the post-war era. This was partly due to the expansion of employment in vehicles and mechanical and electrical engineering: 64 per cent of Coventry's labour force was devoted to these sectors in the mid-1950s, and 30 per cent of Birmingham's (Sutcliffe and Smith 1974, p. 156). The concentration was also partly due to the lack of new industries and the failure of others which had been temporarily imported in wartime:

'one looks in vain for new firms from 1930–1970. Aero engineering, introduced in Birmingham in wartime, was of temporary duration. The new science-based industries did not even gain a foothold.'

(Sutcliffe and Smith 1974, p. 470).

It was partly due to the failure of old industries, such as Coventry's textiles, unable to pay the high wage rates offered in the motor industry; even Coventry's old-established aircraft industry, based on Siddeley, declined in the face of US competition (Richardson 1972, p. 140). It was due also to the relatively weak growth of the service and distribution sectors in the conurbation. These sectors showed employment growth throughout the 1950s and 1960s (Crompton and Penketh 1977, p. 111), but even in Birmingham, the regional capital for service provision, services remained poorly developed by comparison with the national average (Sutcliffe and Smith 1974, p. 163).

Dependence was deepening on industries which were increasingly exposed to competition and to changes in the conditions which had made them prosperous. As consumer- and export-related industries, the county's leading sectors depended on national prosperity and the expansion of their international markets; conversely, they were hit hard by governments' attempts after 1950 to regulate the growth of the economy and to restore the balance of payments with 'stop–go' economic management policies which often involved purchase tax and higher purchase restrictions on their sales. As industries which had grown up through a long period of protection, they were highly vulnerable to the changes which were to beset them from the mid-1960s—the reduction of tariffs on industrial goods with the Kennedy round of the General Agreement on Tariffs and Trade; the corresponding reduction and eventual elimination of Commonwealth preferences; direct exposure to free trade with competitor's on entry to the EEC; changes in production processes and transport costs which exposed the domestic market to imports from newly industrializing countries. The West Midlands industries were also vulnerable to their own success in the sense that post-war domestic regional policy sought to discourage new industrial development and expansion in what were regarded as the prosperous areas and to shift expansion to development areas of the country; a combination of financial inducements and controls through the issue of industrial development certificates was created in the 1940s but came more fully into force in the 1960s. These are among the factors considered in later chapters.

Changes in internal organization

Having outlined the broad changes in the county's industrial base and in its place in the national economy, we shall now pick out the changes which occurred in the internal organization of the local economy—that is, changes in the organization of production between and within firms, and changes in the geographical location and articulation of economic activity. On the whole, there was a shift from a local economy which was rather introverted, with a good many loose forms of integration between a multiplicity of geographically scattered small firms, to one which was both more focused on certain leading firms, sectors, and localities and more open to linkages with firms and trading partners in other parts of the country and world.

Changes in industrial organization

Associated with the increased sophistication of production and the widening of markets since the 1880s have been:

(*a*) the concentration of producers into fewer, larger units with a national and international scale of operation
(*b*) a delocalization of ownership
(*c*) new forms of interlinkage in which small firms become more dependent on the large and the large become more independent of the small.

A rough sketch of the situation from the middle to the late nineteenth century would identify two main categories of production unit—on the one hand, the large integrated concerns mining and processing the coal and iron reserves and, on the other, a large number of very small establishments of skilled workers concerned with metal-working and other craft trades (Allen 1929, p. 444). The small workshops were linked by intermediaries (often factors) to a complex system for the supply of materials, credit, and steam-power, the creation of composite products, and marketing. There was no sudden shift to the integrated factory system in the West Midlands, and when this did occur it was initially with carry-overs from a more loosely integrated past, craft workers frequently remaining semi-independent, and over-hands, or subcontractors, standing between factory owners and workers. Moreover, the 'horizontal integration' of the production process, in which specialized firms depended on each other to create a composite product, persisted as a characteristic of West Midlands industries.

The twenty-five years before the First World War saw a more thorough going generalization of the factory system under pressure of recession and competition, with the opening-up of large-scale markets and the new opportunities for mechanization created by cheap steel and gas power. The limited-liability legislation of 1856, 1861, and 1862 had given industrialists access to the long-term capital market and to industrial expansion and acquisition. This was the period in which many well-known companies distinguished themselves, by their own growth or by amalgamation, from the profusion of small family firms which had characterized the Black Country and Birmingham (the 'city of a thousand trades'): Cadbury, Avery, Lucas, Wolseley, Guest Keen & Nettlefolds, the Birmingham Small Arms Company (BSA), Stewarts & Lloyds, Austin. Dunlop migrated to Birmingham from Dublin in 1910 and Courtaulds moved into Coventry in 1905.

The motor-vehicle industry had to wait longer for the emergence of the modern pattern of dominant companies. Apart from Austin, which had 2000 employees by 1914, the industry in Coventry and Birmingham was characterized by a plethora of small firms which were generated not only out of existing businesses but also, especially in the case of Coventry, by an influx of entrepreneurs from elsewhere. Fifty-one car manufacturers operated in Coventry at some time between 1918 and 1931; the Depression narrowed this number down to eleven in 1931—Armstrong-Siddeley, Alvis, Daimler, Rootes (Hillman, Humber), Jaguar, Morris, Riley, Rover, Singer, Standard, Triumph. The introduction by Morris Motors in 1929 of low-cost cars began the transformation of the car industry into a mass-production business. Even then, it remained dependent on a large number of smaller firms as components suppliers (Richardson 1972, p. 44–56).

The inter-war years saw a massive growth in the scale of productive units and the concentration of ownership not only in the West Midlands but in the country as a whole: 'in 1914 Britain was perhaps the least concentrated of the great industrial economies, and in 1939 one of the most' (Hobsbawm 1968, p. 180). Under the stimulus of First World War government orders, the development of flow production, mechanization, and the demands of the new consumer industries, followed by the competitive environment of the slump, small firms in some sectors (for example, non-ferrous metals) drew together in trade associations for joint manufacture and sale, and large firms were increasingly drawn into large national combinations (Briggs 1952, p. 83; Allen 1929, pp. 413–30) or local combinations of national importance. Cadbury combined with Fry (1919); Vickers bought local railway-rolling-stock companies (1919); ICI bought into local metal companies during the 1920s; the General Electric Company (GEC) established a factory for telephone equipment in Coventry (1921) and bought up local radio manufacturers; Courtaulds extended its manufacturing interests from Coventry to the

Continent; Morris acquired Wolseley Motors in 1927 and BSA amalgamated
with Lanchester in the 1930s; Rootes took over Hillman and then Humber in
the late 1920s.

This agglomeration was taking place in a local economy historically
characterized by its horizontal integration, that is the independence of many
firms across different industries. Highly localized, specialized, and interdependent industries and firms continued to be a feature of the county into
the 1930s (West Midlands Group 1948, pp. 105–20). This network of interrelated industrial processes was said to give Birmingham and the Black
Country the advantages of a large single plant while retaining the flexibilities
of separate firms (Florence 1948). However, the entry of large self-contained
firms into the county's economy was already regarded by local planners in
the 1940s as a threat to this interdependent system (Florence 1948; West
Midland Group 1948, p. 136).

As we have seen, the Second World War and post-war period created the
conditions for a further expansion of the main firms in the leading sectors.
The British Motor Corporation (BMC) was formed out of a merger of Austin
with the Nuffield organization, including Morris, in 1952; Austin had itself
bought Fisher & Ludlow which in its turn had previously expanded by
acquiring small companies. BSA continued its practice of buying up supplying companies and competitors and selling off unprofitable firms; Alfred
Herberts acquired BSA's machine-tool interests. West Midlands firms were
in many cases becoming part of a nationally and internationally integrated
process of production, as specialist centres within a larger whole; for
example, Coventry became the centre of Massey Ferguson's tractor production and of GEC's concern with telecommunication equipment.

It is not clear whether the process of combination and the growth of big
firms affected the county more than other areas, but by 1973 it was no longer
true that the West Midlands was characterized by an unusually high proportion of small firms. Indeed by comparison with the national average, the
county had a lower proportion of smaller firms (with fewer than fifty
employees) and a higher proportion of large firms employing more than
1000. In employment terms, the county relied 'to an above-average extent
upon the very large firms' (Crompton and Penketh 1977, p. 117). This was
especially the case in Coventry.

The effects of the changes in firm structure and inter-linkage can be summarized as follows:

(*a*)   ownership was diffused as family firms were replaced by limited com-
       panies with a large number of shareholders—managers took over con-
       trol of firm policy from individualist entrepreneurs
(*b*)   ownership and control were delocalized by mergers which drew local
       firms into national and international combines—'One effect of these
       mergers was to diminish the economic independence of Birmingham

industry. Many decisions affecting the city's factories came to be taken elsewhere . . . '(Sutcliffe and Smith 1974, p. 166)

(c) the scale of production increased and became a nationally (and internationally) and not just locally integrated process;

(d) the larger firms were increasingly vertically integrated, or self-contained, with more of their production and marketing being carried out within the same company (Allen 1929, p. 331; Briggs 1952, p. 287).

The implication for the more specialist components suppliers was increased dependence on orders from fewer dominant companies. Inter-firm linkages remained particularly important in the motor industry. Although even here there was a tendency towards a reduction in sub-contracting from outside firms, car companies were still essentially assemblers of components produced elsewhere (Briggs 1952, pp. 287–8; Richardson 1972, p. 56). In the case of Austin in the 1950s, the suppliers of most of its components were clustered in a ten-mile radius around its Longbridge plant (Sutcliffe and Smith 1974, p. 158).

By the 1950s wide sections of manufacturing had therefore become dependent as suppliers and sub-contractors on the competitiveness, acumen, and salesmanship of a narrow range of companies. This was especially true in the case of the car industry, which directly and indirectly supported a high proportion of local employment. Such a relationship of dependence rather than interdependence might be stable in prosperous conditions—smaller firms benefiting from the success of larger ones and the latter benefiting from the competition between their suppliers. But in times of change and increasing competition, this arrangement could easily collapse as the large assembly firms lost markets or sought alternative suppliers.

The conditions which made West Midlands industry vulnerable to change were accumulating well before the crisis became obvious in the late 1970s. Over the previous fifty years, not only had the economy tended to become more narrowly based on certain leading sectors and companies, but also changes in ownership, scale, and interlinkage had reduced the commitment of those companies to development within the conurbation. Mergers into large national and international agglomerates made it less likely that technological innovations and investment would be followed through in existing local production units and more likely that they would go to new or already existing plants elsewhere. Increased self-containment, or vertical integration, of the production process within large companies freed them from the need to stay near local suppliers. Leading companies within industries (such as motor vehicles) which remained horizontally integrated with components firms might seek alternative non-local suppliers or subcontractors which conformed better with their production requirements. 'Shopping around' became an alternative to the more difficult task of negotiating changes in practice among existing suppliers or sub-contractors.

The spatial distribution of economic activity

Since the 1870s a two-stage, though overlapping, process can be observed, first of a growing dominance of Birmingham within the regional economy and then of a tendency for industry to disperse to the periphery of the city and beyond. The dominance of Birmingham, and secondarily of Wolverhampton, over the Black Country became clear by the mid-1870s with the collapse of raw-material production and old metal trades and the development of new, more integrated factories which undermined the interlinkages between specialized local producers. New transport networks freed producers of finished goods (located primarily in Birmingham) from dependence on local suppliers and markets.

By the turn of the century, transport networks had also made it possible for larger-scale and more self-contained firms, such as Cadbury, to locate themselves on more spacious sites away from the city centre, and tramways and bicycles allowed workers to reach them. The main lines of industrial expansion were into areas then on the outskirts of the city—Ladywood, Smethwick, West Bromwich, Selly Oak, Bournville, Stirchley, Balsall Heath, Bordesley, Small Heath, and so on.

In the inter-war years further dispersal occurred with the development of consumer durables and light engineering industries. Their mass-production technologies implied large-scale operations and therefore new 'green-field' locations. Such development occurred particularly around Coventry and Birmingham though with different implications in each case. Coventry's relatively abrupt industrial development from the turn of the century attracted outside investors (Daimler, Courtauld, Singer, Hillman, Humber, Rudge, Bettman, etc.) who were able to find open sites relatively near the city centre on the old commons and the Cheylesmore estate, and in Foleshill Rural District Council within two miles of the city centre. Birmingham's more continuous development left a series of concentric rings of industry from successive periods. Briggs (1952, pp. 298–300) describes five rings: a central core of nineteenth-century industries (jewellery, guns, brass-works), an inner ring of specialist workshops, a middle ring built-up around the turn of the century (breweries, food processing, railway rolling stock, gas, paint, metal works), an outer ring of new factories, especially along the Tame Valley (electrical and engineering equipment, advanced metal manufacture, tyres, plastics), and outlying areas, including Longbridge, focusing on vehicles.

The effect of the concentration of economic growth on Birmingham and Coventry and then of its dispersal to the periphery of these cities was to leave the old urban centres with the more traditional and specialist producers. This applied to the inner, older areas of Birmingham and Wolverhampton, and more generally to the smaller towns of the Black Country. Figure 1.2 shows their continued dependence in 1931 on the heavy and secondary metal processes; within that general category traditional specialisms persisted—saddlery and leather in Walsall, iron and steel tubes in West Bromwich, bolts, nuts, rivets, and screws in Smethwick. Such industries, with highly skilled labour forces but obsolescent technology and premises, were very vulnerable to changes in demand from the finished-manufacturing firms. None of the county boroughs of the conurbation had developed a strong service sector to compensate for this stagnation in industrial employment in the urban centres. Even Birmingham, a regional centre in education, commerce, medicine, law, finance, and public administration had below the national share of employment in the service sector (West Midlands Group 1948, pp. 104–17).

Dispersal was already occurring, but *policies* for dispersal emerged first out of the experience of the 1930s depression and the generation of a governmental commitment 'to limit the growth of Britain's largest cities, and redistribute industry to the benefit of the depressed areas' (Sutcliffe and Smith 1974, p. 57). Special areas were designated in 1934, and Birmingham City Council recognized their 'prior need for new industry, and voluntarily toned down the efforts of the municipal Information Bureau, which had been set up in 1930, to attract firms to Birmingham' (Sutcliffe and Smith, p. 120). The Second World War gave further impetus to dispersal policy by the enforced removal of shadow factories (munitions, aircraft, and military-vehicle) to outlying areas of Coventry, Birmingham, and Wolverhampton. A post-war consensus developed which favoured the dispersal of future development, supporting the Barlow Commission's recommendation (1940) of focusing expansion outside the major areas, which included Birmingham, Coventry, and Wolverhampton but not the Black Country. The Abercrombie–Jackson plan for the West Midlands recommended that no new industry should be permitted except that linked to existing activities. In 1951 Birmingham's public-works committee accepted the policy but pressed for some increase in land designated for industry, with prescient reservations:

'Bearing in mind the importance to its [Birmingham's] workers of the maintenance of opportunities for employment, the key position of the City's industries from a national point of view, and the inherent danger of a disturbance of the City's industries leading to a retrogression, the City Council feel that the question of dispersal of industry is one which should be approached with caution'.

(Sutcliffe and Smith 1974, p. 129)

There were other factors than dispersal policy to encourage firms to leave the conurbation—among these were congestion, old premises, and the cost of land—but the evidence is that firms did not so much shift as stagnate or die. Smith (1977) shows that the old-core industrial area of Birmingham (of nineteen postal districts) lost 42 per cent of its plant between 1956 and 1966, 17 per cent by moving out of the inner areas and 25 per cent by simply disappearing. Only 17 firms had moved into the nineteen postal districts, while

262 had moved out; 160 had been 'born' there during the ten years, while 515 had died. Dispersal occurred largely through the differential growth or decline and birth or death of firms rather than through physical moves.

By 1960 employment in the conurbation as a whole was still growing, but the major increases were occurring in the peripheral ring just inside and outside the conurbation (Joyce 1977, p. 5). Nevertheless, until 1960 the distribution of industry remained similar to the pre-war pattern, with established firms preferring to retain their linkages and access to skilled labour rather than move to new sites. Many small specialist firms remained in the central areas of Birmingham and Wolverhampton until they were affected by urban-renewal programmes in the 1960s.

The West Midlands in 1960 appeared to be frozen in a state of prosperity. The leading Coventry and Birmingham industries were doing well, carrying with them the more technologically backward suppliers of the Black Country and the inner rings of Birmingham. Austin, for example, was largely supplied by parts manufacturers within a ten-mile radius of Longbridge (Sutcliffe and Smith 1974, p. 158). Investment in new plant was officially discouraged, and to avoid shifts in location many firms preferred to adapt and contain themselves within existing premises. Underlying change was apparent in the differential growth which was leading to a *relative* decline in employment in the inner areas and an increase on the periphery of the conurbation and in the wider region.

The Experience of the Labour Force

The work available

The nineteenth century structure of small workshops emphasized a hierarchy of artisans over workers in terms both of skill levels and work-place organization. Self-employed artisans were initially incorporated into the evolving factory system as semi-independent 'overhands', 'piecemasters', or 'butties' who contracted with employers to produce a certain output at a fixed sum and to engage and pay workers (Allen 1929). Mechanization and the introduction of mass production in the first part of the twentieth century undermined the skills and privileges of artisans. Old crafts lost their place, and, to the extent that new skills were generated, it was in the intermediate processes of tool-making and tool-setting rather than in the production of finished articles, which became a matter for machine operatives. Bicycle, car, and electrical-engineering production in turn began as small-scale highly skilled processes which changed over to mass production in the inter-war years. Craft unions in Coventry and Birmingham were unable to resist being 'squeezed by the collapse of high class work at the bottom of the depression in 1931–3 and the rise of new techniques such as all-steel bodies and cellulose spray painting which eliminated many of their crafts' (Tolliday). Testimony to the relatively low levels of skill which then prevailed lies in the weakness of training provision in the West Midlands vehicle and engineering industries (compared for example with apprenticeship arrangements in ship-building and steel) and in the history of direct recruitment into these industries.

Wages in the leading sectors of West Midlands Industry have been high, due not so much to skill levels as to the high levels of productivity and profitability of firms. The importance of engineering and vehicle production, and the conditions of post-war full employment, allowed the benefit of relatively high manual wages to be passed on to other associated suppliers. Toolroom agreements in Coventry after the Second World War set the pace for engineering workers in vehicle manufacturing and the large components suppliers in Birmingham and the Black Country. Wage levels, fixed by national agreements, were also high in the remaining large Black Country iron- and steel-smelting plants. Through the post-war period and into the 1970s the county was therefore among the highest-earning areas of the country (see Figure 1.4).

This general distribution of earnings hid a differentiation between large firms in the leading sectors, mainly in Coventry, Birmingham, and Solihull, and the numerous medium and small metal-components suppliers and sub-contractors spread throughout the Black Country and in the central areas of Birmingham. Smaller firms were in general left with the more skilled and labour-intensive stages of production and shorter special runs, while the leading companies took the higher-added-value and more capital-intensive mass-production stages. In effect, large firms were able to keep a part of 'their' labour force at arms length, in competitive units, and therefore at lower wage rates. Fragmentation of the labour market, especially of the Black Country, was reinforced by the role of local firms as specialist sub-contractors for castings, forgings, and other parts. This fragmentation and the consequence variations in employment conditions and prospects were reflected in the highly divergent unemployment rates experienced by the different towns of the conurbation.

The Black Country also received a lesser share of employment in office work which grew through the inter-war and post-war years. While the county as a whole remained below the national average in service-sector employment, managerial, professional, and clerical work grew to about the national average levels (about 24 per cent of the working population by the end of the 1960s) with the expansion of administration in both the public sector and the larger private companies. Hobsbawm (1969, p. 244) shows that such occupations, which nationally had accounted for about 7 per cent of all employment in metal manufacture, vehicle production and engineering in 1907, by 1951 accounted for about a quarter of jobs in these industries.

By the 1950s there were signs of a shift of the employment base away from manufacturing. In 1951 more than 60 per cent of the workers in the county

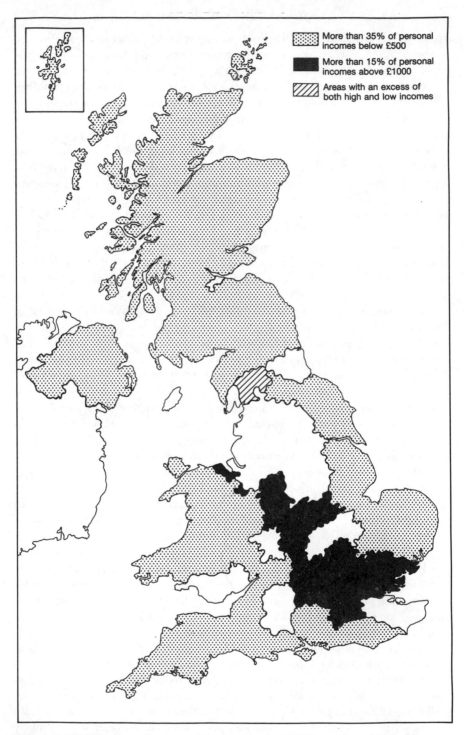

More than 35% of personal incomes below £500

More than 15% of personal incomes above £1000

Areas with an excess of both high and low incomes

Fig. 1.4. Distribution of personal income in the UK by region, 1959–60.
Source: Hobsbawm (1968).

were employed in the manufacturing industries. By 1961 there had been no fall in the absolute numbers so employed in the county as a whole, but in Birmingham manufacturing employment had dropped by about 10 per cent. There was a more than compensatory rise in service-sector employment throughout the county but particularly in Birmingham. However, there were two qualifications—in all areas of the county, service employment remained at below the national average (compare Figure 1.3), and many of the new jobs created in this sector were part-time and low-paid.

The introduction of light and mass-production industries, the growth of office work, and the development of the service sector all favoured the increased employment of women, especially in Birmingham. Female employment has been relatively high in the West Midlands since at least the 1920s, but was given further impetus by the conditions of war and of post-war full employment. The proportion of female workers in the economically active population reached 35 per cent in the West Midlands conurbation (the WMCC area excluding Coventry) in 1951 against a national average of about 32 per cent. This contributed to a situation where, by 1961, not only were wage earnings among the highest in the UK but also household incomes in the West Midlands were even higher than those of London and the South-east (Sutcliffe and Smith 1974, p. 170).

Population growth and labour recruitment

Corresponding to the period of its greatest economic growth and prosperity, between 1911 and 1951 the West Midlands metropolitan area experienced a faster growth of population than any other conurbation. Over the forty years, Birmingham and the Black Country grew by nearly 40 per cent to reach a population of 2 260 000 and Coventry grew by more than 100 per cent to 270 000 (Rugman and Green 1977, p. 52; Richardson 1972, p. 64).

Birmingham and the Black Country had experienced rapid growth since 1800 with increases in the population of between 22 and 35 per cent every ten years until 1861. Thereafter, increases slowed down from around 15 per cent between 1861 and 1871 to about 11 per cent between 1901 and 1911 (Allen 1929, p. 458). These gross percentages disguise the difference between the continued rapid growth of Birmingham and Wolverhampton and the stabilization and even decline in population which followed the effects of the 1875–86 depression on Black Country towns such as Dudley, Tipton, and Wednesbury. Thereafter, these towns tended to remain rather small and circumscribed, with most local expansion taking place in surrounding semi-rural areas (Raybould 1973, p. 126).

Coventry's demographic, like its economic, growth was more abrupt than that of Birmingham, taking place mainly during the first half of the twentieth century. It doubled in the first ten years of the century and then increased at about 15 per cent per decade until 1941; between 1941 and 1951, as a

The Industrial Heartland

Table 1.1. *Population Change in the West Midlands County, 1951–1961*

	Population 1961	Change 1951–1961 (%)
Birmingham	1 183 200	1.9
Coventry	318 400	17.7
Dudley	254 200	9.8
Sandwell	339 500	−1.0
Solihull	128 200	58.0
Walsall	264 800	14.1
Wolverhampton	273 200	7.3
England and Wales	46 104 500	5.4

Source: Rugman and Green (1977).

recipient of 'overspill' from Birmingham, it increased by 34 per cent and then by 18 per cent between 1951 and 1961.

Birmingham's population continued to grow, though at a relatively modest rate, until the 1950s, with an increase of 11 per cent between 1931 and 1951. Thereafter, it was stable until the end of the 1950s and then began to fall. Even before the 1960s, the central areas of the city had begun to experience a massive loss of population in a shift towards the periphery of the city and beyond. Slum clearance and voluntary emigration reduced the population of the central wards by 27.3 per cent between 1951 and 1961, while the middle ring declined by 3.7 per cent and the outer ring increased by 6.7 per cent (Sutcliffe and Smith 1974, p. 184).

The population of the West Midlands County as a whole continued to grow, but the growth areas had switched from Birmingham to the outlying areas of Solihull, Sutton Coldfield, Walsall, and even parts of the Black Country, including Dudley and Wolverhampton (see Table 1.1). Such shifts of population (as well as industry) to areas on the periphery of the old conurbations, where land was available for resettlement, were occurring throughout the country, and indeed Birmingham's population decline came later than that of such cities as Liverpool and Manchester (Sutcliffe and Smith 1974, p. 185).

Historically, the population of the West Midlands County has built up not only through high birth rates but also through immigration. The range and sources of recruitment into the labour force have varied considerably over time and, it is argued, have affected the traditions of local labour mobility and organization. There were three main sources—the surrounding rural counties, the depressed industrial areas of Britain, and overseas countries—which acquired importance in different phases of the county's industrial expansion.

Rapid growth in the nineteenth century was largely due to immigration into Birmingham and the Black Country from the surrounding counties of

Shropshire and Worcestershire, although there were also influxes from Ireland. These migrants came from conservative rural areas without experience of industrial wage labour and without the tradition of non-conformity which was associated in the north of England with working class organization. They joined a labour force which was fragmented into small firms divided further by specialisms between towns. The many traditional industries established their own parochial and specialist labour forces by absorbing local suppliers and contractors into larger factories. Coventry's ancient industries, such as ribbon and watch-making, were even more bound, by guild rules, to recruit on local and inherited lines. Attachment of labour to particular industries and residential areas is evident from the unemployment figures which in the 1880s and 1930s were highly divergent across the county.

These relatively parochial patterns of migration and labour recruitment changed between 1920 and 1937, when the population balance between the north and south of England was reversed as the old industrial base declined. Whereas in 1923 the North contained 54 per cent of the population, by 1937 the South was predominant. Birmingham and Coventry (as part of 'the South') experienced an expansion equivalent to that of the South-east, though much of the Black Country was losing population to the expanding districts of the West Midlands (Thomas 1938). In the case of Birmingham, much if not all of the growth was due to natural increase, emigration matching immigration until 1935 (Walker 1947). Coventry was expanding out of natural increase and a net gain of migrants.

To both cities, the sources of immigration extended in this period from the surrounding rural counties to include the depressed industrial areas of Britain, and especially South Wales and the North-east of England. Wales lost 10 per cent of its economically active population to the South-east of England and the Midlands between 1920 and 1937. There were especially high rates of immigration to Coventry and north Warwickshire, with their new and vigorously expanding industries. Proportionate to its size, there was somewhat less movement to Birmingham, which already had a large population of industrial workers, but in absolute terms it absorbed the larger number (Thomas 1938). The wider range of migration in this period meant that the large-scale growth industries of the inter-war years recruited workers who brought with them experience of trade-union organization and struggle (Zeitlin 1984).

War-time and post-war labour shortages resulted in more deliberate campaigns for the recruitment of workers. During the war, central and local government supported schemes for the training of workers, the recruitment of women, and the transfer of 'directed workers', many of them women, from the depressed areas of the UK. Recruiting agents were sent to Eire by private firms, such as ICI and Austin (Sutcliffe and Smith 1974, pp. 43–4).

Eire and Northern Ireland remained important sources of overseas immigrants throughout the 1950s and were, indeed, the predominant birth places of the population born overseas until the late 1960s. Immigration from the new British Commonwealth (mainly the Caribbean) was increasing in importance but by 1961 still accounted for only 1.4 per cent of the population of the West Midlands County or 2.6 per cent of that of Birmingham. The main areas of settlement of these new immigrants within Birmingham were in the middle ring around the central areas of the city. The relative stability of the total size of population in such areas as Sparkbrook, Soho, and Handsworth disguised the beginnings of a major shift as the original population began to move out and the new residents to move in (Sutcliffe and Smith 1974, pp. 203–8; Rugman and Green 1977, pp. 69–70).

Labour organization

Through most of its industrial history, the West Midlands has had a reputation both for weak trade-union organization and for worker control on the factory floor. This paradoxical combination is explained not only by changes over time or variations between parts of the local economy but also by the relationship between skilled and less skilled workers.

The compliant tradition of the nineteenth- and early-twentieth-century labour forces of Birmingham and the Black Country can be attributed to several of the factors already mentioned: the conservative rural origins of immigrants, the division of workers into small firms divided further by specialisms between towns, the parochial work-forces which grew up around particular industries and even firms, and the opportunities for self-employment for skilled workers. This situation can be compared, for example, with that of Manchester (Roberts 1978) with its immigrants from surrounding semi-industrialized textile villages joining a labour force in large factories with similar working conditions throughout the city and small opportunity for self-employment. Sheffield, another city with strong trade-union organization, had received its immigrants from a semi-industrialized countryside with a liberal, non-conformist tradition; a large part of the labour force was grouped with similar levels of skill in relatively large steel plants across the city (Boughton 1984).

Workers in Birmingham and the Black Country before the First World War did not commonly face great capitalist oligarchies of the type found in Manchester (Briggs 1952, p. 55); with few exceptions, such as Lord Dudley's ironworks (Raybould 1973), the distinction between employer and employee was much less clear, confused by a multiplicity of small owners, semi-autonomous artisans, and different levels of skill. This meant, on the one hand, that there was a less open confrontation between employers and employees, and, on the other, that labour's ranks were themselves strongly divided. Craftsmen were differentiated from other workers not only by their skill but also by, firstly, their ability to protect their trades through exclusive craft unions, secondly, the role they frequently adopted as semi-independent

supervisors or sub-contractors of labour, and, thirdly, the possibility of transferring their skill to other employers or starting out on their own. Skilled
workers' wages in the traditional industries of Birmingham, the Black
Country, and Coventry were held high (Briggs 1952, p. 57), while unskilled
workers, without union protection, found their wages driven low by under-
cutting between competitive firms. The compensation for the unskilled was
in the dynamism of the local economy which was creating expanding
employment.

Such relationships had a certain persistence into the inter-war years and
even after the second World War, not only in the traditional craft industries
but also in the rising ones. The pattern of sub-contracting between competitive suppliers in the leading sectors (such as the engineering and motor-
vehicle) continued to limit the scope for labour organization and demands.
Divisions between skilled and unskilled workers undermined unity between
and within trade unions particularly between the wars. A tradition of
involvement by skilled workers in shopfloor management remained a feature
particularly of industry in Birmingham (Briggs 1952, pp. 55–63, 281). Part
of that tradition had been built on employers' respect for the rights of skilled
workers to control the work process. Two features of shop-floor control had a
peculiar persistence not only in Birmingham but also in Coventry's most
modern industries such as car and aircraft production—piecework, originating in the domestic system where semi-autonomous workers were paid
according to the numbers of jobs completed; and the gang system, where a
skilled employer, often an elected shop steward, controlled a group of
workers (Richardson 1972, pp. 113–15). Such traditional practices were, on
the one hand, a form of collaboration with management and, on the other, a
source of conflict with management about control.

In the inter-war period, the craft basis of union organizations came under
increasing pressure with the development of mechanization and mass production. There was an expansion of the work-force, and many tasks which
had previously been skilled became available to semi-skilled workers.
Especially in the case of Coventry, where industrial development was more
abrupt, the rising industries drew heavily on recruits from depressed areas
with traditions of trade-union organization. There was, however, no quick
transformation of union organization in motor and engineering industries
from a craft to a mass membership. In Coventry, the skilled workers' Amalgamated Engineering Union (AEU) declined from 13 115 members in 1920
to 3 035 in 1925, and the National Union of Vehicle Builders (NUVB) lost
50 per cent of its membership later in the recession between 1931 and 1933.
In spite of this decline, until the late 1930s local branches of both unions only
reluctantly opened their doors to semi-skilled workers, although the latter
were in the great majority in the work-place. Less skilled workers were able
to join the Workers Union and, when that collapsed in the recession, the
Transport and General Workers' Union (TGWU), but their demands were

expressed more through shopfloor action and company strikes than through formal union channels (Tolliday; Turner, Clack and Roberts 1967).

Union weakness in the electrical, motor, and cycle companies between the wars can be attributed to the divisions of interest in the inherited union structure; to relatively high wage rates in the leading sectors; to the threat of recruitment of lower-paid workers for declining industries; to high levels of female employment; to insecurity of employment, especially in the motor industry where seasonal 'lay off' was normal and skill levels were generally low; and to the hostility of management concerned to wrest control of the shopfloor from the skilled workers (Boughton 1984).

The conditions of the Second World War, and of the immediate post-war economy, transformed the position of the unions. The threat of unemployment, seasonal lay-offs and the possibility of replacement by lower-paid workers disappeared in a full-employment economy, employers conceded full union recognition; industrial plant increased in scale; shop stewards became more fully involved in shopfloor production agreements; wages rose, giving credibility to the unions; and membership of those unions (particularly AEU and TGWU) which were able to dispense with attachment to archaic specialisms rose rapidly (Croucher 1982; Hastings 1959).

Out of these conditions came a post-war struggle which gave the West Midlands labour force a reputation for militancy which was in no way typical of its earlier tradition. The unions were defending not only recent gains in wages and working conditions but also the related question of their influence over the work process. Management in the major engineering and vehicle firms sought to assert control by attacking the piecework system, the division of workers into gangs, union influence over recruitment, job assignment, and the pace of work, and the practice of sharing work rather than allowing redundancy. Most of these were in fact issues of local or plant control and therefore involved an attack on the role of shop stewards. The strikes which developed in the motor industry in the 1950s were not only over wage levels but also over attempts by management to change working practices and control shop stewards. A succession of disputes culminated 'between 1959 and 1961 when twenty-three major stoppages occurred in Birmingham, all but two of them in motor and associated concerns' (Sutcliffe and Smith 1974, p. 174).

What was regarded as shopfloor encroachment on managerial prerogative can be seen instead as the extension into the post-war period of a Midlands tradition in which skilled workers collaborated with employers in the management of production. The development of mass unionism in the 1950s clearly weighted the relationship more than before in favour of the unions. The response of management was not to build new forms of worker-participation (as in West Germany, Japan, and Scandinavia) but to exclude labour organizations from decision-making (Tylecote 1982, p. 61). The response hardened further in the 1960s and 1970s with the arrival from outside the Midlands of new owners and managers in the shape of Chrysler and British Leyland[2].

Conclusion

The West Midlands economy adjusted successfully to the recessions of 1870s and the 1930s and to the changes in demand which occurred after the two world wars. Its diversity had allowed new growth sectors to emerge and its interdependence meant that the benefits of growth were widely diffused. However, conditions which made it vulnerable to change were accumulating well before the crisis became obvious in the 1970s. Over the previous fifty years, industry had become larger-scale, less diverse and less locally inter-dependent. Success in the internationally leading sectors of vehicle manufac-ture and light engineering had apparently led to an increasing concentration on those sectors, stymying the development of new industries and the service sector. This less flexible economic structure had come to depend on a pros-perous domestic market and low levels of international competition. The conditions were also growing, through merger, increasing international trade, and increasing capital mobility, for firms to choose to expand outside the UK; by the 1950s government policy was itself encouraging such disper-sal from the West Midlands and discouraging incoming investment.

The prosperity of the post-war economy of the West Midlands disguised a vulnerability which its earlier heterogeneity had avoided. A large number of supplier, sub-contractor, and specialist firms were dependent on the demand generated by a few major assembly companies. In particular the manufactur-ing firms in the inner areas of Birmingham and in the Black Country towns were losing their links with the increasingly autonomous and peripherally located major companies. A high-wage post-war economy was built on the prosperity of the West Midlands's leading sectors and on the spread effect of full employment, semi-skilled and unskilled labour benefiting in wages and security of employment from labour scarcity and mass unionism. In these temporary conditions of generalized prosperity, shopfloor control, which had been a matter of collaboration between employers and skilled workers, became a focus of conflict.

Notes to Chapter 1

1 This approximate figure (quoted in Liggins 1977) is for the West Midlands Region, consisting of the counties of Hereford and Worcester, Warwickshire, Staf-fordshire, Shropshire, and the West Midlands.

2 'After the abrupt dismissal of Mr Adam's predecessor, Mr Derek Robinson, $4\frac{1}{2}$ years ago, the company moved swiftly to impose its own working practices by scrapping the so-called "mutuality agreements" under which shop stewards were involved in almost every decision at plant level' (*Guardian*, 15 June, 1984).

2

The Economic and Social Impact of Population and Employment Change

The purpose of this chapter is to portray recent significant changes in the West Midlands economy within a wider social environment. In carrying out this purpose it develops three themes. They are population change, unemployment and employment, and quality of public service as provided by local government.

Job opportunities are inextricably linked with the changing number, type, and location of jobs relative to an individual's degree of accessibility to such employment in terms of perceived skills, residential location, and propensity to seek work. There is greater competition where jobs are scarce and unemployment rises to significant levels. Such competition results in certain individuals or groups of individuals being less able to secure work. Spatially this will be reflected in differential local unemployment rates. In addition, those young people who are entrants to the job market will find greater difficulty gaining employment. Those with redundant industrial skills for example, in many metal and engineering trades, will find difficulty gaining new employment, especially if they are older and unable to develop other skills. Such pressures can also result in a relative depression of rates of pay.

Hence the movement or non-movement of population plays an important role in the economic fortunes both of individuals and of particular locations. As well as differentiating between areas of population growth and areas of decline, it indicates where much or little new residential and associated infrastructure investment has taken place. We shall focus attention first on relative population growth and decline in the West Midlands Region and County.

Population Change

Change in residential population within the West Midlands Region, particularly within the West Midlands County and its extension through Travel to Work Areas overlapping the county boundary (county TTWA), has been examined over the period 1961–81, based on census data and using post-1974 local-authority boundaries (Smith 1983b). (See Table 2.1). The pattern of change is as follows: a general decline in population of 3 per cent in the West Midlands County (with Solihull as a major growth point); an overall growth of 8.2 per cent in the West Midlands Region (as against some 6 per cent in

Table 2.1. *Population Change in the West Midlands Region, 1961–1981*

	Population 1981	Change 1961–1981 (%)
West Midlands County	2 648 939	−3.0
Birmingham	1 006 527	−14.9
Coventry	313 815	−1.4
Dudley	299 741	+17.9
Sandwell	307 992	−9.3
Solihull	199 261	+55.4
Walsall	267 042	+8.2
Wolverhampton	254 561	−2.7
County TTWA	3 346 569	+4.7
County TTWA excluding county	697 630	+49.9
West Midlands Region excluding County	2 499 406	+23.4
West Midlands Region	5 148 345	+8.2

Source: Smith (1983*b*).

England and Wales); and a concentration of growth (some 50 per cent) in that part of the region immediately beyond the West Midlands County boundary but within the county TTWA. The rest of the region, beyond the county TTWA, grew by 15.5 per cent.

Population decline began in the early 1960s and has continued since then in Birmingham and Sandwell. Birmingham's population declined by 3.9 per cent in 1961–6, by 9.5 per cent in 1966–71 and by 8.4 per cent in 1971–81. Much of this loss was from the inner wards of the city and was due to redevelopment and relocation of households both within and beyond the city boundary. By 1971 signs of population decline at local-authority level were limited to this fall in Birmingham and to minor decline in Sandwell.

Between 1971 and 1981 population decline was both much more widespread and substantial. The population of the West Midlands County fell by 5.2 per cent, and decline was evident in Birmingham, Coventry (6.8 per cent), Sandwell (6.8 per cent), Wolverhampton (5.4 per cent), and Walsall (2 per cent). The concentration of decline was in the older, inner residential areas. Thus in Birmingham the Inner City Partnership (BICP) core area[1] lost 17.6 per cent of its population between 1971 and 1981, with a reduction from 330 246 to 271 985. Over the same period the outer Partnership area had lost 12.7 per cent of its population, with a reduction from 749 845 to 654 733 (BICP 1984*a*, p. 48). Birmingham's population decline was earliest and fastest. In the 1980s Walsall and Dudley joined this sharper decline.

Between 1961 and 1981 population shift redistributed some 6 per cent of the region's population. From 1971 to 1981 regional growth was only 38 740 and the population of the West Midlands County declined by 144 350, indicating a massive relocation. The county's population loss compares with a total population loss of only 43 750 in the county TTWA. Thus some 100 000 of the county loss moved, in net terms, into the periphery of the county TTWA (Smith 1983*b*; p. 32).

Population growth has to be viewed against the stability of population in the West Midlands Region and in England and Wales during 1971–81 (0.8 per cent and 0.2 per cent respectively). Yet over 1961–81 some 390 700 additional persons were located within the region. All the region's counties except the West Midlands County shared this growth, and its main location was in that peripheral belt of the county TTWA beyond the county boundary. Here population grew 49.9 per cent between 1961 and 1981, but only by 16.9 per cent in the latter decade. This compares with 15.5 per cent growth between 1961 and 1981 and 4.8 per cent growth between 1971 and 1981 in the rest of the region outside the county TTWA. Thus the prime growth lay in existing settlements close to the edge of the West Midlands County (Smith 1983*b*, p. 31).

Of these settlements Cannock, Rugeley, Lichfield, and Tamworth were subject to town-development schemes, while Redditch had new-town status. These areas were designed to receive overspill population from Birmingham and, to a lesser degree, from the Black Country. Other areas expanded but not as a result of planned overspill. These include Bromsgrove, Bewdley, Stourport, Kidderminster, and Bridgnorth (pre-1974 boundaries). Each of those towns with a population of 34 000–60 000 in 1961 (Cannock, Kidderminster with Bewdley and Stourport, Redditch, Bromsgrove), had grown by about 20 per cent (range 17.9–24 per cent) by 1971, while those towns with a population of less than 34 000 (Rugeley, Lichfield, Tamworth, Bridgnorth) grew by 58.9 per cent. Within the remaining, rural areas of the peripheral county TTWA, population growth was 19 per cent. Thus in 1961–71 the towns of the county TTWA grew by 32 per cent, the rural areas by 19 per cent, and the rest of the region, outside the county TTWA, by 10 per cent (Smith 1983*b*, pp. 28–9).

Between 1971 and 1981 the main local-authority growth areas in the region (post-1974 boundaries) were these urban authorities closer to the West Midlands County. Growth rates were: Redditch 64.3 per cent, Tamworth 58.3 per cent, the Wrekin 28.5 per cent (outside the county TTWA, but a new town drawing people from the north of the conurbation, especially Wolverhampton) South Staffordshire 17.5 per cent. Redditch and Tamworth dominated growth in this decade, with growth rates in other local-authority areas on the edge of the conurbation being lower: for example, Bromsgrove 14.2 per cent, Bridgnorth 3.7 per cent, Cannock Chase 7.9 per cent. However, these growth rates should be considered against a higher 1971 population base and the low overall growth of 0.8 per cent within the region.

The other key area was Solihull (post-1974 boundaries). A population of 128 000 in 1961 grew to 199 260 by 1981, the bulk of this growth coming in the period between the 1966 and 1971 censuses. Between 1961 and 1971 the growth rate was 49.8 per cent, but from 1971 to 1981 only an additional 7190 people were recorded, giving a rise of 55.4 per cent over the twenty years. The rapid growth in the late 1960s was due to Birmingham's overspill Chelmsley Wood housing-estate development, which accommodated about 45 000 people. In 1985 Solihull remained the authority with the largest amount of undeveloped land in the West Midlands County, and between 1981 and 1984 saw the largest percentage increase in housing stock of the county, at 3.5 per cent, compared with the county average of 1.5 per cent (WMCC 1985c, p. 45). Of all the district councils in the county only Solihull showed slight growth over 1981–3: the rest continued to lose population.

Population projections in 1985 for 1986 and 1991 indicated that decline was likely to be heaviest in Coventry, with Solihull starting to decline and Dudley experiencing a little growth, especially in the late 1980s (WMCC 1985c; p. 30).

The most striking feature of the changing population pattern is that nearly 230 000 more people lived in the peripheral areas of the county TTWA in 1981 compared with 1961 (a 56 per cent increase), reflecting both voluntary and official movement. The whole of the county TTWA contained only 150 000 more people in 1981 than 1961. These had generally been redistributed, in net terms, from inner to outer areas. Thus it can be argued, rather than a population decline in the West Midlands, population dispersal to a widening city region is taking place.

In linking population movement to employment, we need to compare such population change with changes in the levels of employment and unemployment. Evidence on this (Smith 1984d) can be placed alongside the population profile. We do so below, after some initial discussion of the changing pattern of employment and unemployment in the West Midlands.

Unemployment and Employment

The rising level of unemployment in the West Midlands Region, and the West Midlands County in particular, is one of the clearest indications of decline in the capacity of the local economy to provide jobs for its population. The year 1966 provided a watershed. Since then unemployment in the West Midlands has increased at a greater pace than national unemployment. The current local high unemployment levels are not a new phenomenon but part of a process of change which can be traced back to the mid-1960s. The issue of whether local changes in employment fortunes are a temporary phenomenon or part of a more fundamental change in job opportunities in the West Midlands County and region is crucial. The conclusion that unemployment will decline pro rata to a national economic recovery produces different policy prescriptions from the view that unemployment is part of a longer-term structural change in the economy and the economy's ability to provide jobs for those in the labour market. The evidence indicates that since 1966 there has been a shift towards the latter argument (Taylor 1984, p. 1).

Before the mid-1960s a prosperous national economy indicated an even more prosperous West Midlands regional economy, while in times of recession the regional economy was less seriously affected than the national economy (Liggins 1977). The West Midlands unemployment norm at this time was broadly half the national rate. The region moved into recession ahead of the country and picked up again ahead of the country (WMCC 1975, p. 14). A labour shake-out in 1966 together with a spending squeeze in July of that year affected the West Midlands with 5000 redundancies in the BMC (Crompton and Penketh 1977). This led to a knock-on effect among suppliers of components, leading to further redundancies over the next few years. During the slump of 1971–3 the region, particularly the West Midlands County fared badly, contrary to past experience, and was slower to recover than the country as a whole (Taylor 1984, p. 7).

Since the late 1960s, the regional unemployment rate has risen in stages, increasing substantially during each recession, then failing to drop to the previous rate in the subsequent upturn. This has especially been the case in 1971–3 and 1975–6 and since 1979. Thus with each economic downturn the region's earlier, more favourable position, has been eroded. By 1983 the regional unemployment rate was 23 per cent above the average for Great Britain. Between June 1978 and June 1982 unemployment in the region increased by some 184 per cent (227 000) compared with a national increase of 113 per cent. The regional contraction in the employment base between 1980 and 1983 (June to June) was 358 000, or 16 per cent. This was the worst performance of all regions in Great Britain, where the average was a 10.9 per cent contraction (BCIC 1984, Table 4).

The West Midlands economy, especially that within the West Midlands County, has been heavily dependent upon a few key manufacturing industries. Once the basis of growing prosperity, this dependence has led to exacerbated economic collapse in the recession since 1979. The process has accelerated because of the high levels of interlinkage and interdependency between manufacturing firms (higher in the West Midlands than in any other region in Great Britain). Nationally the industrial base has been vulnerable, with decline swiftly transmitted through the manufacturing economy. Manufacturing industry has taken the brunt of the recession. Hence the West Midlands, with the highest dependence upon manufacturing industry of any region, has been affected particularly severely.

In 1978, 48.6 per cent of employment in the West Midlands County was in manufacturing industry (32.1 per cent nationally), while the service sector accounted for 46.5 per cent (52.6 per cent nationally). Within manufacturing industry, four key sectors accounted for some 70.6 per cent of the county's total manufacturing employment. These were: vehicles, 23.9 per cent; metal goods, 20.6 per cent; metal manufacture, 14.6 per cent; and mechanical engineering, 11.5 per cent. Meanwhile, employment performance in the service sector has been poor. Between 1971 and 1978 the West Midlands County saw a growth of 10 per cent, on a low base, compared with 21 per cent nationally. Similarly, between 1978 and 1981 there was a decrease of 3 per cent in service-sector employment in the county compared with a national growth of just under 2 per cent. Hence growth in service-sector employment failed significantly to match the decline in manufacturing jobs. While the loss of jobs in manufacturing was mainly by men working full-time, the gain in jobs in the service sector was mainly by women working part-time.

Loss of jobs, especially in manufacturing industry, has continued. Of the notified redundancies between 1 January 1981 and 31 August 1983 (155 578) some 82.3 per cent were in manufacturing industry. Of notified redundancies in manufacturing industry some 82.2 per cent were in five key sectors. They were: vehicles, 26.3 per cent; metal goods, 18.7 per cent; metal manufacture, 15.7 per cent; mechanical engineering, 14.6 per cent; and electrical engineering, 10 per cent. Thus it is the very heart of the county's manufacturing industry which is shedding jobs rapidly. Between December 1979 and June 1982 manufacturing employment in the region fell by 24.1 per cent (230 000 jobs), while, in the decade to 1981, the vehicle industry alone lost more than 82 000 jobs (40 per cent). A similar rate of loss applied in metal manufacturing over the same period.

Analysis for the period 1971–8 both indicates the base upon which the more marked job loss since 1979 is founded and demonstrates important contracts within the individual TTWAs making up the county. Several points stand out (Smith 1984*a*):

(*a*)   the severity of decline in employment in Coventry, which contrasts with growth in employment in all sectors in the TTWA for outer Birmingham with Solihull

(*b*)   the mixed record in inner Birmingham, with job losses overall, especially in manufacturing, but job gains in the public and mixed sectors (in fact, inner Birmingham during this period had a better rate of job gain than the average for Great Britain)

(*c*)   the strong contrast between the inner and outer areas of Birmingham with Solihull, where there was a 9 per cent decline in jobs in inner areas and a 23 per cent growth in jobs in outer areas (excluding Selly Oak from both groups as it overlaps inner and outer areas), but the weak contrast between inner-urban and outer-urban areas in the Black Country; in the latter, a decline of 3 per cent in jobs in inner-urban areas was associated with a growth of only 1 per cent in outer-urban areas; both decline in inner-urban areas and growth in outer-urban areas was on a small scale in the Black Country compared with Birmingham

(*d*)   within the West Midlands Region, the redistribution of jobs from the inner-urban areas of the county, especially inner Birmingham, to the outer part of the county, outer ring of the county TTWA, and the rest of the region; the inner West Midlands lost 7 per cent of its jobs, while the outer county and the rest of the region both had a gain in jobs of 5–6 per cent; the most marked growth, as with population, was in the areas contiguous to the outer edge of the West Midlands County, where there was a 16 per cent increase in jobs

(*e*)   growth in jobs in the public sector occurred in government administration rather than in public industry or other public services provision (such as health care); however, the latter did grow by some 43 per cent in the outer ring of the county TTWA, beyond the county boundary, and by some 12 per cent in the inner areas of the West Midlands County.

After 1978 the effects of the recession on unemployment deepened, the main shift in the picture created above being a much more rapid relative growth in unemployment in many of the inner-urban areas of the Black Country (areas which—unlike Coventry and Birmingham, with their greater dependence upon vehicles—had suffered less acutely than the rest of the county).

Table 2.2 compares changes in population with changes in the economically active population, the employed population, and the unemployed population for various areas over the period 1961–81, based upon census data. It highlights areas of employment growth and decline relative to population change, though the scale of the increases in unemployment rate is proportionally different to that of the other changes (Smith 1984*d*). All these data for the region and its sub-areas reflect a greater increase in unemployment than in England and Wales as a whole. The heart of the decline lay in Birmingham (rather than Solihull), with the Birmingham–Solihull area suffering a decrease of 14 per cent in the number of economically active persons and a decrease of 24 per cent in the number of employed persons compared to a decrease of 8 per cent in population. Unemployment rose sharply by 617 per cent, but was below that for the Black Country and Coventry, at 732 and 724 per cent respectively. The Black Country gained 2.5 per cent in population and lost only 3 per cent of its economically active persons, but lost nearly 15 per cent of its employed persons. Presumably because of this margin, the Black Country experienced a more severe increase in unemployment than the Birmingham–Solihull area. Coventry closely paralleled the Black Country (though its unemployment rate rose more sharply earlier in the 1970s).

The key growth area in terms of numbers of economically active and employed persons was the periphery of the county TTWA, beyond the county boundary, with a 48 per cent increase in the number of economically active persons and a 37 per cent increase in the number of employed persons. Yet this area still witnessed a 489 per cent increase in unemployment rate.

Table 2.2. *Population and Employment Change in the West Midlands Region, 1961–1981*

	Overall population change (%)	Change in no. of economically active persons (%)	Change in no. of employed persons (%)	Increase in unemployment rate (%)
Birmingham–Solihull TTWA	−8.1	−14	−24	+617
Black Country TTWA	+2.5	−3	−15	+732
Coventry TTWA	−1.4	−2	−15	+724
West Midlands County	−3.0	−8	−20	+676
County TTWA	+4.7	−0.3	−12	+623
West Midlands Region	+8.2	+4	−6	+557
Region excluding county TTWA	+15.5	+14	+6	+391
Region excluding county	+23.4	+22	+13	+414
County TTWA excluding county	+49.9	+48	+37	+489
England and Wales	+6.1	+6	+1.5	+369

Source: Smith (1983*b*, 1984*d*).

The rest of the region, outside the county TTWA, experienced less increase in the number of economically active and employed persons, but also less growth in unemployment. The latter reflected distance from the main manufacturing base of the region and hence from some of the main contractions in manufacturing jobs, and a more diversified employment structure.

Given the varied nature of the West Midlands County, the dominance of local labour markets by a small number of key industries or even key firms, and the concentration of unemployment within particular areas of the conurbation, it is important to consider unemployment trends by smaller geographical units than Travel to Work Areas or Counties.

Within the West Midlands County there has been considerable variation in the proportion of unemployed by employment-office areas. For those for which data are available for the whole of the 1973–83 period, the rate of increase ranged from 33.5 per cent in Aston (Birmingham) to 423.4 per cent in Cradley Heath (Sandwell). Those areas reflecting an above-average increase in unemployment over this period were concentrated within the older industrial areas of the Black Country. Besides Cradley Heath (with an increase in unemployment rate more than eight times that of Great Britain as a whole), areas with increases more than three times the national average were Halesowen, Oldbury, and Willenhall, while Bilston, Brownhills, Dudley, Tipton, West Bromwich, Solihull, and Chelmsley Wood (the last two outside the Black Country) recorded increases of more than twice the national average (Taylor 1984, pp. 31–3). Over 1973–1982 the greatest increase was in the inner-urban areas of the Black Country and the lowest increase in inner Birmingham. However, this largely reflects the relatively high unemployment levels of inner Birmingham in 1973 and the relative prosperity of the Black Country at that time.

This low increase in unemployment in inner Birmingham does not indicate that unemployment in inner Birmingham was low. Indeed inner Birmingham wards had the highest proportions of their economically active population without work in the early 1980s. In 1981 wards in the county with more than 30 per cent unemployment were all in inner Birmingham (Deritend, Sparkbrook, Soho, and Aston). Recent post-code data from the Department of Employment (DE) show wards with very high employment rates. For example, in September 1983 seven wards had unemployment rates of more than 40 per cent (affecting men more than women). These were Deritend, Handsworth, Duddeston, Small Heath, Soho (all in inner Birmingham), Blakenhall (Wolverhampton), and Soho and Victoria (Sandwell) (Taylor 1984, p. 35).

New ward boundaries in Birmingham (39 replacing 42) and Dudley (24 replacing 22) affects the basis of ward unemployment rates at December 1984. Figure 2.1 maps these ward unemployment rates and clearly indicates the concentrations of the highest levels of unemployment in inner-city areas. If we compare this pattern with the pattern of unemployment rates in 1981, what emerges is increasing levels of unemployment in wards spreading outwards by December 1984 from the core areas of April 1981, with other concentrations of high unemployment rates on some of the council-housing estates beyond the inner-urban areas.

Brief analysis of these ward unemployment data of December 1984 is presented in Table 2.3, reflecting wide variations in unemployment rates both between and within local-authority areas. It is the core area of the BICP zone where the greatest concentration of unemployment is found. The same gradient of unemployment rate in Birmingham was reflected in the 1981 census, when 9.8 per cent were unemployed in Great Britain, 15.2 per cent in Birmingham, 18 per cent in the BICP area, and 24.2 per cent in the BICP core area. This last figure represented an unemployment rate among men of 27.5 per cent and among women 18.2 per cent. In 1981 this core area contained 27 per cent of Birmingham's population of just over one million, while the BICP area as a whole contained 65 per cent (BICP 1984a, pp. 2, 48). It was particularly the young and men who were numerically most affected by unemployment in 1981 and who continue to be so affected (though any significant increase in the propensity of women to register as unemployed would have an impact upon these figures). Table 2.4 shows unemployment rates by sex and age in 1981.

Though high unemployment is concentrated in inner-city locations, there has been a pattern of wider unemployment dispersal among the young, so that the overall pattern begins to reflect the distribution of the young economically active, hence the concentration of high unemployment rates in some of the more peripheral council-housing estates. This concentration partially reflects differential employment change within the BICP area compared with Birmingham as a whole. Between 1971 and 1983 the number of persons in employment in the BICP area saw a decrease of 46 per cent in manufacturing (against decreases of 40 per cent for Birmingham and 32 per cent for Great Britain); an increase of 4 per cent in the service sector (as against no change for Birmingham and an increase of 11 per cent for Great Britain); and a decrease of 41 per cent in construction (as against a decrease 3 per cent for Birmingham and 19 per cent for Great Britain). The loss of jobs in the construction industry has particularly hit the inner city (BICP 1984a, p. 2).

At the same time residents of the BICP core area in work in Birmingham in 1981 were much more dependent upon buses (43 per cent) and foot (19 per cent) as means of travel to work than residents in the city as a whole (34 per cent and 13 per cent respectively). They were also much less dependent upon the use of a car and its implied flexibility of work location: 28 per cent of residents of the BICP core area used a car to travel to wrok compared with 45 per cent in Birmingham as a whole (BICP 1984a, p. 2).

The socio-economic structure of the inner city is biased towards those occupations which are more likely to suffer as a result of differential employment contraction. Table 2.5 provides relevant data. The greater incidence of

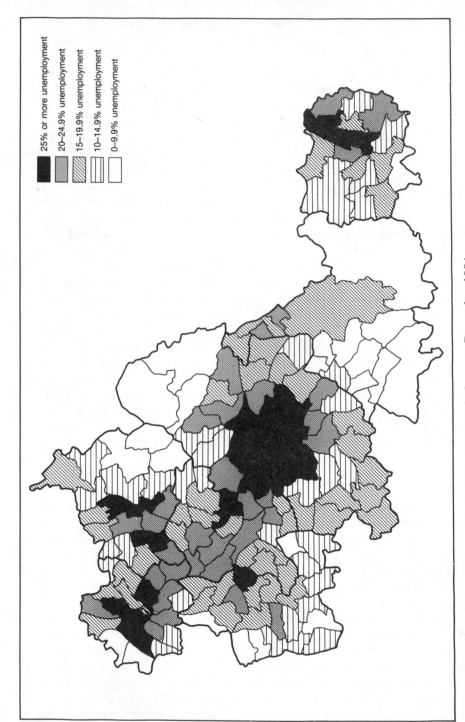

Fig. 2.1 Ward unemployment rates, in the West Midlands County, December 1984.

Source: WMCC (1985*c*), based on DE data.

25% or more unemployment

20–24.9% unemployment

15–19.9% unemployment

10–14.9% unemployment

0–9.9% unemployment

Table 2.3. *Ward Unemployment Rates in the West Midlands County, December 1984*

	Average unemployment rate (%)	Unemployment rates, showing no. of wards in each range					Total no. of wards
		40% or higher	30–39%	20–29%	10–19%	less than 10%	
Birmingham	20.5	1	4	11	20	3	39
Wolverhampton	19.8	0	2	8	8	2	20
Sandwell	19.4	0	1	9	14	0	24
Coventry	18.8	0	2	5	10	1	18
Walsall	16.2	0	1	6	10	3	20
Dudley	14.4	0	0	3	16	5	24
Solihull	11.9	0	0	2	5	10	17
West Midlands County	18.3	1	10	44	83	24	162

Source: WMCC (1985c, Table 4.8).

Table 2.4. *Unemployment Rates by Sex and Age in Birmingham and the West Midlands County, April 1981*

	Age group								Total		
	16–19		20–24		25–44		45–pension				
	Male	Female	Male	Female	Male	Female	Male	Female	Male	Female	M and F
BICP core area	39.8	36.3	30.2	24.3	25.5	15.1	26.4	11.1	27.5	18.2	24.2
BICP excluding core area	27.4	22.8	21.1	13.7	14.5	7.8	16.8	6.7	16.9	9.6	14.0
Birmingham	29.5	25.1	23.3	15.8	15.9	8.6	17.2	6.8	18.2	10.6	15.2
West Midlands County	25.5	22.6	22.2	15.0	14.7	8.1	16.6	6.4	16.9	9.7	14.2
Great Britain	19.3	17.4	16.5	11.6	9.8	6.0	10.5	5.0	11.4	7.6	9.8

Source: BICP (1984a, p. 4).

semi-skilled, unskilled, and other occupations, and an equal proportionate share of skilled occupations in the BICP core area compared with other areas have rendered inner-city residents particularly vulnerable to unemployment.

In April 1981, 43.1 per cent of the population of the BICP core area were in households whose the head was born in the New Commonwealth or Pakistan (compared with 21.3 per cent for the BICP area as a whole, 15.2 per cent for Birmingham and 4.5 per cent for Great Britain. This provides a racial dimension to the regional pattern of unemployment. Ethnic-minority groups are highly concentrated both within Birmingham and within its inner-city core area. Data on unemployment rates among these groups are available for the BICP area. They show rates of unemployment among ethnic-minority groups to be more than 50 per cent higher than the rates for corresponding white groups within the BICP area. For Bangladeshi households the rate is more than 100 per cent higher, closely followed by high rates for Pakistani households (BICP 1984*a*, p. 9). There is thus a more acute unemployment problem among these ethnic-minority groups within the BICP core area. In Sandwell and Wolverhampton, and to a lesser extent in Walsall and Coventry, this same close relationship between high inner-city unemployment and ethnic minorities is found. In August 1982, 54.4 per cent of registered unemployed Commonwealth or Pakistani origin within the West Midlands County were to be found in Birmingham. When the exercise of racial discrimination in the allocation of jobs is also taken into account, this means that ethnic-minority groups are at an extreme disadvantage in obtaining work (WMCC 1983*a*, pars. 3.1.22 and 3.1.24).

Employment-office data show that in October 1982 five offices in the county drew more than 25 per cent of their registered unemployed from these ethnic-minority groups. Four were in Birmingham and one just outside. Handsworth employment office drew 50 per cent of its registered unemployed from these groups, while Sparkhill, Aston, Small Heath, and Smethwick (Sandwell) drew between 25 and 29 per cent (Taylor 1984, p. 42).

Within the county's five TTWAs those unemployed from manual occupations accounted for 70–5 per cent of the unemployed in each TTWA in June 1982. This was reflected in the ratios of numbers of unemployed to job vacancies. For all occupations this ratio in June 1982 for the county was 57.1 : 1, some 2.7 times the national average. It was 3.3 times the national average for craft and similar occupations, at 75.2 : 1, 3.5 times the national average for general labourers, at 699.4 : 1, and 5.4 times the national average for other manual occupations, at 80.4 : 1 (Taylor 1984, p. 43).

In May 1982 more than 40 per cent of the registered unemployed from the industrial sector in the country TTWA had been previously engaged in metal goods (17.7 per cent), motor vehicles (11.4 per cent), metal manufacture (6.4 per cent), and mechanical engineering (4.7 per cent). Other significant unemployed groups by previous occupation were: construction, 12 per cent;

Table 2.5. *Percentages of Population in Birmingham Economically Active by Occupational Group and Sex, 1981*

Occupational group	BICP core area		BICP		Birmingham		Great Britain	
	Male	Female	Male	Female	Male	Female	Male	Female
Professional	2	0	3	1	4	1	6	1
Managerial	5	3	8	4	11	5	15	7
Intermediate	8	36	13	45	15	48	17	52
Skilled	36	7	38	6	37	5	36	7
Semi-skilled	26	33	22	29	21	27	16	23
Unskilled	11	9	8	9	7	8	6	7
Other	13	11	8	7	7	6	5	4

Source: BICP (1984*a*, p. 2).

distributive trades, 10.3 per cent; instrument engineering, 4.7 per cent; public administration, including defence, 3.4 per cent (Taylor 1984, pp. 45–6).

Typically the level of unemployment among women has been lower than that among men (see Table 2.4). However, this hides the fact that unemployment among women has been growing faster than that among men. If we compare average rates of increase in unemployment from June 1973 to June 1983 in the five county TTWAs by sex, the following pattern emerges. Birmingham's annual average increase in unemployment among women was 132.4 per cent (54.5 per cent among men). Similar respective data for Coventry were 84.8 per cent and 64.3 per cent, for Sandwell–Dudley 243.3 per cent and 101.7 per cent, for Walsall 225.9 per cent and 99.8 per cent, for Wolverhampton 105.4 per cent and 63 per cent, and for Great Britain 76.4 per cent and 39.5 per cent (Taylor 1984, p. 47). Coventry provides an exception with a rate of increase in unemployment for women only slightly above that for men. In 1973 Coventry's number of registered unemployed women was closer to the figure for men than in any other county TTWA. Thus economic decline has had a greater proportionate impact upon women workers than upon men. However, since 1980 the rate of increase in male unemployment has generally exceeded that of female unemployment, no doubt due to the impact of the post-1979 recession upon the manufacturing sector which is dominated by men (Taylor 1984, pp. 47–8).

Before 1979 economic slumps had particularly boosted female unemployment. Within the county TTWA the unemployment rate for women was 90 per cent of that for men in 1971 compared with 74 per cent in 1961 and 60 per cent in 1981. Outside the county, ratios of unemployment growth among women to that among men were consistently higher than they were within the county over the period 1961–81 (Smith 1984, pp. 105–6).

Long-term unemployment is of particular concern, indicating a structural change in industrial-sector job opportunities and producing higher personal and social costs, such as illness and divorce, than short-term unemployment. In July 1982 38.6 per cent of those unemployed (men and women) in the West Midlands Region had been without work for six months or more. This was the highest regional rate of long-term unemployment in Great Britain, and compared with a regional rate which was the second-lowest in Britain in 1974 (Taylor 1984, p. 49). The region has fared particularly badly in long-term unemployment, and the pace has accelerated. In October 1983 some 48.4 per cent of unemployed men in the region had been unemployed for more than a year, including 25.6 per cent for more than two years. Both figures were again the highest regional figures in Great Britain (Spencer 1985, par. 48). This reflects the very rapid growth locally and to a lesser extent nationally in long-term unemployment. The employment distress of the West Midlands is particularly highlighted by these figures, and the concentration of long-term unemployment within the region falls particularly within the West Midlands County (Ball 1983). It has been argued that long-term unemployment is a much more significant criterion of relative economic stress than short-term unemployment, and that its incidence is changing the location of job opportunities in the UK (Ball 1983; Green 1984). Ball's work shows the spread of long-term unemployment from the Birmingham, Coventry, and Wolverhampton TTWAs. Particularly since 1980 its incidence has become very pronounced in the Dudley–Sandwell and Walsall TTWAs. Indeed this trend has extended beyond the conurbation, with Redditch, Stoke-on-Trent, Oakengates (Telford), and Burton-on-Trent witnessing rapid growth in long-term unemployment (Ball 1983).

Long-term unemployment is concentrated among those over 45 years of age. In July 1982 some 74 per cent of the county's unemployed in this age-band were classified as long-term unemployed. For younger workers, job-creation and training schemes played a critical role in keeping the long-term unemployment rate lower than would otherwise have been the case. Nevertheless, the rate for the 16–18 age-band, based on six months' unemployment or more, was 27 per cent in July 1982 (Taylor 1984, p. 52). The figure was significantly higher for those in their early twenties.

Data for January 1984 place all the West Midlands County TTWAs on the list of the ten TTWAs having the highest rate nationally of long-term unemployment (of more than one year). Liverpool had the highest rate at, 50.3 per cent; Wolverhampton the second-highest at 48.7 per cent; Birmingham the third-highest, at 47.6 per cent; Dudley–Sandwell the fouth-highest, at 46.9 per cent; Walsall the sixth-highest, at 45.6 per cent; and Coventry the tenth-highest, at 44.1 per cent (BCIC 1984, Table 2). Within the BICP area the rate of long-term unemployment was 49.9 per cent. Data were not available for the BICP core area, but it would be expected that the rate would be much higher in that zone and hence likely to affect ethnic-minority groups to a greater extent (BCIC 1984, Table 6). The West Midlands Region, and the county in particular, have been affected by long-term unemployment to a greater degree than elsewhere in Great Britain. This change in fortunes has occurred rapidly and remains an extremely serious problem within the local economy, creating a multitude of connected emotional, financial, and social problems.

Local-authority Service Provision

The growth in unemployment and the differential socio-economic migration outward from the older residential areas, combined with reduced relative earnings, the fiscal stress increasingly felt by local authorities, and government policies restraining public expenditure, have led to enhanced financial problems for many in the West Midlands. We consider first earnings, then fiscal stress, social polarization, and problems facing key local-authority services.

From our study of earnings (reflecting levels of individual and household self-sufficiency) the following main points emerge (Smith 1984*b*). Between 1970 and 1983 relative earnings in the West Midlands fell from being the highest of any region in Great Britain in the early 1970s to being almost the lowest of any region by the early 1980s, a dramatic shift which particularly applied to earnings of male manual workers. No other region experienced such a sharp or consistent fall in men's earnings. Within the region the gradient of manufacturing earnings shows a general decline with distance from the West Midlands County, reflecting lower wages in the growing areas of the region. Three other regions with high and rising unemployment, Scotland, and north and north-west England experienced a rise in relative earnings, thus confounding any simplistic theory that labour surplus alone is the key to declining earnings. In the West Midlands the slackening of demand for labour has had some impact on eroding earnings of both men and women and in many industries. In particular, the significant reduction in both jobs and relative earnings in the motor-vehicle industry increased, if it did not cause, the fall in men's relative earnings.

The region moved down the regional rankings for relative earnings in two swift falls, losing six places in 1974/5 and a further three in 1979/80. The timing and scale of these falls closely match rises in unemployment in the region. At the same time the West Midlands experienced a greater decline in overtime working, a lower increase in payment by results, a decline in shift working, and persistently lower annual increases in earnings than other regions. This implies that the region was more affected than others by lack of intensification of work and reduced capacity. This has significance for local costs. Thus supply and demand in the labour market provides a broad explanation for the fall in relative earnings in the West Midlands, while that fall was accentuated by the significant decline in the size of the motor-vehicle workforce and rapid decline in their relative earnings.

One can argue that higher unemployment would lead more people to become self-employed and resolve their unemployment. Our evidence established no relationship between levels of unemployment and levels of self-employment. Changes in self-employment do not indicate any resurgence of small business in the region either to compensate for unemployment or to create new opportunities within the economy (Smith 1984*c*, p. 11).

The reductions in income described above mean greater costs and pressures falling upon central- and local-government services at a time of significant reduction in the resources available to local government. This leads to local fiscal stress, which we have analysed for local authorities within the West Midlands County (Flynn 1983).

Fiscal stress is defined as increasing demands on services not being matched by an increasing resource base. The county and district councils have undergone demographic and ecconomic decline which have increased pressures on local-authority services. Decline can reduce demand on services; it can also increase unit costs where there is an increasing proportion of lower income groups. The pattern of fiscal stress stems from a reduction in government grant, not from a declining local resource base.

From 1977/8 there was no significant decline in the local resource base until 1982/3. If county and district government block grants (at constant prices) are added together for the financial years 1979/80 to 1982/3, there was a decline of 16.7 per cent from £492.58 million to £410.26 million. The result has been a combination of price increases, rent increases, and cuts in services. Rates have increased but failed to compensate for grant loss. Cuts in expenditure have had a negative multiplier effect upon the community. In the case of Birmingham, loss of grant to the city and to the county council (in respect of city services) between 1981/2 and 1982/3 resulted in a reduction of £23.1 million in expenditure in the private sector. Loss of jobs in local government can often result in a switch of expenditure from one government department to another, for example, from the D.o.E. to the DHSS. These changing pressures on local government are giving rise to new challenges and opportunities in management (Spencer *et al.* 1985).

By 1984 one in three households in the West Midlands County lived at or below the official poverty line, while the number of persons claiming supplementary benefit in the county had risen 50 per cent since 1980. At the same time as pressure is felt on public resources, prospects for private-sector investment are not good. Many of the UK's biggest thirty-one pension funds, for example, are considering withdrawing investment from the county because of poor prospects for rates of return compared with elsewhere (WMCC, EDU 1984*b*). Thus both public and private resources are being squeezed in the county, decreasing further the prospects of future investment.

Social polarization in Birmingham is more marked than in other areas of the West Midlands County. The contrast between the inner and outer areas, on economic, social, and housing indices, is also more marked than in any other large inner-city-partnership area nationally (D.o.E. Inner Cities Directorate 1983*a*, p. 4). This particularly reflects the concentration of ethnic-minority groups in the inner city. Indeed the degree of socio-economic polarization is greater than anywhere else in the country except Teesside (Eversley and Begg 1986). At the same time the BICP area was in 1983 the most disadvantaged of all inner-city-partnership areas in Great Britain (D.o.E. Inner Cities Directorate 1983*a*, p. 1). Those indicators which were higher in 1981 for the BICP than for any other inner-city partnership area were unemployment, ethnic minorities, unemployment among 16–19 year-olds, low skill, and particularly overcrowded households. At the other extreme, the BICP had the lowest proportion of pensioners living alone (due in part to the frequency of extended family households among those of Asian origin) (D.o.E., Inner Cities Directorate 1983*a*, p. 3). The concentration of ethnic-minority groups is the cause of the strong polarization. It is correlated with high unemployment, low socio-economic structure, and poor educational attainment. Much of the movement out of the inner-city area has been by white people, leaving behind housing which has been taken up by second-generation members of ethnic-minority groups. Businesses run by and catering to members of ethnic-minority groups are found in many of the inner-city areas—for example, food shops, butchers, mosques, temples, banks, travel firms, clothing shops—increasing the attraction of these areas for ethnic-minority groups.

As regards housing, the inner-urban area of Birmingham compares more favourably with other inner-city areas in England (Eversley and Begg 1986), but this conceals the much wider extent of older housing in other parts of Birmingham. It also indicates the early-post-war housing redevelopment and active residential renewal programmes undertaken by the city. But problems remain. A survey of housing conditions in the West Midlands County under-taken in 1981/2 indicated that 45.1 per cent of the pre-1919 dwellings in Birmingham were in the BICP core area, 42.9 per cent of all unfit housing in the city was in the core area (most of it in owner-occupation), and 29.5 per cent of dwellings in the core area were unfit. By 1982 the core area contained twenty-two of the city's twenty-four Housing Action Areas and forty-five of its fifty-three General Improvement Areas (BICP 1984a, pp. 28, 34, 35). It thus remains an area of acute housing problems, especially in terms of over-crowding, and in the light of major reductions in public expenditure on hous-ing. At the same time the core area contained only 13 per cent of the public open space in the city, while containing 27 per cent of the city's residents (BICP 1984a, p. 28).

Other inner-city areas, in Wolverhampton, Sandwell, Walsall, and Coventry, had less adverse indicators in 1981; nevertheless they had prob-lems, albeit on a smaller scale. These areas '[showed] a very similar deficit with regard to favourable factors [in 1981], which means that in terms of their prospects they [did] not differ so much from inner Birmingham' (Evers-ley and Begg 1986).

Given the scale of these problems and their growing significance there has been rationalization of priority areas to fit resources available and to enable reduced resources to have an impact. In the late 1970s three types of priority area were defined within the county-structure-plan process, using 1971 cen-sus data: social priority areas, job priority areas, and environmental priority areas (WMCC 1983a, para. 2.2.2). With 1981 census data, these were reviewed. What has emerged, in effect, has been a tightening of defined prior-ity areas to concentrate resources in those areas of greatest need and where an impact could be made, for example, Industrial Improvement Areas. These more closely defined priority areas in aggregate cover a lesser area than previously. At the same time within the BICP an inner crescent of acute disadvantage and poor environment within the BICP core area has been defined. The purpose of this is to limit the impact of increasingly limited resources to a more confined area, thus producing greater impact and visibility (see Chapter 8). The problem remains, however, that the extent of disadvantage on various indices is increasing not contracting. Fiscal stress leads to greater concentration of resources on those areas with very acute problems, but lack of adequate intervention elsewhere will soon lead to magnified problems in other zones. Redefinition of priority areas for treatment merely redefines a problem and makes it appear more manageable. In reality, problems are growing, resources are inadequate, and the spiral of decline continues.

Lack of investment of both public and private resources is leading to deteriorating housing conditions. Current levels of investment are inadequate to reduce the need for housing improvement. Despite the decline in population in West Midlands County in 1971–81, the number of households increased by 37 400, reflecting smaller household size (WMFCC 1983, p. 10). Annual investment programmes and the county's own survey of housing conditions in 1981/2 show concentrations of poor housing in Birmingham, Sandwell, and Wolverhamptom, but also significant quantities in Coventry, Walsall, and Dudley (WMFCC 1983, p. 10). Poor housing is concentrated in pre-1914 housing in areas of poor environment and associated social and economic problems. Significant problems are also visible and emerging in the inter-war housing stock and in some newer council housing.

Housing finance has suffered most in the cutbacks in public expenditure, with capital expenditure falling faster than revenue. Expenditure on housing nationally fell by 63 per cent in the ten years to 1983/4 (WMFCC 1983, p. 11), and 40 per cent from 1979/80 to 1982/3. As a result, 'there is clear evidence that the rate of deterioration is exceeding the level of improvement and that more people, particularly the poor and disadvantaged groups, are trapped in poor housing conditions, while many of those who can afford better housing conditions are leaving the older areas' (WMFCC 1983, p. 14). Such migrants are largely white.

The result of lack of resources could well be that those with greatest housing need 'will increasingly live in deteriorating housing and environmental conditions' (WMFCC 1982, p. vii), leading to yet greater overcrowding. It also reinforces the polarity between social and ethnic groups, already accentuated in Birmingham. Investment by the private sector is not substituting for the lack of public-sector resources. In Birmingham the racial polarization of the inner-city market in owner-occupied housing means that Indian subcontinent Asians and, to a lesser extent, West Indians, bear the brunt of problems, notably concerning loans, and maintenance and improvement costs (Karn 1983, p. 3). The 1980s have seen a reversal of the steady improvement in both public and private housing which was achieved in the 1960s and 1970s. Deterioration combines rising costs with falling standards and 'is hitting the poorest and the black first and hardest, whether they are owner-occupiers or council tenants' (Karn 1983, p. 6). Thus housing-market mechanisms and the operation of the public sector are, because of reduced public and private resources, accelerating the spiral of decline in the inner-city areas.

Without higher levels of housing improvement and new construction, many will be trapped in poor conditions and, with the lack of employment opportunities, will find it difficult to gain access to better housing and environmental conditions (Johnson 1982, p. 198).

The provision of educational and social services is affected by retrenchment and, in the former case, by declining school rolls (though many inner-city rolls remain stable). The level and quality of service provided are in many cases declining. Maintenance and repair of older schools is inadequate; 24.6 per cent of primary schools and 16.3 per cent of secondary schools in the BICP core area were built before 1903 compared with 13.1 per cent and 7 per cent for Birmingham as a whole (BICP 1984a, p. 82). Schools are increasingly looking to their local communities for support, which leads to disparities between affluent and poorer areas. The proportion of free school meals and the rate of absenteeism/truancy are higher in the inner-city areas (BICP 1984a, p. 82). Budgets for school equipment have been reduced, and the West Midlands County has a low rate nationally of pupils staying on and gaining A levels. In terms of job competition this lower level of qualification of West Midlands school-leavers is disadvantageous in a situation where high unemployment among young people leads 'to young people taking work which does not match their education at a time when educational attainment levels are increasing' (Beacham 1984, p. 13).

Increased unemployment, lower incomes, and increases in the proportion of households at or below the poverty line, rates of divorce and marriage breakdown, alcoholism, drug abuse, longevity, single-parent families, and the crime rate all put pressure on the various personal social services. The widening tasks undertaken by social services have not been matched by an appropriate level of resources. The result is greater rationing and selectivity, as well as greater dependence upon individuals or households to resolve their own problems.

Housing, education, and social services, which accounted for between 78.8 per cent (Sandwell) and 87.1 per cent (Walsall) of district councils' total expenditures in the county in 1984/5, all have a direct impact upon the quality of life of those who are disadvantaged. Amelioration of many of the problems facing the disadvantaged in inner-urban areas will depend upon public resources, to which some private resources may be attracted. Investment by the public sector in jobs, the environment and improving quality of life is critical. Its erosion is leading to deteriorating conditions, primarily but not exclusively within inner-city areas. There is no mechanism at regional or city level for monitoring the effects of declining investment on urban services and on individuals, social groups, households, yet the evidence would suggest such monitoring is vital (Stewart 1981).

Note to Chapter 2

1 The Birmingham Inner City Partnership is a joint programme involving central government (through the D.o.E.), Birmingham City Council, the WMCC (before its abolition in Apr. 1986), and the Birmingham health authorities. Since its establishment in 1978, as an element of government policy dealing with inner-city problems, it has operated on the basis of a core area and an outer Partnership area, as defined in Fig. 8.1. A brief appraisal of the BICP is included in Chapter 8.

3

From Boom to Slump:
Economic Change in the West Midlands County

The area which now makes up the West Midlands County entered the 1960s as a vibrant, prosperous economy. The first half of the 1960s witnessed the culmination of the West Midlands post-war economic boom. All the requisites for high levels of output that had been evolving during the earlier post-war years reached their peak: population growth, immigration, employment, construction, and so forth (Wood 1976). In the mid-1960s high wages and high activity rates led to above-average family incomes. Unemployment was generally well below the national average (except during recession), and at times the rate fell below 1 per cent. Yet within only fifteen years the West Midlands County was experiencing levels of unemployment exceeding those recorded in some of the traditional 'depressed' regions of the UK economy. By 1983 more than 40 per cent of the economically active in the core of the conurbation were registered as unemployed. The economy of the West Midlands County had shifted from being one of the most prosperous in the UK to being an economy in crisis and decline.

This chapter traces the transition of the local economy from the prosperity of the 1960s to the rapid decline of the late 1970s and early 1980s. It begins by outlining how the role of the West Midlands as the industrial heartland of the UK shaped its fortunes from the mid-1960s onwards. In particular, it highlights the fact that those features of the local economy which underlay its growth were the same features and characteristics which were viewed as weaknesses in later years. It goes on to describe changes in employment, output, productivity, and investment between the mid-1960s and mid-1980s, establishing which of the indicators are important and when they changed.

The purpose of this chapter is, therefore, to place the present recession in the local economy in its evolutionary and historical context, for it is clear that the origins of the transition from prosperity to decline can be seen in the mid-1960s.

Although the present slump is of unrivalled magnitude in the post-war period, indications of the economy's weakness have been evident over at least two decades. For example, the West Midlands Economic Planning Council outlined the problems of the regional economy as early as 1965 and warned that 'national and world demand . . . may well continue to rise but whether this is reflected in the order books of the West Midlands will depend increasingly on the extent to which the region's firms keep up in research mindedness, invention, innovation and productive and marketing efficiency' (Department of Economic Affairs 1965). Shortly after its formation in 1974 the WMCC argued that 'A highly specialised, tightly-knit industrial area, consisting of a small number of large firms served by a large number of small firms is likely to be more vulnerable to external economic forces than a diversified balanced industrial area' (WMCC 1975, p. 18). This question of the industrial specialization of the economy is taken up in the following section.

The Industrial Structure of the West Midlands County

As Chapter 1 illustrated, the wealth and prosperity of the local economy in the immediate post-war years was built upon its manufacturing industries. The West Midlands was the industrial heartland of the country. As such, employment has been concentrated within this sector. As Table 3.1 illustrates, a higher proportion of total employment was to be found in the manufacturing sector in the West Midlands County than nationally throughout the period 1961–81. Consequently the West Midlands was hit by the deindustrialization of the national economy. In 1961 almost 65 per cent of the West Midlands County labour force was employed in manufacturing compared to 39 per cent in Great Britain as a whole, in 1971 the figures were 54 per cent and 36 per cent, and in 1978 they were 49 per cent and 32 per cent.

By June 1981, despite heavy job losses, more than 42 per cent of the workforce of the West Midlands County was still employed in the manufacturing sector compared to 28 per cent nationally. ·

Within manufacturing, a high degree of concentration was to be found in a small number of key sectors: vehicles, metal goods, metal manufacture, mechanical engineering, and electrical engineering. These five industrial sectors provided 80 per cent of manufacturing employment consistently throughout the period from 1961 to 1981, despite shedding some 320 000 jobs.

At a more disaggregate level, the West Midlands County economy is disproportionately dependent upon a small number of industries as defined by the Minimum List Headings (MLHs) of the Standard Industrial Classification (SIC). As Table 3.2 illustrates, more than 60 per cent of manufacturing employment was to be found in only fourteen MLHs in 1971, 1978, and 1981. Two of these, motor-vehicle manufacturing and metal industries not elsewhere specified, alone accounted for around a third of manufacturing employment.

Examining this same question of industrial specialization by reference to LQs, Table 3.3 lists those MLHs in the county with an LQ greater than 2. This means that the West Midlands County has at least twice the national concentration of employment within these ten MLHs. Those MLHs with the highest concentration and hence highest LQ are again involved in traditional metal-based industries.

Table 3.1. *Broad Industrial Structure: Percentage of Employees by Sector in the West Midlands County and Great Britain, 1961, 1971, 1978, and 1981*

Sector	1961		1971		1978		1981	
	WMC	GB	WMC	GB	WMC	GB	WMC	GB
Agriculture	0.28	2.55	0.16	1.94	0.16	1.67	0.17	1.75
Mining	0.49	3.28	0.26	1.82	0.22	1.58	0.19	1.58
Manufacturing	64.49	39.31	54.46	36.42	48.61	31.95	42.30	28.01
Construction	4.92	6.61	4.50	5.65	4.52	5.30	4.46	5.15
Services	29.73	48.26	40.42	54.18	46.49	59.29	51.24	63.51

Source: DE, *Annual Census of Employment.*

Table 3.2. *Key Minimum List Headings in the West Midlands County, 1971, 1978, and 1981*

MLH	No. employed		
	1971	1978	1981
Motor-vehicle manufacturing	151 658	127 560	92 959
Metal industries n.e.s.[a]	102 467	89 574	64 056
Other electrical goods	28 359	22 996	17 605
Iron and steel general	25 116	21 031	11 599
Copper, brass, and other copper alloys	24 847	21 522	16 008
Bolts, nuts, screws, rivets	24 326	17 499	10 469
Iron castings	23 326	21 411	13 389
Metal-working machine tools	21 479	14 909	10 572
Industrial plant and steelwork	19 670	17 744	10 394
Aerospace equipment	19 426	15 353	12 416
Steel tubes	19 380	17 344	12 249
Telegraph and telephone apparatus and equipment	17 716	12 472	14 488
Other mechanical engineering	17 268	15 017	13 685
Rubber	16 201	11 421	10 358
Combined share of manufacturing employment (%)	*65.3*	*63.7*	*62.1*

Note: [a] Not elsewhere specified.

Source: DE, *Annual Census of Employment*.

Table 3.3. *Industrial Sectors in the West Midland County with a Location Quotient Greater than 2, 1981*

MLH	LQ
Bolts, nuts, screws	6.8
Copper, brass, and other copper alloys	5.5
Steel tubes	4.3
Jewellery and precious metal	3.7
Metal industries n.e.s.[a]	3.3
Iron castings	3.3
Metal-working machine tools	2.9
Motor-vehicle manufacturing	2.8
Aluminium and aluminium alloys	2.6
Other electrical goods	2.3
Telegraph and telephone apparatus and equipment	2.2

Note: [a] Not elsewhere specified.

Source: DE, *Annual Census of Employment*.

Thus, the overall picture is of an economy heavily dependent upon a few key industries, with a level of specialization much greater than that of the national economy. It was upon this specialization within metal manufacturing and engineering that the prosperity of the West Midlands in the post-war period was built. In a period of decline, it was this same specialization which contained the seeds of local economic crisis. This problem of an economy specializing in a few key industries has been compounded by the high level of interlinkages and interdependence between industries and between a small number of large firms and a large number of small firms.

Linkages between industries and companies are strong both within the conurbation and extending out into the region (Wood 1976; Florence 1948). Central to the manufacturing base is the car industry, which not only directly employed more than 20 per cent of the West Midlands County's work-force in 1978 but also, through its purchases in other sectors, influenced and sustained employment in a wide range of industries (House of Commons Expenditure Committee 1975). A recession in a downstream part of these industries means a reduction in demand upstream. As the following sections indicate, it is reduced employment in the vehicle and other key industries which underlies the decline of the wider economy. Furthermore, this problem of the poor performance of key industries has been exacerbated by the failure of the economy to diversify, and by the under-representation in the county of 'growth' industries.

Employment Change in the West Midlands County

From the mid-1960s there was an erosion of the manufacturing base of the West Midlands County which accelerated through the 1970s. The number of manufacturing jobs in the county peaked in 1966 (WMCC 1978). From then manufacturing employment has been in decline. Between 1965 and 1981 some 369 500 jobs were lost, with particularly dramatic falls in employment between 1974 and 1976 and during the recession between 1978 and 1981 (see Figure 3.1). During this period almost 25 per cent of jobs in the manufacturing sector in the county were lost, a rate of job loss significantly higher than that occurring nationally (Taylor 1983).

This contraction of the manufacturing base was the end result of employment decline within the key industrial sectors of the economy. As indicated in Chapter 2, employment in the vehicle industry alone contracted by some 40 per cent between 1971 and 1981, while more than 40 per cent of the jobs in metal manufacture have also gone. Decline has been almost as great in the metal-goods and mechanical-engineering industries (Flynn and Taylor 1984).

Although the scale of job loss in manufacturing has been dramatic and a continual feature of the local economy since the mid-1960s, concern for the future of employment was not voiced until the rapid rise in unemployment experienced by the county in the late 1970s. In part this was due to an expansion of employment in the service sector; the gain of 58 945 jobs in this sector between 1971 and 1978 partly compensated for the loss of 108 427 jobs in

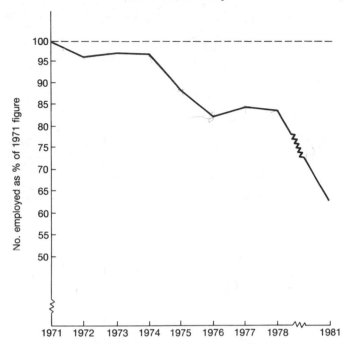

Fig. 3.1 Manufacturing Employment change in the West Midlands County, 1971–81.

Source: DE, *Annual Census of Employment*.

manufacturing. When adjusted for demographic changes, such as the fall in the number of economically active persons in the county, the rate of unemployment, although higher than that experienced in the 1960s, remained close to the national average up until 1978.

However, with the acceleration of decline within manufacturing and the cessation of expansion of employment in the service sector after 1978, unemployment has risen dramatically. In the three years to 1981 total employment in the West Midlands County declined by almost 12 per cent, very nearly twice the national rate of decline. The rate of manufacturing decline has already been discussed, but perhaps of greater note is that in contrast to earlier periods service employment also fell. This was in opposition to the national trend which was a slight increase in service employment (see Table 3.4).

Thus, the present malaise affecting the West Midlands economy is the result of a sustained period of decline in the core manufacturing industries of the county. Their decline did not represent a fundamental shift in the character of the economy away from its metal-manufacturing and vehicle-related origins upon which post-war prosperity was built towards a greater involvement in service or more technologically advanced industries. Rather, the past

Table 3.4. Employment Change by Percentage per Year in the West Midlands County and Great Britain, 1961–1981

	1961–1969		1971–1978		1978–1981		1971–1981	
	WMC	GB	WMC	GB	WMC	GB	WMC	GB
Agriculture	−4.7	−5.9	−1.1	−1.6	−1.4	−0.2	−1.2	−1.2
Mining	−7.4	−4.6	−2.8	−1.5	−7.0	−1.6	−3.7	−1.5
Manufacturing	−0.8	−0.1	−2.0	−1.4	−7.7	−5.6	−3.4	−2.5
Construction	0.9	−0.3	−1.1	0.03	−4.3	−3.7	−2.0	−1.1
Services	1.3	0.9	1.5	1.8	−0.9	0.5	0.7	1.2
Total	0.03	0.13	−0.57	0.4	−3.92	−1.68	−1.53	−0.23

Source: DE, Annual Census of Employment.

Table 3.5. *Numbers Employed by Sector in the West Midlands County, 1961–1981*

Sector	1961[a]	1969[a]	1971[a]	1978[b]	1981[b]
Agriculture	3 956	2 454	2 291	2 019	2 019
Mining	6 855	2 775	3 633	2 910	2 295
Manufacturing	892 283	837 774	759 402	650 975	499 858
Construction	68 060	73 063	65 523	60 515	52 679
Services	411 289	452 914	563 636	622 671	623 514
Other	991	11 255	1	27	1 313
Total	1 383 434	1 380 235	1 394 486	1 339 117	1 181 678

Notes: [a] Using 1958 SICs.
   [b] Using 1968 SICs.
Source: DE, *Annual Census of Employment*.

two decades have witnessed the failure of the local economy to diversify. The overall pattern of change was one of employment decline within the key manufacturing sectors of the local economy, the rate of decline being more rapid in the county than that experienced by these industries nationally. This drop in manufacturing employment was partly offset by an increase in service employment, although the county's employment performance was poor when compared to national trends. As Table 3.5 illustrates, the West Midlands economy remains highly specialized in manufacturing and under-represented in services.

A shift-share analysis of employment change in the West Midlands County, 1971–1981

Shift–share analysis breaks down employment change over a period into three major components—the national component, the structural component, and the differential component. The *national component* is defined as the change that would have occurred had local employment changed at the same rate as total national employment and if the local economy had an industrial structure exactly the same as the nation. The *structural component* is defined as the change in local employment that would have occurred had local employment in each industry changed at the same rate as in each industry nationally. The sum of the national and structural shifts gives a hypothetical 'expected' change, expected in the sense that, all other things being equal, a locality and its industries would grow at the same rate as the nation. The final component, the *differential component* represents the residual local employment change not 'expected' on the basis of national and industrial changes.

If a locality has a high proportion of its employment in national growth industries this favourable industrial structure will be reflected in a strong positive structural component. A high proportion of its employment in declining sectors would be reflected in a negative structural component. A

Table 3.6. *Shift-share Analysis of Employment Change in the West Midlands County: Number of Jobs Affected by Sector, 1971–1981*

Sector	Component			Actual change
	National	Structural	Differential[a]	
1971–1981				
Agriculture	−2 680	2 408	0	−272
Mining	−3 299	2 750	−799	−1 348
Manufacturing	−123 177	−57 521	−78 846	−259 544
Construction	−8 215	1 188	−5 817	−12 844
Services	120 329	−37 896	−22 555	59 878
Total	−17 042	−89 071	−108 017	−214 120
1971–1978				
Agriculture	−3 812	3 551	80	−182
Mining	−3 338	2 949	−334	−723
Manufacturing	−42 055	−31 736	−34 636	−108 427
Construction	−186	348	−5 170	−5 008
Services	89 847	−18 621	−12 281	58 945
Total	40 450	−43 509	−52 340	−55 369
1978–1981				
Agriculture	883	−893	−80	−90
Mining	−122	−19	−474	−615
Manufacturing	−82 845	−26 299	−42 333	−151 117
Construction	−7 434	808	−1 210	−7 836
Services	30 482	−19 275	−10 274	933
Total	−59 036	−45 678	−54 371	−157 439

Note: [a] The differential shift represents the residual after the national and structural shifts have been deducted from the actual changes in employment. Figures do not add precisely because of rounding etc.

Source: Calculated from DE, *Annual Census of Employment* data using 1968 SICs.

strong differential component may indicate the importance of factors other than industrial structure, although it should be noted that these other factors cannot be identified or assumed from the shift–share analysis. Shift–share is a descriptive not an explanatory technique. However, it may provide clues to explanations of employment change and it is an alternative way of examining the raw data.

A shift–share analysis has been carried out for the West Midlands County based on SIC categories for the period 1971–81, and the periods 1971–78 and 1978–81 to see if the area performed differently prior to and during recession. The results are summarized in Table 3.6.

The purpose of the shift–share technique is to analyse actual employment change in such a way as to isolate as far as possible the effects that can be considered to reflect:

(a) the national rate of growth of employment overall or by sector (the national shift or component)
(b) the national rate of growth of employment in each industry (here at order level), thus taking into account the effects on local employment of the mix of local industries, but still assuming growth in these industries at the national rate (the structural shift or component)
(c) other influences on local employment (the differential shift or component).

The differential component is simply a residual. It is considered to indicate 'indigenous performance', including any net inward movement of industry, though this is not an important item in the West Midlands County.

From Table 3.6 it is evident that the structural and differential components in overall employment have been similar in size in each period, with the differential one a little larger in each period (10 000 jobs larger in the shorter periods; 20 000 larger over 1971–81). It is actually the national component that switches from positive in 1971–8 to negative in 1978–81, and the figure is larger for the latter, shorter period. In consequence, the national component is negative and small for 1971–81 and far outweighed in its effect on actual employment in the West Midlands County by the structural and differential components. Thus, the county's employment record is shown to have been better than the national one over 1971–8 but markedly worse over 1978–81. The structural mix was adverse throughout the 1970s with an even more substantially adverse differential component, implying poor indigenous performance.

Turning to manufacturing employment change, we find a distinct difference by period. A massive actual loss in manufacturing of just over 100 000 jobs between 1971 and 1978 and just over 150 000 jobs between 1978 and 1981 is involved. For 1971–8, all three components for manufacturing are negative and about the same size (30 000–40 000), with the national shift the largest of the three at −42 055. For 1978–81, the three components differ from each other and from the earlier period. All are still negative. The national component, at −82 845, is roughly double what it was for the earlier period and much larger than the other two components for the later period. It is almost double the differential component at −42 333 and almost treble the structural component at −26 299. Thus the West Midlands County had fared worse than the national economy in manufacturing in both periods, but far worse in 1978–81. In both periods, the differential component, i.e. indigenous performance, was substantially negative, outweighing the structural component, and being almost double the structural component in 1978–81.

In the service sector, the base was quite different from that in manufacturing because there was an overall growth in jobs between 1971 and 1981, though this growth occurred almost entirely in the 1971–8 period. Overall, while manufacturing lost more than 250 000 jobs, services grew by almost 60 000 jobs. However, the shift–share analysis shows this growth to have been entirely due to the national component. That was large, at 89 847, for 1971–8 and still substantial, at 30 482, for 1978–81. Thus, in services, the West Midlands County bettered the national economy's growth record. Both the other components were negative in both periods and not dissimilar in size. In both periods, the (negative) structural component was larger than the (negative) differential component by about 50 per cent—in contrast to manufacturing, where the differential exceeded the structural.

Thus, the local industrial structure in the West Midlands County was more disadvantageous to the service sector than to manufacturing relative to local influences reflected in indigenous performance (though the structural component was smaller in absolute terms in services than in manufacturing).

In manufacturing the West Midlands County scored badly compared to the national economy, and in services it scored well. In manufacturing, the county scored worse in the later period, 1978–81; in services, it scored better in the earlier period. Overall the West Midlands County did relatively worse in 1978–81, and cumulatively for 1971–81 ended with negative components all round. Thus between 1971 and 1981, the differential component of −108 017 explained half of the overall actual loss of 214 120 jobs, but the 1978–81 fall in jobs was more significant.

The Economic Performance of the West Midlands

The poor employment performance of the West Midlands reflects the area's poor performance on other economic indicators. In both County and region there have been low levels of net output, a poor investment record, and low levels of productivity.

To begin with investment, although data are only available for the West Midlands Region, Table 3.7 shows that investment in manufacturing has been consistently below the region's share of manufacturing employment. Furthermore, investment in manufacturing per capita has been the lowest of any region. It has been suggested that this low level of investment was due to the region's industrial structure (see D.o.E. 1975). However, in their analysis of individual industry reports for 1970–2 from the Census of Production the WMCC concluded: 'The results show quite clearly that the poor employment performance of the West Midlands cannot be simply related to its industrial structure. Indeed over the three years this would have led one to expect it to have recorded some £127 million more investment (an increase of over 21%) than it actually did' (WMCC 1978, p. 27).

The region's poor investment record did not change after 1972. Net capital expenditure per employee in manufacturing was consistently below the

Table 3.7. *The West Midlands Region's Shares of Manufacturing Investment and Employment as Percentages of UK Totals, 1961 and 1971–1981*

	1961	1971	1972	1973	1974	1975	1976	1977	1978	1979	1980	1981
Manufacturing investment	10.6	10.2	9.8	11.2	11.6	10.6	10.2	10.3	10.5	10.1	10.8	9.7
Manufacturing employment	13.8	13.6	13.5	13.6	13.6	13.6	13.4	13.5	13.5	13.4	13.3	12.8

Source: Business Statistics Office, Business Monitor, *Census of Production* (London, 1961, 1971–81).

national average in the period up to 1981. In fact, the West Midlands's performance marginally deteriorated. With the exception of the food, drink, and tobacco industries, the level of investment per employee in the West Midlands was generally less than the national average across the spectrum of broad industrial groups. Only in 1976 did the crucial engineering and allied industries record a level of net investment per employee in the West Midlands greater than the national average (see Table 3.8).

Thus investment in manufacturing in the West Midlands, 'falls far short of what is required, and as a result much of the region's capital stock has not been renewed and has become increasingly obsolete' (Miller 1981). Given the poor investment record of the UK as a whole relative to rival industrial economies, the implications for the international competitiveness of local industry are serious.

This poor record of investment has been reflected in low and declining levels of productivity across all manufacturing industry. The work of Mawson and Smith (1980) has illustrated that the West Midlands Region has been consistently low ranked when net output per employee across all UK regions is analysed. Furthermore this poor performance extended across all manufacturing industries. Throughout the 1970s net output per employee in the region was some 13 per cent below the UK average (see Figure 3.2). In addition the region's share of total net output by manufacturing industry in the UK has been declining since 1974. Thus by 1981, whereas 12.8 per cent of the nation's manufacturing work-force were to be found in the West Midlands, they produced only 11.2 per cent of national net manufacturing output.

The net result of all these factors is that regional gross domestic product (GDP), the value of all currently produced goods and services for final demand, has been falling relative to the UK average and as a share of the UK total. In the early 1960s GDP per head of the regional population was nearly 10 per cent higher than in the UK as a whole. The region was second only to the South-east of England in terms of relative prosperity (Mawson and Taylor 1983). Although there is some evidence that this advantage was declining slowly through the 1960s, the period from 1970 to 1976 witnessed a fall in the region's share of the UK total GDP. The cumulative effect of this fall in GDP per head was to bring the region more in line with the estimates for Scotland, the North of England, the East Midlands, and Yorkshire and Humberside in 1976 (see Table 3.9).

However, after 1976 the region's relative position worsened dramatically. Between 1976 and 1981 the West Midlands experienced the greatest change in GDP per head as a percentage of the UK average of any region: a fall from 98.1 per cent in 1976 to 90.6 per cent in 1981. The region had shifted from being second only to the South-east in economic prosperity in 1976 to being the poorest region in England in 1981. Nationally only Northern Ireland and Wales had a GDP per head below that of the West Midlands.

Table 3.8. *Net Capital Expenditure per Employee, Broad Industrial Distribution, West Midlands Region and the UK, 1973, 1976, 1978, and 1981*

	Food, drink, and tobacco (III)		Coal, petroleum, chemical products, and metal manufacture (IV–VI)		Engineering and allied (VII–XII)		Textile, leather, clothing (XIII–XV)		Other manufacturing (XIII–XV)		Total manufacturing (III–XIX)	
	£	Index (UK=100)	£	Index (UK=100)	£	Index (UK=100)	£	Index (UK=100)	£	Index (UK=100)	£	Index (UK=100)
1973												
UK	475.8		551.5		193.9		215.5		310.0		291.5	
West Midlands Region	549.1	115	267.1	48	165.7	85	164.1	76	323.8	104	224.2	77
1976												
UK	685.0		1553.7		352.4		238.9		419.4		537.6	
West Midlands Region	774.5	113	507.3	33	367.7	104	188.6	79	430.3	102	412.3	76
1978												
UK	1149.7		1872.7		592.9		346.7		714.6		805.1	
West Midlands Region	1336.5	116	634.0	34	578.2	96	304.3	88	577.0	81	613.1	76
1981[a]												
UK	1341.0		1930.5		899.0		336.0		683.5		951	
West Midlands Region	1534.0	114	975.5	50	801.0	89	248.0	74	598.0	87	719	75

Note: [a] The figures for 1981 are not strictly comparable with earlier figures as they are based on the revised 1980 SICs.

Source: Business Statistics Office, Business Monitor, *Census of Production* (London, 1973, 1976, 1978, 1981).

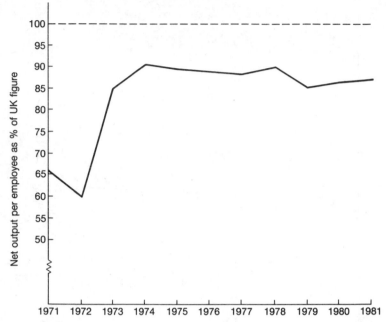

Fig. 3.2. Net output per employee in the West Midlands Region compared
with the UK, 1971–81.
Source: Regional statistics, 1983.

Thus the decline of the West Midlands economy has been characterized by
a fall-off in investment, productivity, output, and employment. All these
economic indicators performed badly from the late 1960s onwards and
caused the local economy's malaise in the late 1970s and early 1980s. The
present downturn in the West Midlands is not therefore a response to the
cyclical slump in the national and international economy but part of a long-
term, structural decline in the economy. Recovery nationally may not produce recovery locally.

Corporate Structure and Change within the West Midlands County

Reference was made in Chapter 1 to the major features of the organization of
economic activity within the West Midlands County. In particular, the move
towards the concentration of economic power in a small number of large
companies was highlighted. The 1960s and early 1970s saw the culmination
of this process of concentration and centralization of industry as the merger
boom which was affecting the whole of the UK economy took effect locally.

In the car industry, increased competition both domestically and world-
wide sparked off a series of defensive and offensive mergers and takeovers.
Leyland, the truck company based in the North-west region, for example,

Table 3.9. *Gross Domestic Product per Head in UK Regions as Percentage of UK GDP per Head, 1971–1981*

Region	1971	1972	1973	1974	1975	1976	1977	1978	1979	1980	1981
West Midlands	102.8	101.1	100.3	100.3	99.9	98.1	97.0	97.2	95.7	92.6	90.3
North	86.9	88.7	90.2	91.5	94.1	96.2	95.7	93.3	92.8	93.9	94.5
Yorkshire and Humberside	93.3	93.1	93.0	95.1	94.6	94.6	95.6	95.1	93.7	93.4	92.4
East Midlands	96.6	97.8	98.2	96.1	96.4	96.3	96.9	95.5	96.2	96.6	95.5
East Anglia	93.6	92.2	94.3	92.4	92.3	93.8	95.2	95.0	94.2	96.3	96.9
South-east	113.7	113.7	113.0	113.5	113.3	112.7	112.6	113.8	115.3	115.5	115.9
South-west	94.8	95.2	94.4	93.4	90.6	91.0	91.9	92.2	93.4	94.4	95.3
North-west	96.2	96.9	96.8	96.5	96.1	96.3	97.3	98.3	96.4	96.6	95.1
Wales	88.3	88.6	88.8	87.0	89.3	89.9	89.1	87.3	87.0	85.8	84.6
Scotland	93.0	92.8	94.9	95.5	96.4	97.8	96.4	95.1	94.8	95.0	98.6
Northern Ireland	74.3	71.5	72.2	73.2	75.6	75.1	74.0	72.4	72.6	72.6	75.5

Source: Regional statistics, 1983.

bought out an ailing Standard Triumph in 1961. The company then went on
to acquire Aveling Barford and later Rover. At the same time the BMC (itself
the result of a merger between Austin and Morris in the 1950s) merged with
Jaguar to form British Motor Holdings (BMH), which in 1968 joined with
Leyland to form the British Leyland Motor Corporation.

Behind these major mergers lay a series of other changes in ownership and
control. Jaguar, for example, had taken over Guy in 1962, Daimler in 1960,
Coventry Climax in 1963, and Henry Meadows in 1964. BMC had also taken
over Pressed Steel Fisher & Ludlow, who specialized in bodywork, while
Standard–Triumph brought Mulliners (another body specialist) to Leyland
after acquiring Rover and took over Alvis, a military-vehicle specialist. In
addition, Rootes was taken over by the American-owned Chrysler in 1967.
This succession of defensive and offensive mergers had a profound effect on
both the UK car industry and the local economy, leaving only one major car
manufacturer not in foreign ownership and placing the fortunes of the key
industry in the West Midlands largely in the hands of one company, British
Leyland.

Elsewhere in the economy, acquisition and merger further centralized and
concentrated control. By 1977 twenty-five companies represented approximately 48 per cent of manufacturing employment in the county. Given the
high degree of industrial interlinkage within the economy, their importance
in shaping the fortunes of the West Midlands would be considerable. Thus,
as Liggins (1977) argues, the West Midlands had become an over-specialized
economy dependent on a much smaller number of very large firms.

In addition to this concentration of employment within a smaller number
of companies, employment in the county was also concentrated in a small
number of large plants. Although the majority of industrial establishments in
the West Midlands County are in the small employment-size-bands—62.3
per cent of units in the county in 1981 employed fewer than 50 employees—
most manufacturing employment was concentrated in the 500-and-over
employment-size-band. In 1978, 52.1 per cent of manufacturing employment
in the county was in plants employing more than 500 persons, compared
with only 39.4 per cent nationally.

The significance of this characteristic is illustrated in the components-
of-change analysis constructed by the Department of Industry (DI) Regional
Data System for the study area. If change in manufacturing employment is
broken down into its component parts for the periods 1975–8 and 1975–81, a
number of noteworthy features emerge (see Table 3.10). First, not surprisingly, the deterioration in employment opportunities worsened in the period
1978–81 relative to the period 1975–8. Second, employment decline has been
heavily concentrated in the 500-and-over employed-size-band, with decline
within these plants being the dominant process of change. Third, the only
increases in manufacturing employment were in plants employing fewer than
200 in the early 1975–8 period, with greater growth in the 21–50 band. These

Table 3.10. *Manufacturing Industry. Employment Change by Plant Size in the West Midlands County, 1975–1978 and 1978–1981*

Size band	Change in employment level (%)	
	1975–1978	1978–1981
11–20	−4.0	−24.7
21–50	+3.5	−13.9
51–200	−0.4	−19.5
201–500	−4.7	−25.0
500+	−9.1	−32.9
Total	−5.7	−28.4

Source: DI, Regional Data System.

observations should, however, be viewed with caution, given the potential for bias within the DI Regional Data System.[1]

Thus economic growth during the post-war period created a regional economy dominated by large plants and corporations. While this was a reflection of the pre-eminence of the West Midlands as the industrial heartland of the nation, it also meant that the regional economy was increasingly dependent upon the fortunes of a small number of large corporations. As will be discussed in Chapter 5, given the nature of change in the international economy, the increasing internationalization of production, and the growth of transnational corporations, the local economy was opened up to the global corporate strategies of a small number of transnational companies. Decisions about local plants were therefore influenced more by concern with global corporate profit than by concern with the individual efficiency or profitability of specific plants.

Economic Decline

The picture that therefore emerges from this discussion of change in the West Midland County's economy, is that decline has evolved into crisis. The narrow range of metal-based industries on which the post-war prosperity of the local economy was built have been on the downturn since the mid 1970s. Manufacturing employment has been falling since the mid-1960s and the 1980s recession has merely accelerated a more fundamental process of decline. Nor can this decline be explained by national trends or solely by the industrial structure of the local area. For as the shift–share analysis illustrated, these two factors were responsible for only part of the loss of employment in manufacturing. It is the unexplained differential component that is of crucial importance: why did the manufacturing sector in the West Midlands perform so poorly compared with manufacturing in the UK as a whole? The scale of problem facing the local economy is magnified when the UK's poor showing against other national economies is recognized.

Table 3.11. *Distribution of Employment by Sex, in the West Midlands County 1971 and 1978*

Sector	No. employed				Employmentchange 1971–1978 (% per annum)	
	Male		Female			
	1971	1978	1971	1978	Male	Female
Primary	19 225	14 974	12 034	9 542	−7.59	−6.79
Manufacturing	557 295	480 878	202 107	170 097	−1.96	−2.26
Construction	59 657	53 182	5 866	7 333	−1.56	3.57
Services	270 169	269 783	293 467	335 440	−0.02	2.04
Total	892 162	820 816	502 324	518 801	−1.14	0.45

Source: DE, *Annual Census of Employment.*

Part of the answer obviously lies in the local economy's poor performance on other economic indicators. Investment in manufacturing in the West Midlands has been low compared with the national average, even when industrial structure is taken into account. This has led to low productivity and a fall in the share of UK GDP in the region. However, this still begs the questions: why was investment not forthcoming and why was net output per employee not improved? It is to these questions that the next section of the book turns.

The other crucial question that also needs to be answered is: why did the local economy fail to diversify? Nationally the growing service sector has been the major arena of job generation. Although the West Midlands benefited to some degree from this process, its releative performance was again poor. Service employment did increase but not at the national rate. The recent fall in service employment against the national trend is a cause for concern, particularly since jobs in the service sector may be filled by new entrants to the labour market, who may be part-time rather than full-time, and may be more likely to be filled by women. This was certainly the case in the period of growth in the West Midlands (see Table 3.11). Thus an emphasis on developing service industries may not be the panacea for manufacturing decline.

The net result of all these trends is that fewer jobs have been available to those seeking work. Before the late 1970s demographic change helped to disguise the scale of problems facing the county, but recently the large influx of young workers into the job market has raised the level of unemployment. Thus in the county TTWA in 1981 the total economically active population was about the same as in 1961, but the employed population had actually fallen by 12 per cent since 1961. Chapter 2 has shown the relationship between population change, employment change, and unemployment.

Thus two processes of change have been occurring. Firstly, there has been decline in the numbers employed, while stability in the numbers of economically active persons (although the number of economically active men has fallen, the number of economically active women has increased) has led to a steady increase in job scarcity and rising unemployment. Secondly, there has been a redistribution of both population and employment from the conurbation to the surrounding areas. This urban–rural shift has been a feature of economic change throughout the UK in the post-war period (Fothergill and Gudgin 1982).

The year 1966 can be viewed as a watershed for the local economy in so far as 'that year saw the peak in many statistical indicators of economic health in the County' (Smith 1978*a*, p. 13). After 1966 local unemployment worsened relative to that in the UK as a whole, and since 1978 the county unemployment rate has been steadily rising relative to the national average.

Thus the unprecedented high levels of unemployment being experienced by the West Midlands County in the mid-1980s (see Chapter 2) are not the result of cyclical downturns in the national economy, as in the past, but are the result of more fundamental changes. The scale of industrial dereliction and the wholesale closure of industrial plants bear witness to the depth of the crisis which the West Midlands's industry is experiencing. Many of the famous company names of West Midlands industry no longer exist or are shadows of their former selves, having been forced to rationalize drastically their operations in order to survive. The landscape of the West Midlands has been fundamentally altered. An upturn in the national economy would not by itself solve the problems of the local economy or lead to a massive reduction in unemployment in the West Midlands. The industrial capacity no longer exists there. The industrial heartland of the UK economy is slowly becoming an industrial wasteland.

Note to Chapter 3

1   The Regional Data Bank has a number of limitations. Notably there is a potential for under-recording openings and a bias in the lower employment-size-bands, as the 1981 figures are based on the Census of Production for which only a sample survey is undertaken for units employing fewer than 100 persons, with very little sampling of units employing fewer than 20.

4

Some Explanations for Local Economic Change

This chapter examines some of the available explanations for the economic changes which have been recorded in earlier chapters. This theme of explanation is continued in Chapter 5, which concentrates upon the behaviour of the large firms in the local economy, and part of Chapter 6, which deals with the effects of central-government policy on the local economy.

The present chapter focuses on those explanations which can throw some light at both the inter-regional and intra-regional levels upon the spatial distribution of decline and change within the West Midlands. It is based on a condensation of two working papers which have specifically addressed this issue of explanation (Smith 1984 and 1985).

Approaches to explanation relating to business performance in the West Midlands are considered. It is poor performance in holding and winning markets at adequate profits that has given rise to the shift of industrial employment and plants away from the West Midlands County to the rest of the region, other parts of the country, and abroad. This spatial shift reflects the relative disadvantage in operating conditions in the West Midlands County and its inner-urban areas.

Urban–rural shift in the UK as a whole involves the large cities in losing manufacturing industry to their surrounding medium-sized and smaller towns as well as to rural communities (Fothergill and Gudgin 1982; Goddard and Champion 1983). This trend has also been noted in the USA and parts of Europe (Keeble Owens and Thompson 1983; Hall and Hay 1980).

Four elements can be disaggregated from this shift:

(a) the impact of national and international competition, producing changes in corporate policies to redress uncompetitiveness; this rationalization and restructuring is manifest spatially as firms appraise their various locational options

(b) conditions in the big cities which lead to disinvestment. Massey and Meegan (1978, p. 287) emphasize labour as the crucial factor in de-industrialization of the cities

(c) a reduction in employment per unit of factory space but increased capital investment in industrial plants, which increases pressure on floor space and industrial-land supply

(d) the shortage of vacant, good industrial land and buildings in the big cities.

All these elements work to generate the urban–rural shift out of the West

Midlands County and work through the factors identified in the explanations elaborated below. Nine types of explanation are to be considered. Each is discussed in turn, with reference made to subsequent chapters where explanation is further developed.

Locational, Environmental, and Natural Resources

The proposition here is that the size, location, accessibility (Clark 1966; with critique in Brown 1972, pp. 160–2), terrain, climate, and resources of an area may influence its decline if they cease to remain appropriate for continued development. Such a proposition does not seem to fit the West Midlands with its central position in the UK and improving nodal transport position. However, wider trading changes have reduced the significance of these and exposed their limitations (for example, the lack of a motorway to the East-Anglian ports). The key challenge is the counter-urbanization trend (Berry 1976) which implies a fundamental devaluation of large city environments and amenities by both people and industry. This has reinforced economic decline in the West Midlands County.

Industrial Structure

The argument here is that the industrial structure of an area influences its growth or decline according to whether its industries, especially the dominant ones, happen to be growing or declining in demand nationally (Brown 1972, p. 85). This emphasis on demand contrasts with an emphasis on supply when factors of production are being considered. In practice, uncompetitiveness leading to loss of markets is more common than falling demand *per se*, with some loss of jobs resulting from labour-saving where orders have been retained.

There has been controversy recently about the continued influence of industrial structure on the growth or decline of an area, partly deriving from differences in the measures, dates, scales, and locations used in the descriptive technique of shift–share analysis (Fothergill and Gudgin 1979, pp. 167–9; Keeble 1976, pp. 42–5; Chisholm and Oeppen 1973) and partly from differences in findings. As Danson, Lever, and Malcolm (1980, p. 202) suggest, if a favourable industrial structure such as they found in eight conurbations (including the West Midlands) in the 1960s was associated then with loss of jobs, it would be unwise to rely on that explanation in subsequent years. It is worth noting that shift–share comparisons are invariably made with national, not world, trends, hiding the fact of national decline. (See Chapter 3 for shift–share analysis for the West Midlands.) There has thus been a move to find explanations other than industrial structure for local decline. The concern has been with lack of self-sustaining indigenous economic growth. Attention has turned to the more subtle effects of industrial specialization in large capital-intensive firms and industries (see Chapter 5) and to the formation of new firms and innovation in business products (Segal 1979; Checkland 1981; Cousins *et al.* 1974). In the West Midlands the industrial structure was favourable to growth until after 1966 (Tyler 1980, p. 161). Keeble (1978, p. 104) pronounced it as having the second most favourable structure in the whole country in 1959.

The conclusion is that performance rather than structure is crucial (see also Chapters 5 and 6) and it is in this that conurbations and inner-urban areas have been defective (Lloyd and Dicken 1982, p. 9). Notwithstanding this, in the West Midlands County and its inner-urban areas, the industrial structure became adverse to employment maintenance, let alone growth, after 1967 and has remained adverse into the 1980s. There is therefore a strong possibility that structural disadvantage is an explanation for decline in the West Midlands. However, it is a descriptive rather than causal explanation. It is necessary to go behind industrial structure to find out why West Midland (and UK) firms have failed to sustain their share of world markets through lack of competitiveness.

Factors of Production

This explanation suggests that the factors of production available in the West Midlands County have been relatively uncompetitive. Making some allowance for satisficing, environmental standards, and corporate considerations, businesses are likely to seek to locate where costs are likely to be low, profits high, and prospects good. The West Midland County and its inner-urban areas were competitive and attractive locations for manufacturing until the 1960s. Is an explanation for decline simply that local factors of production have ceased to be competitive, so that industry is draining away via closure, shrinkage, and transfer? If so, was there a big change in the national competitiveness of local factors of production around 1967 and around 1979? Factors of production are examined under four sub-headings.

Land and premises

The factor of production land and premises is the central issue in the explanation of urban–rural shift put forward by Fothergill and Gudgin (1979 and 1982), and Fothergill, Gudgin, Kitson, and Monk (1984), and Fothergill, Kitson, and Monk (1985). The argument turns on two national economic trends: 'The first is the decline in the number of workers per unit of factory space . . . The second . . . is the increase in industry's demand for floor space' (Fothergill, Kitson, and Monk 1985, p. 2). Both trends constrain industrial development and modernization in the cities and push firms and jobs out to places where space is more readily available and existing firms are able to expand more easily than those in the cities. According to this view, it is the constraint on space that has caused decline in employment in cities rather than the economics of city locations (Fothergill, Kitson, and Monk 1985, pp. 15–17). With that theory in mind, we look at land and premises separately.

Land   Many factors (history, competition for land, dereliction not cleared by market forces, the Green Belt, the Industrial Development Certificate (IDC)) constrain or constrained industrial-land supply in the West Midlands County. The pressure of demand has not been strong enough to break through these. The supply of industrial land is particularly limited in Birmingham. Within the West Midlands County in 1983 there were only twenty-five vacant sites of more than 8 hectares of which only 182 hectares were available immediately. Demand was running at 65–190 hectares per annum between 1974 and 1982 (WMFCC 1985*b*). These limitations on supply are confirmed by other recent research (CURS 1984). Sites are being provided in surrounding counties and are proposed in the Green Belt on the edge of the county. Outside the county, abundant green-field sites exist in the surrounding counties to tempt industry across the Green Belt. Fothergill, Kitson and Monk (1985, p. 54) calculate that availability of industrial land per 1000 manufacturing employees in 1982 was five times greater in the rural areas and two and a half times greater in the small towns of the West Midlands Region than in the county.

But the industrial-land situation did not suddenly change for the worse in 1967, when IDC policy began to bite (see Carter 1977). The major change was the suspension of the IDC control in 1979, though policy implementation was relaxed in 1971–2. Considerable efforts have been made to ease the industrial-land problem: the building of industrial estates, both public and private; the designation an Enterprise Zone in Dudley; science parks beside the universities; reclamation of derelect land (though clearance is not keeping up with dereliction); planning efforts to find more sites and to market existing sites (City of Birmingham 1984*b*). On the other hand, the release of some industrial land for housing where industrial development is considered unlikely is also occurring (WMCC 1983*a*, pp. 57–8). Thus land supply is limited and choice constrained in the county.

Premises   The second element in the Fothergill–Gudgin thesis concerns floorspace densities and the quality of existing industrial buildings. They see buildings as an even greater constraint on industrial development in the county than land supply. Supply and quality of industrial floor space are considered first, density later.

At first sight, the supply of vacant industrial floor space in the West Midlands seems more than adequate. In 1982 King & Co., chartered surveyors, reported 19 871 000 sq. ft. vacant; the country reported 29 983 000 sq. ft. vacant, including smaller units than King & Co. (both quoted in WMCC

1983*a*, p. 51). The county figure represents a vacancy rate of only 7.5 per cent for industrial floor space in the county (Fothergill *et al.* 1985, p. 22). This compares with vacancy rates of 7.4 per cent in Walsall and 13.2 per cent in Wolverhampton (9.5 per cent and 18.2 per cent respectively in terms of individual premises rather than floor space) in 1984 (CURS 1984).

The critical factor of vacancy-rate levels in relation to likely usage is the quality of the vacant stock. The WMFCC (1985*b*) declared one-third to be unusable. In Walsall we found that 45 per cent of vacant premises had been built before 1945, including 26 per cent before 1919, while 29 per cent were in poor condition. In Wolverhampton, the proportions were respectively 40 per cent, 13 per cent, and 28 per cent. Premises of 4 000–8 500 sq. m. (43 000–92 000 sq. ft.) were much more likely to be of pre-1945 construction (CURS 1984).

Williams *et al.* (1980, p. 22) examined individual buildings in the BICP core area. Its data, converted into whole factories, is quoted by Fothergill, Kitson, and Monk (1985, p. 26) as showing that 63 per cent of factories had been built before 1945 (29 per cent before 1919); 74 per cent of establishments in the BICP core area operated on more than one storey compared with only a quarter in rural areas.

The quality of the stock and of vacant premises has implications both for the costs and productivity of the businesses operating in such buildings and for the attraction of vacant property on to the market. Apart from presenting problems as regards age and number of storeys, premises are often in a poor state of repair and sites are deficient in access for lorries, car-parking space, and capacity for modernization and expansion (see Fothergill, Kitson, and Monk 1985, p. 27), being hemmed in by canals, roads, and housing. Fothergill *et al.* (1985, pp. 28–9) conclude:

Factories in cities therefore have not only less room for physical expansion within their existing sites but also fewer opportunities to expand on adjacent land . . . Densely developed sites, older buildings and multi-storey production are each associated with above average job losses . . . Modern factories on spacious sites are associated with growth wherever they are located; older factories on cramped sites are associated with decline.

Clearance policies and industrial-improvement areas, of which there were some fifteen in the West Midlands County in 1985, in addition to the county's new industrial-priority areas, can help a little, while English Industrial Estates was brought into the county by central government in the mid-1980s to help stimulate the market. New and modern premises came on to the market as speculative factory-building became legal when IDC control was abandoned in 1979. Before that IDC permission had been given to construct some replacement units and warehouses on separate curtilages. Very large modern factories are in short supply, but local authorities and developments have made special efforts to provide small units (for example, nursery units, enterprise workshops) in the last decade. Efforts are also being made to improve landscaping, access by road, and marketing of vacant premises through property registers.

Density   The amount of industrial floor space required per worker has been rising. This increases pressure on floor space and thus on industrial land (Fothergill, Kitson and Monk 1985,, pp. 18–23). It also reduces the employment than can be accommodated in the industrial buildings and sites in the West Midlands County.

The density issue has two aspects: site coverage by buildings (with coverage reduced by parking, turning space and landscaping); and floor space per worker (with much space now occupied by training schools, canteens, computers, turning bays, and, above all, labour-saving equipment and conveyors). Between 1964 and 1982 the average number of workers per 1000 sq. m. of industrial floor space fell from 36 to 21, or by 3 per cent per annum. (Fothergill, Kitson, and Monk 1985, p. 18). This increase in floor space per worker pushes firms into demand for extra space which may entail them moving and so bring them up against the shortage of sites and premises in the county. A great deal of additional accommodation in the county is required if manufacturing employment is to be restored to anything like previous levels. Fothergill and Gudgin (1982, p. 21) put great emphasis on this factor: 'The employment associated with the change in the stock of floor space accounts for the whole of the urban–rural difference in manufacturing employment change'. They find loss of employment *in situ* in capital-intensifying industries particularly significant.

Prices, rents, and rates   One of the assumptions behind explanations for industrial dispersal from cities is that rents and prices of land and premises are lower in the more rural areas of the regions and the UK. The higher city prices reflect competition for land use which manufacturing may no longer be able or wish to meet. On land prices, Fothergill, Kitson and Monk (1985, p. 35) show the price per hectare in the West Midlands county in 1982 to be £153 000. The WMFCC (1985, p. 12) mention £173 000 per hectare in Birmingham compared with £135 000 (12 per cent less) in small towns and rural areas in the region.

With regard to the rent of premises, a differential of 30 per cent between Birmingham and Telford and 10 per cent between Birmingham and Redditch was found to exist in the late 1960s but none at all between these locations and the Black Country (Smith 1972, p. 37). More recently, a differential of 23 per cent existed between Birmingham and Worcester but little between Birmingham, Manchester, and Glasgow (*Birmingham Post*, 4 Feb. 1983, p. 14). Rents in Birmingham have not kept pace with the retail price index since 1973/4 (Debenham, Tewson & Chinnocks 1984).

Conclusion   The higher price and the inadequacy (in quantity, choice, and quality) of industrial land and premises in the West Midlands County combined with pressure on floor space is, for Fothergill and Gudgin, the key to employment loss in the county and the shift in employment to places where constraints are fewer. For firms already in the area this is the 'constrained location theory' mentioned by Keeble, Owens, and Thompson. (1983, pp. 406–7). An incoming firm with strong preferences about tenure, location, size, and condition of either land or premises will find choice very constrained in the county and may be forced elsewhere. Fothergill, Kitson, and Monk (1985, p. 16) argue that 'the supply of land and buildings, not firms' preferences, ultimately sets the ceiling for the city's industrial development'.

Constraint on choice of land and premises does indeed set the ceiling for existing industry and influence its performance to a degree, but, we suggest, as a hindrance not as an overwhelming force. The theory does little to explain the weakness of external investment through new firm and branch plants. Constraint on land and premises has negligible influence on loss of markets and lack of diversification in existing firms where management, design, quality of product, and marketing are all strong independent factors. Thus, we rate problems with land and premises as a contributory and reinforcing factor in decline. Nevertheless, adequacy of land and premises is an important enough issue to be addressed with determination by policymakers, because land supply is often neither competitive nor satisfactory to existing, incoming, or newly created firms in the county.

Labour

Labour costs are becoming more significant compared to other production factors and their costs. Massey and Meegan (1978, p. 287) emphasize labour as the crucial element in de-industrialization, while other writers point to labour-cost differentials between inner-urban and rural and small-town locations as important (Moore, Rhodes, and Tyler 1980; Keeble, Owens, and Thompson 1983).

Skill is interlinked with training (whether formal or through experience), which needs to develop specific appropriate skills to match vacant jobs. The record of the West Midlands County shows long-established weaknesses in training at all levels. Among school-leavers even before 'economies' in training and Youth Training Schemes, relatively low proportions entered apprenticeships, especially in Birmingham, and high proportions took jobs with no training (Smith and Smith 1977, p. 17). Among adults there is a shortage of apprentice-trained men skilled in traditional metal skills (CBI 1984; *Birmingham Post*, 13 June 1985). More recently, a dearth of 'new' skills to facilitate adoption of new technologies has been uncovered. This is local evidence of a national problem, confirmed by evidence of inadequate spending over many years on work-force training (DE 1968; *Employment Gazette*, Sept. 1977, pp. 927–40, and May, 1983, pp. 188–94). There is also evidence that managers rate Birmingham as a less desireable place to live and work in than smaller towns like Redditch and Worcester (Cochrane 1984, p. 235, 263, 332). Moreover, differential migration has polarized labour supply and skill between inner and peripheral areas. Although the perception of such a shift in jobs is greater than the reality for those with manual skills (Smith 1977, p. 45), perception may be enough to induce employers to transfer their operations from an inner area, perhaps in combination with a change to female labour and replacement of skilled workers by machinery.

Such a move is also likely to permit a reduction in wage rates. Taking average gross weekly earnings for men manual workers as an indicator, in 1968–73 a firm could have cut its wage payments by 6 per cent by relocating from the older industrial areas to the county periphery, or by 18 per cent by relocating to the rural west of the region. In 1983 a firm could still have saved 8–9 per cent by relocating in Shropshire or Hereford and Worcester (7 per cent on women's wages, or 36 per cent if it switched from male to female labour at the same time as relocating) (Smith 1984, pp. 8–9). However, by 1983 there were few other regions and counties with such significant differentials compared to the West Midlands County. This reflects the massive decline in the ranking of male manual earnings in the West Midlands Region *vis-à-vis* other regions and the national average in the 1970s (see Chapter 2). This fall has not generated a significant flow of manufacturing firms into the West Midlands Region to take advantage of its lower earnings.

Industrial movement, out of rather than into the West Midlands County, may reflect two other facets of labour: militancy and productivity. Militancy embraces aspects of labour quality such as flexibility, mobility, and attitude (covering issues like shiftworking, turnover, absenteeism, and industrial relations). An objective, though misleading, test of industrial relations concerns the incidence of disputes—misleading because even in the heyday of strikes in the 1970s, they were concentrated in half a dozen plants in the car industry, often in Coventry (Smith, Clifton, *et al.* 1978). Evidence indicates the impact of unionization on pushing up wage levels (Mulvey 1978, p. 112). Thus location away from stronger urban trade-union influence has clear advantages to industrialists.

Shiftworking and payment by results represent two ways of intensifying the use of labour to cut costs. Between 1973 and 1983 these practices became almost as common in other regions as in the West Midlands. However, they were adopted early in the West Midlands.

Relative productivity is plainly of interest to employers, and labour is often held responsible for differences in productivity despite management responsibility for manning and investment levels. Measuring productivity by net output per employee, it is clear that the West Midland County and region score badly compared with other regions. Moreover, the deficiencies are of long standing (Mawson and Smith 1980, pp. 41–8). The West Midlands has been behind and is falling further behind. Its record of low net output per employee began before 1967 across all industrial sectors and went with high manual earnings before 1974. Together, they constituted an unattractive, uneconomic combination.

Thus labour in the West Midlands County seems to be, and to have been, uncompetitive relative to labour elsewhere. The deficiencies have lain in price, productivity, reputation for militancy, and weakness in training, which often derive from management as well as from labour itself. As with land supply, labour supply in the West Midlands County on its own does not seem to offer an explanation for decline, though it will be a contributory and reinforcing factor in a decline set in process by other factors.

Capital

Capital includes cash for immediate outlay and investment for the longer term. Profitability is very important as a main source of operating finance. Other sources include loans from parent companies, where these exist, bank overdrafts and loans, private venture capital, lease-back arrangements, and from government assistance (local, central, EEC), including tax relief for depreciation and investment, regional and industrial policies under the 1972 Industry Act and subsequent legislation, inner-city policy, and local economic initiatives. The problem is to attract finance from the private sector to projects in the West Midlands, especially given the poor record of profitability. The West Midlands has been disadvantaged by a lack of local banking and financial institutions, and there is a suspicion of avoidance of investment by London financiers.

Has investment in manufacturing in the West Midlands been lower or less effective than that elsewhere in the UK (or among competitors), to account for the area's decline? The very poor record of net output per employee implies inadequate investment, perhaps to a greater degree than nationally. Three tests have been applied to assess investment in the West Midlands Region:

1. Regional capital expenditure per employee in manufacturing has been ranked against that in ten other regions and in the UK as a whole between 1963 and 1982. Of the eleven regions, the West Midlands ranked ninth in 1963 and 1975, tenth in 1974, and bottom in 1968 and 1979–82. The West Midlands had the worst record of all in the first half of the 1980s. Its capital expenditue per employee was only about 80 per cent of that for the UK and 50 per cent of that for the top region.

2. The region's share of national capital expenditure has been compared with its share of national employment between 1951 and 1982. Its share of capital expenditure was consistently lower, at about 80 per cent of its share of employment (Mawson and Taylor 1983).

3. Share of capital expenditure was compared with share of employment in

individual industries to allow for industrial structure. There were a few years from the 1960s to the early 1980s in which one or two industries (food and vehicles most often) showed a share of capital expenditure higher than their share of employment, but none did so in 1979 or consistently. There were many instances of the reverse relationship, with much lower shares of capital expenditure in relation to employment share in metal manufacture, metal goods, and electrical engineering.

The investment record in the West Midlands was retrograde in the 1960s and 1970s and has not improved in the 1980s. The only partial exceptions have been food and vehicles. The backlog in capital stock in the West Midlands must now be very serious, after twenty years of underinvestment. It is little wonder that local manufacturing industry is uncompetitive, unprofitable, and in decline.

Why has investment been lacking? Why has it gone elsewhere? Uncompetitive and unattractive land and labour may be factors, but it seems likely that greater responsibility lies with entrepreneurship and reward and, beyond these, with corporate strategies and agglomeration economies. Capital seems a contributory and reinforcing rather than a causal factor in decline. Nevertheless, policy-makers need to ensure that capital supply is maintained and used and that adequate incentives exist for investment.

Entrepreneurship

Entrepreneurship, featured here as a factor of production distinct from capital has two aspects: first, the generation of new (or updated) ideas and their translation into production and sales: second, the urge to grow through the expansion of existing activities or through new activities. Thus entrepreneurship is concerned with *people* (founders, directors, risk-takers, evaluators, and organizers of ideas) and *ideas* (generated through research and development and inventivenes).

In theory at least, new enterprises have an important potential role in local development (as a seed-bed and as a source of diversification, flexibility, and competition). But the potential is often not realized in the kind of firms that start up (Firn and Swales 1978, p. 202). This may be because they have to climb on to an already 'crowded platform' (Lloyd and Dicken 1982, p. iii). Founders are often 'craftsmen' rather than real 'opportunities' (Smith 1967). There is evidence of swelling numbers of small firms, including self-employed people, and many of these must be new (Smith 1984c). The West Midlands ranks sixth out of eleven on Storey's index of regional entrepreneurship (Storey 1982, p. 196) and as high as third on four of the eleven variables (the South-east of England comes top overall and on many variables; the North of England performs worst). On Oakey's survey of distribution of innovations, the West Midlands ranked seventh and fifth out of ten on the rate of innovation per number of workers and plants in 1980 (quoted in Rothwell and Zegveld 1982, p. 142).

The real test is formation of new firms taken in conjunction with closures. Between 1956 and 1966/7, at a prosperous time, the stock of metal businesses in the conurbation fell by 1000, or 22 per cent. New firms added 9 per cent to the 1956 stock; closures reduced it by 24 per cent.

Comparable evidence for 1963–72 reveals that over this period new, independent, manufacturing firms added 6 per cent to the 1972 stock in the West Midlands conurbation. Firms moving in added 18 per cent to employment in the West Midlands conurbation; this 18 per cent was part of a mere 13 632 jobs across all new establishments in the 'buoyant' West Midlands compared to 34 456 jobs in 'declining' Clydeside (Firn and Swales 1978, pp. 209–10).

Recent evidence on the surplus of new firms over closures for 1980–3 based on registration of VAT suggests that the West Midlands County and region are holding their own compared with other regions and metropolitan counties. The surplus added 8.8 per cent to the opening stock in the county and 9.6 per cent in the region (compared with 8.4 per cent in the UK) across all industries, and 6.9 per cent and 11.3 per cent compared respectively with the 10.6 per cent in the UK in manufacturing. So the West Midlands Region did relatively well, but the county performed relatively badly in manufacturing, thus confirming the urban–rural shift.

The supply and quality of entrepreneurship do seem to be weak in the West Midlands County relative to its past record and its needs. However, a renewed flow of entrepreneurship, of which there is some evidence, will not solve the problem of decline if, once founded, the new enterprises fail, do not expand, or move elsewhere. The entrepreneur has to be supported by the other factors of production and by other qualities that generate a satisfactory location. Weak entrepreneurship seems to be a contributory and reinforcing rather than a causal factor in decline. But policy-makers should seek to strengthen it.

This section has considered the supply of factors of production in the West Midlands County relative to alternative locations, particularly in the region, as an influence on relative profitability and competitiveness. Many aspects of factor supply have been rated as unfavourable in price or quality in the county. How does all this affect profitability? Is the county (or region) a good place in which to do business? Has it changed in this respect?

If we examine gross trading profits of companies and public corporations (before stock appreciation) in the region between 1967 and 1983, two points emerge. First, trading profits fell after 1975–8 more than nationally. Second, compared to the retail price index, West Midlands profits rose more than inflation between 1967 and 1974 but fell behind in 1975 and again after 1979. Taking 1974 as 100, in 1983 profits stood at 220, while the retail price index had leaped ahead to 326.

Only one study isolates relative profitability in the West Midlands conurbation (Moore, Rhodes, and Tyler, 1980). Profits per employee in the conurbation fell from being 90.5 per cent of the UK average in 1958 to 80.5 per cent in 1968; those in the rest of the region rose from 82.6 per cent to 94.4 per cent of the UK average (quoted in Fothergill, Kitson, and Mark 1984, p. 74). Compared with some other conurbations, the West Midlands was late in losing out to its hinterland. But both the conurbation and its hinterland and the rest of the region were poor even before 1967 compared with the UK average.

Our review of the supply of factors of production depends less on premises, land supply, and quality being the sole problems, though they are undoubtedly important. We find that there is production-factor disadvantage in the West Midlands County. Policy needs to be directed to reducing factor disadvantage in major directions such as provision of land and premises, promotion of training, and a more sympathetic planning regime.

Urbanization

The process of urbanization and agglomeration may, after running for two hundred years or more in the UK, have reversed to a process of counter-urbanization. Centralizing forces are giving way to decentralization. Location and costs in an agglomeration like the West Midlands County have become a disadvantage to some, hence the urban–rural shift.

The concern here is not with internal economies of scale in plants or firms, but with external economies of scale gained by an industry (specialist labour, training, and other facilities, suppliers, and so forth) and the associated economies of a denser urban environment shared by industry, business generally, and the population (for example, housing, schools, banks) (Townroe and Roberts 1980). In combination, these have led to the build-up of cities. But cities are changing in several respects:

(a) age, obsolescence, and disrepair inevitably go with a densely built-up industrial area with a two-hundred-year history; significantly, market forces have failed to rectify those; related to them are the environmental aspects of atmospheric and land pollution and dereliction

(b) there is traffic congestion, with traffic improvements being counterbalanced by larger lorries; congestion represents a cost to business

(c) the social composition of the resident labour force is changing; it is less skilled than it was and often more militant.

It has been argued that the inner city acts as an incubator, nursery, or seed-bed for new small business and so maintains its viability (Cameron 1980, pp. 351–2). Subsequently those firms will move out to find larger and better premises, internalize input supply, and use less skilled labour. They may no longer need the agglomeration services and may be unwilling to pay for them (Hoover and Vernon 1959). There has been controversy over this concept (Nicholson, Brinkley, and Evans 1981; Fagg 1980). The relative rates of formation of new firms identified earlier imply a weakening of the seed-bed hypothesis in the West Midlands. Agglomeration economies may have ceased to exist, become diseconomies, ceased to matter in location decisions given other considerations, or ceased to be confined to the urban core. There seems little doubt that agglomeration and urban economies have ceased to be attractions to the urban core and may even have become diseconomies. The West Midlands County has consequently lost much of its pull as far as manufacturing production is concerned. In policy terms, two points follow: first, the need to recognize the wider catchment area in administration and planning; second, the need to work to reduce the diseconomies of traffic congestion, pollution, dereliction, poor image, and environment.

Corporate structure

The argument here is that the nature of the manufacturing and business concerns in the county and the changes they have undergone, have had particular impacts. They have been conducive to decline in manufacturing employment in the county. This argument is further developed in Chapter 5, but some points need to be made here.

Spread of corporate control and capital-restructuring strategy

This is a much discussed field (Massey 1978 and 1984; Murgatroyd and Urry 1983). In examining its relevance to and impact on the West Midlands County, we shall consider size of plant and organization, then move to the characteristics of large organizations and their corporate strategies, identifying implications for the West Midlands as we proceed.

Size of plant and organization   Evidence indicating restructuring concerns changes in the size, number, and employment of firms. Prior to the 1979 recession, restructuring showed itself through centralization and concentration of employment, floor space, output, and control in the bigger plants and groups. In 1977, 49 per cent (306 000) of manufacturing employees in the West Midlands County worked in 262 plants owned by just 26 corporations; in 1979, 39 per cent worked in plants with more than 1000 employees, though this figure had fallen to 34 per cent by 1983 (Gaffakin and Nickson 1984). The West Midlands economy no longer contains many small independent concerns (Liggins 1977, p. 80). Firms with fewer than 100 employees made up 80 per cent of the manufacturing plants but only 17 per cent of the employment in the county in 1983 (estimated from the Census of Production, 1983).

A second aspect is location of control. In Birmingham, 75 per cent of the firms that employed more than 1000 people in 1984 were controlled from outside the city, 56 per cent from London. Of those with between 250 and 999 employees, the figures were 56 per cent and 22 per cent, and among those with between 20 and 50 employees, 16 per cent and 7 per cent. Outside manufacturing, outside control was almost as high for the large concerns and actually higher for the medium-sized and small employers (CBI 1984, p. 2, tables 1.1–1.3).

Characteristics of large corporations   The two crucial facets of large corporations are their corporate control and their ownership of many plants. Since the corporate decision-makers control plants in different locations and have knowledge of alternative locations (and of their relative virtues), they there-fore have the opportunity of strategic choice in location of investment. The range of alternatives is often national and international, and it is the latter that is beginning to have a serious effect on the West Midlands (Gaffakin and Nickson 1984). It is not a matter of voluntary choice. Competition, even if oligopolistic, forces decision-makers to take a close look not just at absolute profits but also at relative returns and corporate considerations.

These corporate tendencies have been building up for decades (see Chapter 1) but in the 1960s transport, communication, management, and production technology reached the point where it became feasible to operate a worldwide network of plants to produce products for western markets in competition with domestic plants. This development coincides with the cru-cial years when the West Midlands turned into decline.

Corporate organizational and investment strategies   These corporate tendencies have given rise to organizational and investment strategies which, explicitly or implicitly, contain a locational element. The strategies are influenced by selectivity over location in relation to:

(*a*)   where investment and restructuring are to take place, this may entail relocation outside the West Midlands County

(*b*)   matching functions to relevant factors of production at each location (Westaway 1974); the effect of this is to perpetuate the role of the West Midlands County as a core routine manufacturing location despite its decline and the threat from other locations with lower costs; but the county is weak in headquarters, research, development and innovatory units (Firn 1975)

(*c*)   rationalizing units and production to cut the surplus, uneconomic, or misfit production, functions, and units, Massey and Meegan (1978, pp. 281–2) show in their study of electrical engineering that Birm-ingham lost a net 2980 (or 25 per cent) during the restructuring exercise between 1966 and 1972; the older premises and plant, where age has been compounded by poor investment, IDC control, and adverse regional policy, are usually the ones to be closed and are often found in the older, inner areas of the county (*d*) directing spending on overheads and surplus profits drawn out of branches to pay for central services and internal redistribution.

Thus the West Midlands tends to lose finance, functions, and personnel and to keep routine production with lower-level jobs and vulnerability to relocation and competition. Neither of these processes is encouraging for the West Midlands County and its inner-urban areas.

The impact of product and firm life-cycles

The argument here is that products go through a life-cycle, and that each stage in that life-cycle is associated with a different rate of growth (or decline) and requires a different mix of factors of production, which may give rise to relocation possibilities (Hirsch 1967; Vernon 1979). To maintain size and viability, a plant must find new products or new applications of its products at the expansive stage. It is also likely to have lost mature products to more appropriate rural locations in accordance with Thompson's filter-down theory (Thompson 1968 and 1969; Howells 1982, referred to in Keeble, Owens, and Thompson 1983, p. 406).

Obviously there is some overlap between the effects of product life-cycle and the redistribution of functions. Here too, the implications are adverse for the West Midlands County unless it can find a stream of new products to regenerate itself and its infrastructure.

Vulnerability of manufacturing to foreign competition

It is suggested that the economy of the West Midlands like that of the UK, is particularly open to competition from overseas, where low relative costs and high relative efficiency sharpen competition now the protection of transport costs, tariffs, and so on have gone. (See Chapter 6 for a further discussion of this issue.)

Conclusion

There is a strong possibility that corporate structural disadvantage in the West Midlands became severe at just the time when growth turned to decline. It must be seriously considered as the main explanation for economic decline. This argument is developed further, both theoretically and empirically, in Chapter 5.

Government policy

An explanation for decline affecting the West Midlands relatively severely compared with many other parts of the country could be the existence or application of central-government policies that have had ill-effects in the area. Such ill-effects might be due to the area's industrial structure or location. The two policies that warrant closer consideration are regional policy and regional planning.

Regional policy

It is widely held in the West Midlands that regional policy in the post-war period has stifled industrial development in the West Midlands Region, particularly in the county, where the policy was imposed most tightly. The relative concentration of policy on manufacturing focused the impact on the West Midlands among the non-assisted areas. Regional policy operated through the 'carrot' of financial and other assistance tempting firms to the assisted areas and the 'stick' of IDC to restrict industrial building in the West Midlands (Smith 1972; Bentley and Mawson 1985*a*). The policy is considered to have deterred development and hindered diversification in the West Midlands County and diverted it to the assisted areas and local over-spill areas. The strongest attack on the policy and especially on IDCs was by the West Midlands Economic Planning Council ((WMEPC) 1971, pp. 78–9). This policy is discussed more fully in Chapter 6, where the focus is on the impact of government policies in the West Midlands.

Regional planning

Regional planning affects policy choices about the spatial distribution of population and economic activity mainly within the region. It has therefore laid the foundation of development since 1967 and may provide an explanation for economic decline, perhaps through industrial and population movement to, or retention in, locations that hindered competitiveness. Originally, the purpose of regional planning was to facilitate growth and improve standards, negotiating the relocation of additional population and surplus economic activity from the congested conurbation; currently, its purpose is, rather, to cope with economic decline and to assist regeneration with a minimum reduction in standards. The effect of regional planning has been to constrain industrial development within the West Midlands County. This is discussed more fully in Chapter 8.

Conclusion

This section briefly considers two spatial policies of central government as possible explanations, through their bad design, side-effects, or general inefficiency, of economic decline in the West Midlands and the social malaise that goes with it. Regional policy and regional planning have been particularly criticized for requiring the export of manufacturing investment and employment from the West Midlands County over forty years. In practice, alongside the often painful official dispersal of people and firms, private voluntary dispersal has been considerable.

Such an export of the more mobile and active elements from the county must have had some impact on the residual composition and its powers of regeneration. Regional policy and regional planning have certainly been a contributory and reinforcing factor in the decline of the West Midlands County's economic base. Regional policy has had an impact on the whole region, though regional planning has assisted that part of the region outside the county. Inner-city policy and non-spatial policies can hardly hope to compensate.

Planning policy

Local town and country planning policies have been blamed for some of the elements of local industrial decline. However, their role in decline is difficult to specify if allowance is made for their restricted options and central-government influence on resources, not least through regional policy and regional planning. The latter restricted the size of the West Midlands conurbation and the amount of land within it that could be allocated or developed for industry (Smith 1982, pp. 34–5).

The development plans of the 1950s and 1960s were very much concerned with urban reconstruction and redevelopment. The local economy was buoyant and policies at that time were little concerned with safeguarding industry. But slowly that has changed. Strategic planning, assisted by a county-wide remit after 1974, has analysed decline and sought ways of regenerating the local economy through policies helpful to industry and job creation. Until the 1980s this was against a background of the industry-dispersing aims of regional policy and planning. The County Structure Plan approved in 1982 addresses totally different issues from the development plans of the 1950s: population, income, and industrial decline, especially in inner-urban areas, rather than distribution and accommodation of growth.

While local-authority planning policies *per se* cannot realistically be held responsible for local industrial decline, they have impact at the level of the individual firm. A helpful planning regime can assist local economic development. Local economic initiatives are considered in Chapter 7. There is evidence of an industry-neglecting regime in the 1950s and 1960s reflected in policies of redevelopment and road-building and treatment of non-conforming users which caused offence through noise, pollution, and so on, (Smith 1978*b*). These policies were often insensitive to the needs of small businesses. The effect was to disturb and dispossess hundreds of businesses of all or part of their premises, often after protracted blight. This was accompanied by the provision of often inadequate compulsory compensation with which to set up business elsewhere. Such firms were often described and treated as marginal. Now they are fostered. The loss of businesses in the first five Comprehensive

Redevelopment Areas in Birmingham may well have been as high as 64 per cent, as the published evidence only accounts for 690 of the 1654 known officially to have been affected over the decade or so before 1965 (Stedman and Wood 1965, quoted in Smith, 1972, pp. 48–9). Thomas (1976, pp. 237–8) found that 56 per cent of the manufacturing firms in the Newtown Redevelopment Area of Birmingham in 1946 had gone by 1972. Metal-goods firms seem to have been particularly susceptible to the effect of redevelopment on their premises; 46 per cent gave this as their reason for moving in one study (Smith, Ruddy, and Black 1974, p. 14). The shortage of small premises was an exacerbating factor as destruction proceeded; this was not appreciated until the 1970s.

Non-conforming land-use was another contentious issue. The scale of the problem can be indicated in one part of Birmingham, where in 1958–74 roughly half the manufacturing firms were non-conforming users operating on non-industrial land and half the firms on industrial land were non-manufacturing (Smith 1977, p. 35). Foundry and plating firms were particularly affected by community objections on grounds of nuisance, yet those were crucial to many industrial linkage chains. Costs of remedy to the firm could be very high (D.o.E. Inner Cities Directorate 1978). Policy operated with varying degrees of rigour (as the policy was expensive in compensation up to 1970 but thereafter was moderated to action only towards 'bad neighbours', and now encourages light-industrial users in residential areas. However, residents often object strongly to industry in their streets (Apgar 1975).

While planning policies affecting industry have hit individual firms severely and have certainly angered industrialists, they cannot be assessed as a significant factor in decline overall. Moreover, the planners needed to redevelop areas, make road improvements, counter nuisance, and so on and industry enjoyed planning benefits, especially the motorway system.

Social disadvantage

Could an explanation for decline and the poor performance of business in the West Midlands County and its inner-urban areas lie with the resident population? Local population is relevant to local business in two directions: the supply side, as a labour force, and the demand side, as consumers. In both respects, local residents will be supplemented by those coming into the area daily to work or to spend. On the demand side, a fall in relative incomes reduces spending, with impact on local business. Many factors have acted to reduce incomes in inner-urban areas: unemployment, low activity rates, less skilled work, change from manufacturing to service jobs, lack of pressure in the labour market, demographic change, and higher heating and housing costs, among others. Locally generated consumption in inner-urban areas is likely to have fallen relative to other parts of the urban environment.

One can cite as an explanation for decline class struggle over changes in the labour process. This view suggests that workers, particularly in inner-urban areas of working-class solidarity, may resist measures to raise productivity and lead employers to change their investment and employment policies. Friedman's account of the struggles in the Coventry car industry exemplify this point. An apparent victory by workers became hollow because of high costs that made the product uncompetitive (Friedman 1977). Marshall has recently documented the link between class struggle over changes in the labour process and the 50-year business cycles first identified by Kondratieff in the 1920s, in one UK region after another, over the past 150 years. He records the passing of the West Midlands and its car and engineering industries from a propulsive position into decline (Marshall 1985). Therefore, class struggle too could provide a factor in decline in particular unionized and highly paid sectors of the local economy. This view is reflected by employers who search out cheaper, less militant, and more flexible workers in their corporate strategies.

Is industry moving out of urban areas to follow population or vice versa? Industry and population both move out as part of the urban–rural shift, but the sequence is important for causation. The matter is controversial, but Warnes (1980, p. 26) and Stiennes (1982) consider that the jobs followed the people; employers, in other words, had to move outwards to find the employees they needed or preferred.

However, social disadvantage, while it may be increasing in the West Midlands County, is not considered a salient factor in decline. The nature of the resident population, marginally changed by migration flows, is rather a symptom of decline and a factor reinforcing and contributing to decline caused by other stronger factors.

Industrial milieu

By industrial milieu is meant the nature, values, style, social, political, and economic mix of an area, which also takes into account cultural and religious influences. The proposition is that in the West Midlands these factors make up a way of life which is no longer conducive to manufacturing competitiveness. The same can be said of the UK as a whole (Weiner 1981; Olson 1982).

Conclusion

There seem to be three relatively autonomous elements among the explanations of local economic decline:

(*a*)   the advances in transport and technology that have opened up the world market and made the urban–rural shift economically feasible
(*b*)   the obsolescence and congestion inherent in a well-established built-up area
(*c*)   the struggle against changes in the labour process.

The first makes possible, and the second and third make desirable, to manufacturers the urban–rural shift. Conurbations now reflect urban diseconomies.

Small and independent businesses as well as large corporate ones have been dispersing from the county. Thus the urban–rural shift has not *depended* on corporate strategies, but it has been massively assisted by corporate strategies. It can be argued that it was around 1967 that development in transport and technology reached the point at which an urban–rural shift really became attractive to firms in the West Midlands. Population had been shifting outwards from the county for some years though rather later compared with the shift from other cities in the UK. The effects of obsolescence, congestion, and social polarization had been building up. The industrial mix of the economy was to become a liability. Transport and technology were creating a world market; tariffs were being reduced, bringing foreign goods, especially cars, into Britain; corporate strategies were becoming global; the obsolescence of buildings and labour militancy were becoming liabilities. So when foreign competition forced restructuring and cost-cutting on West Midland business at the end of the 1960s and subsequently, corporate strategies were developed for survival. It is to these corporate strategies and to the large firms of the West Midlands economy that the next chapter turns.

5

De-industrialization and Corporate Change

We have drawn a picture of an economy in relatively poor shape to cope with a deep recession. The origin of the present crisis was the inability of the manufacturing sector to make sufficient profit for reinvestment, which led to a progressive weakening in the competitiveness of firms in the West Midlands. Throughout the 1960s and 1970s the symptoms of the underlying crisis in the economy were to be seen in a series of mergers, plant closures, and bankruptcies, and in declining profitability. Survival was achieved by attempts to restore profitability through rationalization, sectoral shifts, shifts in the location of production, and investment in new techniques. Manufacturing decline had its roots in the mid-1960s, but was obscured by growth in service employment and the public sector. Processes of change were therefore in operation throughout the 1960s and 1970s but were greatly accelerated by the severe post-1979 recession. There was not the cushion of relatively high demand, so the impact was deep and rapid.

We will be arguing that the processes of economic change which made the West Midlands economy vulnerable to rationalization and plant closure in the late 1970s and early 1980s evolved in the previous two decades. They had their roots in the nature of the West Midlands economy and, in particular, the dominance of the local manufacturing sector by a small number of large companies on whose fortunes much of manufacturing employment was dependent (see Chapter 1).

However, we will not be arguing that explanations for the local economy's malaise can be found within the West Midlands, but instead will be placing the local economy within its national and international economic context. Attempts to find explanations for decline at the level of the county or the region may ignore critical developments in national and international spheres which may be of at least equal, if not greater, importance than local factors. As Massey and Meegan (1978) argue in their work on manufacturing decline in cities, there is a tendency for problems to be defined in spatial terms and causes of these problems to be sought within the same spatial unit; this can blur issues of causality.

Indeed it has to be understood that 'internal factors' within regions or cities may be important within the overall context of economic change taking place at the international and national level. Such changes form the basis of the discussion which follows.

Responding to Recession

By the late 1970s the regional economy was in poor shape to cope with a deep recession. Markets had been progressively lost over twenty-five years. Profits and therefore investment had been low, which led to relatively high unit costs and an inability to develop new products for existing or new markets.

The recession after 1979 accelerated the process of change and altered some of the operating conditions of companies: very high unemployment produced a fundamental shift in labour-market conditions which allowed stronger managerial control of the labour process; the fall in aggregate demand made pressure of competition very severe and necessitated drastic measures if firms were to stay in business; the expansion of consumer credit despite the recession created opportunities in consumer-durable sectors; the banks launched the lifeboat of short-term credit for companies which might otherwise have gone into liquidation; the value of sterling began to fall after a period of being very high.

In order to assess the response of West Midlands industry to recession we have focused upon the strategies adopted by the largest twenty-six manufacturing firms (in 1977 employment terms) operating in the local economy. Using Lloyd and Reave's term, these 'prime movers' accounted for almost half of total manufacturing employment in the West Midlands County in 1977 (Lloyd and Reave 1982). Given the high degree of industrial linkage within the economy, their importance in shaping the fortunes of the West Midlands generally would be considerable.

It must be recognized that although responses to recession have been kept analytically distinct, in reality many are interlinked and are part of the same process of change. Our categorization begins with the strategy of investment/disinvestment. This involves investing in those areas, plants, markets, sectors, or products where greater profits are expected while disinvesting, reducing output, scrapping capacity, and cutting back the labour force in those sections of the economy where relative profit is low. In a sense this category is similar to Massey and Meegan's definition of rationalization, which, they argue, is the necessary by-product of changing relative levels of profitability as investment flows to those areas in the economy where the return is highest (Massey and Meegan 1982, p. 87). However, a distinction needs to be made between rationalization which is the result of a failure to compete and that which is part of a wider strategy of growth and development.

In part the need for this distinction is a result of our focus on individual companies in contrast to Massey and Meegan's focus on industries. As Townsend and Peck (1984, p. 321) rightly point out,

classifying job losses in terms of output changes pre-supposes that such changes are mostly specific to products, or more broadly to industries, rather than to individual corporations. Consequently, it is fundamental to an analysis of corporate job loss to consider product mix . . . the sites at which corporations produce particular specialities and the structure of corporate divisions, which generally divide activities on a commercial basis.

The second category of responses to recession, reducing costs, is therefore distinguished from the first in that it encompasses a range of strategies by which a company attempts to improve its competitive position while remaining within a particular industry or market. Reducing costs by rationalizing production may be one way of achieving this end (as British Leyland, for example, has done). Other strategies identified include intensification, technical change, changes in sourcing policy, reducing labour costs, and moving production to low-cost locations.

Thirdly, it is important to separate those strategies developed to compete on cost factors from those developed to compete on non-price factors, such as marketing and product design. While strategies in the latter category may not directly influence employment, the ability to develop and market products to meet changing demands in the world market is often crucial to the profitability of companies and industries. As Williams, Williams, and Thomas (1983, p. 48) point out, 'the immediate reason for the decline in the problem industries is not that world demand is declining, but that the British manufacturers in those industries are unable to adjust to the composition of demand'.

In what follows we examine how the 'prime movers' have adapted since 1970 to changes in their economic environment. Firstly, we see how the rationalization of plant and employment has been associated with investment in new sectors and markets as well as with response to declining market share and increased competitive pressures. Secondly, we look at the way companies have responded to their changing economic environment by adopting a series of measures to reduce costs and hence improve their positions in the market. Thirdly, we analyse the importance of product in the success or failure of a company.

Investment/disinvestment

Earlier we argued that the economy of the West Midlands was over-specialized in the engineering and metal-using industries, heavily dependent upon the UK vehicle industry as a final market for its goods, and had a pattern of trade concentrated in the old imperial markets. In the early and mid-1960s the 'prime movers' in the local economy reflected this pattern of specialization and dependence. Yet by 1983 the nature of the operations of a number of these leading firms had changed dramatically. Many were no longer engaged in their traditional activities, products and markets had radically altered, and employment in the West Midlands had fallen substantially.

In new sectors   The specialization of the 'prime movers' in sectors which were susceptible to import penetration and produced poor rates of return caused

many of these companies to look for increased profits in new sectors and
activities. In response to the problem of declining profitability a number of
the leading firms in the West Midlands began to move into new product
areas, diversifying the range of activities in which they were involved and
hence the final market upon which they were dependent. There was also an
attempt to switch from products of low added value to those of high added
value.

Tube Investments (TI), for example, was originally formed in 1919 by a
small group of tube-makers and tube-users, with its early growth centred
largely on the production of steel tubes. Expansion and diversification into
other growth centres got under way in the 1950s, but was given a major
stimulus by the nationalization of steel and of TI's big steel-making interests
in 1968.

The basis of the philosophy of TI through the late 1960s and the 1970s was
that it should be a group involved in making and handling metal, making
machines that did work on metal, and building consumer goods out of metal.
In line with other metal-manufacturing companies, TI recognized the need
to move away from products which were differentiated in the market place
only by price to those that were differentiated by design, quality, and reputation. It outlined this strategy clearly in 1977:

Many of the Group's products are made from steel, which in its simpler forms is a
highly price competitive commodity and in world markets is particularly sensitive to
movements in exchange rates. More stable markets and better opportunities are to be
found by moving forward to more sophisticated and higher added-value products
where design, performance quality and delivery matter as much as price. (TI 1977.)

While such a strategy of diversification led to the rapid growth of TI
through the 1960s and the first half of the 1970s the impact of recession in the
late 1970s also led to a re-examination by the company of its involvement in
its more traditional activities. The years 1979–82 saw TI sell off or close
many of the activities for which it was previously well known, principally alu-
minium- and steel-making. The reasons for these decisions mirrored those for
expanding into new areas of operation. The chairman of TI outlined these
clearly in 1982, following TI's decision to pull out of British Aluminium:

What has happened in the world aluminium industry has demonstrated the vulnerability of businesses with products which, apart from price, are undifferentiated
between suppliers. The vulnerability of such business in times of recession is
increased when there is international trade in the product, when prices are affected by
exchange rates related to factors other than comparative industrial costs, and there
are wide variations in the degree of obligation of different producers to earn profit.
Steel and aluminium have been two industries exposed in these ways, from both of
which TI has now disengaged. (TI 1982.)

Although TI's decision to pull out of British Aluminium did not affect
employment in the West Midlands, the decision to sell Round Oak to the

British Steel Corporation (BSC) in 1981 and its resultant closure led to the loss of 1670 jobs. The restructuring of TI during this period of recession, the disposals and cutbacks undertaken to reverse declining profitability, produced a fundamentally different company to that which existed in the early 1960s. By 1982 consumer products accounted for 40 per cent of TI's business, another 35 per cent was in special engineering products, and only 25 per cent was in steel tubes. Of this 25 per cent a significant proportion was in highly specialized types (TI, 1982). This fundamental restructuring of TI resulted in large-scale loss of jobs within the West Midlands conurbation, plants were closed, and TI's interests in its traditional metal-forming activities reduced.

This process of change was also to be seen in other local companies, such as Guest, Keen & Nettlefolds (GKN). In the early 1960s GKN was no more than a medium-sized West-Midlands-based engineering group with steel-making interests. However, it was to increase its involvement in automotive components, gain a substantial foothold in the overseas component business, become heavily involved in steel distribution, and, despite the nationalization of steel, maintain an important presence in steel (*The Times*, 23 Feb. 1978).

GKN's investment in new manufacturing sectors centred on its push into car components. First, the company shifted the dependence of its foundry and forging operations from the automobile industry to the truck and tractor manufacturers, who during the 1960s and 1970s provided a more buoyant market. Second, it began to expand its involvement in transmission manufacturing, in which it had an important technological lead. This strategy was particularly apparent after 1977 when the newly formed 'management committee' headed by Sir Trevor Holdsworth identified automobile components as an area that would be given maximum support through major investment and acquisition. However, such a strategy for expansion was also linked with an assault upon the European and North American markets and had major consequences for employment in the West Midlands. As the *Financial Times* (29 Feb. 1980) commented at the time, GKN's policy of restructuring the company might well be viewed, 'as a strategy to outwit the decline of British manufacturing industry. As the largest engineering group in Britain, it was becoming obvious during the mid-1970s that GKN was not going to prosper by selling to British industry.'

The second area identified for growth was industrial services and distribution. The move into distribution began in 1968, when GKN increased its involvement in steel stockholding through a series of acquisitions. These culminated in its acquisition of Miles Druce in 1973, which gave GKN 20 per cent of the market in steel stockholding.

However, of greater importance in more recent years to the reshaping of GKN was the move into the market for replacement automotive parts. In 1977 it was this market, together with component manufacture, that was identified as the major area for growth and investment. GKN's increased involvement in the replacement-parts market made sense for two reasons. First, it completed the vertical integration of the activities of the company beginning with the manufacture of metal, which was then formed and assembled into car components for the original equipment. Now GKN could supply the replacement part when the original came to the end of its useful life. Second, the replacement-parts market was increasingly profitable as the stock of cars increased (*Financial Times*, 29 Feb. 1980).

While the development of the replacement-parts business was one of the key strategies for growth from the mid-1970s, this investment was accompanied by disinvestment in other areas of activity. The production of fasteners—nuts, bolts, screws, rivets, and so on—has been one of the traditional activities of GKN. GKN was the principal manufacturer in the industry, and its plants were largely based in the West Midlands. In the early 1970s GKN had a work-force of around 17 000 producing fasteners, which was more than one-third of the total number employed in that industry. Yet by July 1980 this work-force had fallen to 5000 of which approximately 3000 were to be found in the West Midlands (*Financial Times*, 23 July 1980). The reorganization of GKN's fastener activities in the following years led to more than 1500 further redundancies.

The run-down of the manufacture of fasteners by GKN reflected the difficulties experienced by the industry generally. GKN argued that it was unable to compete against the rising tide of cheap foreign imports. This was particularly the case at the lower end of the market. GKN did, however, retain its manufacturing capacity for its proprietary product Supadrive, which sold well in Europe, the USA, and even Japan (*Birmingham Post*, 29 Jan. 1980).

Yet although GKN was disinvesting in the manufacture of fasteners it was investing in its distribution activities in the industry. GKN has always played a key role in the distribution of fasteners, as well as being a major consumer of the product in its own assembly production. In fact the domination of fasteners distribution by GKN led the Office of Fair Trading in 1976 to refer the matter to the Monopolies Commission for investigation. This was an area which GKN began to develop as its manufacturing interests declined.

While GKN was itself a victim of the flow of imports into the UK, it is interesting to note that, in its distribution role, the company also participated in facilitating this flow. At the beginning of 1980 GKN Distributors, the industry's biggest customer, warned that the British fastener industry had a year in which to sort itself out, or the company would increase its sourcing overseas (*Birmingham Post*, 24 Jan, 1980). Having begun its move out of manufacture, GKN could afford to act upon its words.

Elsewhere in GKN, recession produced rationalization and loss of jobs through a defensive restructuring of production. In 1980 three plants were closed by GKN Forging and 2000 jobs lost as capacity was brought in line with demand (*Financial Times* 28 June 1980). GKN Forging had been badly hit by the slump in the UK commercial-vehicle industry. This slump also badly affected GKN Sankey, which was involved in the fabrication of cabs for lorries and tractors. The difficulties suffered by Massey Ferguson compounded the problems of GKN. GKN Axles was also hit by this downturn. The combination of these problems with the slump in UK car production, which hit the manufacture of wheels, forgings, and castings, made a policy of rationalization necessary to ensure the survival of GKN. Between 1977 and 1982 UK employment in GKN fell from 73 196 to 37 231, a loss of more than 49 per cent of the work-force.

The processes of rationalization and investment in new sectors or activities were not confined to these two companies. British Sound Reproducers disinvested in record-changing equipment and invested in electronics in the face of declining profitability (Gaffakin and Nickson 1984, p. 106). Glynwed was another metal-producing and metal-using firm which in the late 1960s and early 1970s diversified into consumer products by the acquisition of companies such as Sydney Flavel (gas appliances) in 1972. Dunlop has attempted to move out of the European tyre market and into producing goods for the leisure market as well as products for the wider engineering industry (Gaffakin and Nickson 1984). GEC was disinvesting in the heavy-engineering side of its business in the late 1960s and early 1970s and investing heavily in electronics, gas turbines, electric motors, and telecommunications in the mid-1970s. Similarly, Metro-Cammell, part of the Laird group, was shifting production away from the manufacture of general railway equipment to buses (Birmingham Community Development Project 1977) Delta shifted from its metals-dominated origins to a broader spectrum of industrial activities (Flynn and Taylor 1984, pp. 94–5).

Thus the mid-1960s to the mid-1980s witnessed a restructuring of the activities of a number of firms with key positions in the West Midlands economy. The recognition that they were too heavily dependent upon a narrow price range in demand-sensitive products spurred companies such as TI and GKN to invest in new areas of activity. In general, this was a shift to goods of higher added value, or a shift from basic and intermediate goods to the consumer market.

In many cases, however, investment was accompanied by disinvestment in the traditional West-Midlands-based activities of these companies. Thus GKN's push into the car-components market and industrial services and distribution was part of a strategy which also led the company to disinvest almost totally in fastener manufacture and run down its interest in foundry and other metal-related activities. The outcome for the local economy was closure of plants, loss of jobs, and redundancy.

In new markets   The steady run-down of British manufacturing industry and the de-industrialization of its economic base from the 1970s (see Blackaby 1978) had major consequences for those manufacturing firms that survived. With the flow of imports also increasing, firms supplying intermediate goods for British manufacturing industry had increasingly to compete for sales in a declining market. In the West Midlands those companies involved in the manufacture and supply of components for the vehicle industry were particularly badly hit by the erosion of the share in the UK and world markets gained by British-built cars. The financial difficulties experienced by British Leyland in the early 1970s would clearly have a knock-on effect within the components sector. The apparent fragility of this important market led many of the major components companies based in the West Midlands to search for new sales outlets for their goods. There was a shift to exploit the expanding European car market which had a profound effect upon employment in the West Midlands, as not only were sales concentrated in Europe but so were manufacturing facilities.

Traditionally, all the major components manufacturers had made market assessments of particular car models and planned their production accordingly. As the group director of GKN's automotive division pointed out in his evidence to the Commons Select Committee on the Car Industry: 'We have generally taken a view on the success or failure of certain models. Therefore, we have not been caught out when demand for a certain product has not been as high as expected'. (*Financial Times*, 13 Mar. 1975.) This assessment was now applied to British Leyland as a whole, and alternative markets were sought. The most important of these was Europe. This move into Europe did not result only in an increased proportion of sales going in exports to Europe, it also saw a growth in investment in manufacturing facility in Europe. The *Financial Times* (5 Feb. 1975) noted: 'as the plight of Britain's car makers hugs the headlines, Britain is quietly but massively moving into the European car components trade'.

GKN, for example, obtained a foothold in Europe when it acquired Birfield. This purchase brought with it an initial 40 per cent stake in the West German components company Uni-Carden (manufacturer of universal joints and propeller shafts), which GKN later (1978) increased to 81.1 per cent. As well as plants in West Germany, Uni-Carden had manufacturing facilities in Italy and France, and these together with GKN's British plants formed the basis of GKN's world-wide strategy for transmission manufacturing. Later, in an attempt to expand the range of its activities in Europe, GKN tried, but failed, to acquire the West German components company Sachs, whose range of products included high-technology electrical and engine parts (*Financial Times*, 23 Jan. 1976).

Lucas Industries had also moved into Europe, first through its association with Dusellier in France, and later through investments in West Germany and Italy. By 1974 Lucas also had full control of Rotodiesel, thereby gaining a considerable slice of the French diesel market (*Financial Times* 29 Nov.

1974). Associated Engineering considerably expanded its operations in France through the 1970s, and in Italy bought a business in the mid-1960s which extended to a work-force of 1600 by 1975. (*Financial Times*, 5 Dec. 1975). Wilmot Breedon (later taken over by Rockwell) also moved into France, and by the mid-1970s, its French associate, Compagnie Industrielle de Mécanismes, was among the most successful parts of the group.

TI's chairman, Brian Kellet, defended overseas acquisitions on the ground that they created new export potential for the UK:

Other things being equal, we would always prefer to manufacture in this country and export to overseas markets. In such circumstances setting up an overseas operation, often with a partner who has a special local knowledge, generates sales and profits we would not otherwise enjoy and often also provides a valuable market for components or equipment exported from our UK companies.

(Quoted in Gaffakin and Nickson 1984, p. 146.)

The shift overseas was not restricted to Europe. GKN, for example, began to move into North America to exploit the shift to front-wheel drive by US car manufacturers. Similarly, Lucas set up manufacturing plants to exploit the increasing popularity of diesel-powered cars following the oil crisis of the mid-1970s (*Financial Times*, 8 July 1980). In the early 1980s Lucas signed a five-year supply and technology agreement with the US electronics company, Motorola, and in May 1982 the company purchased Ledex Inc., a US manufacturer of mechanical electronic equipment, at a cost of £7.5 million (Gaffakin and Nickson 1984).

Overall, then, the period from the late 1960s to the mid-1980s witnessed the growth of overseas production facilities as West Midlands companies attempted to penetrate the previously neglected European and North American markets. Although cost considerations were involved, market considerations were of paramount importance, and the apparent favourable return on capital and sales may have been a reflection of the buoyancy of these markets when compared to that in the UK. Furthermore, it has also been suggested that these overseas activities were developed at the expense of investment in the UK, investment which would have boosted the profitability of UK operations (Gaffakin and Nickson 1984).

While there have been a number of counter-tendencies to this process—for example, the blocking of overseas acquisition by European governments (as in the case of GKN and Sachs) and Lucas's move back to the West Midlands—these give little hope for the future. Increasing competition among the world's leading components companies and pressure from the car assemblers to keep components costs down is accelerating the move towards a trans-European components industry dominated by a small number of large companies producing throughout Europe. Even if the West Midlands is a location for this production, as in the case of Lucas, the need to keep costs down has led to the introduction of new working practices and increased automation which militate against an increase in jobs and are more likely to bring about further redundancies.

Reducing costs

The previous section has shown how investment in new sectors and markets has been paralleled by disinvestment and the rationalization of those areas of a firm's activity which have relatively poor rates of return. This is essentially a strategy of pulling out of a market or sector in which a company cannot effectively compete and concentrating investment in those areas which promise greater profitability. However, a number of 'prime movers' attempted to reduce costs and hence increase competitiveness while remaining in the same market. For example, the rationalization of British Leyland (incorporated as BL in 1978) through the closure of a number of peripheral plants and the concentration of production at Longbridge and Cowley was an attempt to reduce costs and increase sales, and hence boost profitability. However, rationalization of production facilities in this manner was only part of the strategy adopted by the company and was inextricably linked to other attempts to reduce costs.

In some cases, attempts by companies to reduce costs can be viewed as defensive, strategies for survival rather than growth. Rationalization which involves the scrapping of plants in order to reduce output to match demand may be acceptance of failure to compete or a response to a declining market. Birmid Qualcast, for instance, halved its foundry capacity and closed six of its West Midlands foundries between 1978 and 1982 because of increased competition from imported castings and the contraction of its principal customer, BL. However, the company's run-down of productive capacity locally was paralleled by investment in its Derby foundry to create the most mechanized iron foundry in Europe. In addition, productivity was improved in the foundry division, with output per employee increasing from 28 tonnes a year in 1980 to 35 tonnes in 1982, productivity which could rise to 52 tonnes a year if the company operated at full capacity. Thus rationalization and steps to increase competitiveness are often part of the same strategy, and although they are considered separately here they cannot be disentangled when considering an individual company.

Intensification Intensification has been defined as the reorganization of an existing production process, without abandoning capacity and without major investment in new forms of production, in order to increase productivity (Massey and Meegan 1982, p. 31). An increase in output per worker can be achieved by a variety of means, which may include the introduction of small work aids, the increasing fragmentation of tasks, the speeding up of the line in conveyor-belt production, minor mechanization, or simply exhortations and incentives to work harder. As Massey and Meegan (1982, p. 32) argue, although intensification is not a strategy that is inextricably associated with decline or recession, it is probably more likely to be adopted during set-backs than booms, when, of course, it is more likely to lead to loss of jobs. This has been the case in the West Midlands in recent years.

During the recession since 1979 the clear threat of loss of jobs through rationalization has increased management's ability to push through other changes in the organization of production and increase output per worker. Throughout industry in the West Midlands, industrial relations have been transformed and the balance of power between management and unions radically altered in management's favour. Against a background of redundancy and plant closures, new manning levels and working practices have been introduced and pay deals kept to a minimum. *As a Financial Times* headline on 6 July 1980 pronounced, 'West Midlands Bosses Find They Have the Upper Hand'.

The intensification of work and the resultant impact upon employment have nowhere been clearer than in the vehicle industry. In both Talbot and British Leyland, the two major local employers in the industry, higher levels of productivity, have resulted in significant loss of jobs. Talbot introduced new manning levels and work practices at its Ryton assembly plant in spite of union opposition (*Financial Times*, 28 Feb. 1981). As a result of these changes and the rationalization of the company's activities following its take-over by Peugeot–Citroen, which came into effect in 1979, employment in the two main Talbot plants in Coventry has declined rapidly. Whereas in 1974 Talbot (then Chrysler UK) employed 14 500 workers in its Coventry plants, by 1983 this had fallen to only about 5500, a 65 per cent fall (Healey and Clark 1984, p. 25).

At BL a similar process of job loss has been occurring. The rationalization of capacity and the concentration of the car production of the Austin Rover group (the largest car division of BL) at the two major plants, Longbridge and Cowley, has already been discussed. These changes were associated with a run-down of the work-force and an intensification of production within these two plants in order to raise productivity and quality and reduce costs, and hence improve competitiveness.

Within the West Midlands conurbation, changes taking place at Longbridge have been of great importance. The 'productivity miracle' (*Sunday Times*, 21 Mar. 1982) at Longbridge has been achieved by a combination of large-scale job losses, tighter disciplinary procedures, and production incentives. Wage increases have been low. BL claimed in 1981 that Austin Rover had achieved a 40 per cent improvement in productivity over the previous few years and that Longbridge was then running at 'European levels of efficiency', (BL, *Annual Report*, 1981, quoted in Williams, Williams, and Thomas 1983, p. 257). As a result of these changes, together with investment in automated production processes, the manufacturing work-force at Longbridge was cut from 19 400 in 1977 to only 11 000 by mid-1982. Output, however, increased from 158 000 cars in 1977 to around 255 000 in 1982. By 1984 productivity on the Metro line had become the best in Europe (*Engineer*, 9 Feb. 1984).

The intensification of production experienced by workers in the car-assembly industry began to spread to the components sector. In 1984 Lucas announced the introduction of new flexible working practices at its Birmingham plants. Under the threat of plant closures and a ballot of the workforce, unions at Lucas reluctantly agreed to changes in the organization of production designed to lead to the loss of some 700 jobs and the closure of two plants at Solihull and Shirley (*Birmingham Post*, 10 Apr. 1984).

Thus the intensification of the production process has been a dominant strategy pursued by many of the 'prime movers' in the West Midlands County. The balance of power between unions and management has shifted, as unemployment has risen and trade-union membership declined in the county. The outcome is a more productive industrial base. Whereas the poor productivity record of the West Midlands was blamed for its decline, the 'productivity miracle' in key companies is now seen as an optimistic signal for the future. However, for those that remain in work in these productive plants the experience of work has radically altered, and their compliance with new working practices in the future is not assured, given the increasing frustration of workers as witnessed by the Longbridge riot of 1980 and Cowley strike of 1983. On the other hand, the failure of recent industrial action highlights the shift in the balance of power towards management and the disorganization of the once powerful trade-union movement in the car industry.

Technical change   Allied to the intensification of the labour process has been the introduction of new technology. Investment in new production capacity normally involves major reorganization of the production process, resulting in a substantial reduction in the amount of labour required for any given level of output. This has happened in the recession since 1979. Two industries identified by Massey and Meegan (1982) as intensifying industries were iron and steel, and aluminium.

In the case of iron and steel the dominant process of employment change within the West Midlands has been rationalization not technical change. However, as Massey and Meegan argue, the definition of the main form of production reorganization taking place may depend on the scale of the geographical area being examined. When an industry is going through a period of technical change, it may well be that new investment occurs in one area and closure of out-of-date factories in another. Plant closures in the iron and steel industry in the West Midlands were part of BSC's Ten Year Development Plan of 1973 which proposed a major growth in capacity based on a few large integrated steel complexes on or near the coasts of Wales, Scotland, and England. The policy was one of investment in new methods in selected locations and closure of older, small-scale, and poorly located works (Taylor

1983, p. 152). BSC's major plant in the West Midlands, Bilston, was classified as marginal under this plan and was closed in 1975. Thus rationalization locally was inextricably linked to investment and technical change elsewhere. A change in production technology led to new locational requirements and undermined the West Midlands's position as a favourable location for iron and steel production.

The aluminium industry in the West Midlands has benefited from the shift from the use of iron to the use of aluminium for some car components. Aluminium production is capital-intensive, and there has been substantial investment to improve productivity. As a result, output can be expanded with very little extra labour. Indeed there have been significant redundancies despite increased orders, because the latter have not matched the industry's capacity. Further loss of jobs appears likely as more firms begin to use robots in the labour-intensive finishing end of the production process (Brady and Liff 1983, p. 61).

Investment in new production processes and automation has been increasing. Major retooling took place at Longbridge in 1979 and included the installation of robotic systems. This increased automation at Longbridge explains in part the plant's lead in productivity and was one response by the company to intense international competition. The pattern of production within the vehicle industry—variable forms, large volumes, batch production, variation in models, and so on—is ideal for robotization especially since it is accompanied by appropriate processes, such as spot welding, paint spraying, loading transfer, and so on, for which standard robotic systems are commonly available. The high degree of rationalization in production and the development of complete new lines for new models have also strongly facilitated the introduction of robots (WMCC, EDU 1984*a*, p. 86).

However, the introduction of this new technology has not in itself drastically displaced labour. The WMCC (1984*a*, p. 43), estimated that direct displacement of labour due to the use of robots in production ranged from 0 to 6 persons per robot with an average of 2.6. Even if job loss occurred at the top of this scale, only 300 workers would have been displaced by the 50 robots installed at Longbridge. This is insignificant when compared with the approximately 40 000 jobs lost in BL plants in the West Midlands County between 1977 and 1984. However, where the introduction of new technology is allied to radical changes in established work practices, as in the case of BL, the impact upon employment can be drastic.

Elsewhere investment and technical change have been associated with loss of jobs. Cadbury-Schweppes, for example, announced a £125 million programme to modernize its chocolate and confectionery division in 1980. More than 3000 jobs were lost, the majority at Bournville in Birmingham with redundancies concentrated amongst part-time women workers (Gaffakin and Nickson 1984, p. 110).

Similarly, at GEC investment in new production facilities has taken place following the company's switch to the manufacture of the new System X tele-communication equipment by the mid 1980s. Unlike the manufacture of the old equipment which was essentially labour-intensive, the production of the new equipment is a capital-intensive process. Jobs have therefore been lost. In 1971 the five Coventry plants of GEC Telecommunications employed more than 15 000 workers. By 1981 this had been reduced to some 11 000, and a year later to fewer than 10 000 (Gaffakin and Nickson 1984, p. 124). To a large extent this cutback in jobs during the 1970s was part of the company's large-scale rationalization programme which also hit plants in other parts of the West Midlands (Massey and Meegan 1978). However, since 1982 redundancies have been linked very closely to the introduction of System X. At the end of 1982 GEC Telecommunications announced 1150 redundancies at its Coventry factories, blaming its decision on British Tele-com's accelerated change-over to System X (*Financial Times*, 2 Dec. 1982). By 1985 future job losses in GEC and British Telecom appeared likely.

Investment in new methods of production has therefore begun to have an impact on employment in the West Midlands. In many cases the introduc-tion of new manufacturing systems has been linked to other processes of change, principally rationalization and intensification. High unemployment in the West Midlands and the threat of job loss has made it easier for man-agement to undertake changes in the labour process with little union oppo-sition. Although new manufacturing systems are the exception rather than the rule in the West Midlands in the mid-1980s, there is evidence to suggest that they are beginning to spread into the components sector. The compo-nents companies have been major recipients of aid under the Support for Innovation Scheme since 1982, which suggests that rapid technological advances in products and processes are now occurring. Such advances will have a negative impact on employment in the West Midlands in future years.

Shift to low-cost locations Companies have not confined their attempts to reduce costs to changes in their plants in the UK, however. A number of the 'prime movers' have shifted production overseas to those parts of the world where labour and other costs are significantly lower than in the West Mid-lands.

The region and its work-force have been increasingly integrated into the global production of its transnational 'prime movers' (Lloyd and Shutt 1983). A number of the West-Midlands-based companies have traditionally owned subsidiary companies overseas, notably in the same British Common-wealth countries in which sales of their products were high. The period from the mid-1960s to the mid-1980s witnessed a new phase of overseas develop-ment. We have discussed the move by some companies into Europe to exploit markets; others shifted production overseas to exploit cost advantages. Most notable amongst these was British Sound Reproducers (BSR).

BSR, although originally set up in 1932 as a manufacturer of medical equipment, grew rapidly through the 1960s and 1970s as a result of the success of its production of automatic record-changers. By 1976 the company was being hailed as a very successful producer of a low-cost, high-volume product and had gained 60 per cent of the world market in record-changers. Profits increased, reaching a record £28.9 million in 1976. However, a change in consumer tastes, a move away from record-players to cassette-players, and increased competition from overseas producers, notably Japanese, led to a turn-round in the fortunes of BSR. In 1979 BSR's pre-tax profits fell from £15.2 million to £3.9 million, and by 1980 the company was ranked the tenth-biggest loss-maker among the top 1000 UK companies (Gaffakin and Nickson 1984).

The response of BSR's management was two-fold. First, there was a switch to new product areas, principally electronics, and a run-down of the audio division. Second, the company concentrated investment and production in the low-cost area of South-east Asia.

While BSR was expanding in the Far East, it was retrenching its activities in the West Midlands. Between 1980 and 1982, 10 000 jobs were lost as the company rationalized its production facilities at home (*Financial Times*, 16 Feb. 1982). Further redundancies occurred throughout 1983 and 1984. By 1985 the focus of its production had clearly shifted to the Far East. Its world headquarters are no longer to be found in the Black Country but in Hong Kong. As Gaffakin and Nickson (1984) argue, BSR has effectively become a Far Eastern electronics group, with new products and a new geographical base.

BSR has not been alone in developing production in low-cost locations. Dunlop, Glynwed, Birmid Qualcast, and Delta have all built up capacity in low-cost locations. However, it would be wrong to overstate the importance of this process of change as an explanation of job loss in the West Midlands. While the internationalization of production has been a dominant feature of change amongst the 'prime movers' of the West Midlands economy, the growth of investment overseas has been determined as much by market considerations as by cost.

New sources of supply   The final strategies adopted by companies in order to reduce costs were to change their policies towards their sources of supply or to put pressure on their components suppliers to keep down prices. Given the high degree of vertical integration within the economy of the West Midlands and the high proportion of companies involved in the production of basic and intermediate goods, the policy adopted by the small number of companies involved in final assembly is of strategic importance. A decision to purchase components elsewhere can seriously undermine the profitability of a supply company. For example, the decision of BL to acquire a number of components from single sources in the late 1970s was a crucial factor in the financial difficulties of Rubery Owen and Wilmott Breedon (Flynn and Taylor 1984,

p. 120). At the same time the purchase of components from the cheapest possible supplier may be the only way for a company such as BL to keep costs down and survive.

As a result the relationship between BL and its component suppliers has become aggressive in recent years. BL has threatened to turn to overseas sources if prices are not kept down and quality maintained. As part of this strategy of reducing the cost of parts bought in, BL undertook in 1984–5 a world-wide survey of components which, it claimed, showed that it could purchase 70 per cent of these parts outside the UK at prices on average 20 per cent lower than in the UK. However, BL has used the threat to turn to overseas sources as a lever to push down prices and in the mid-1980s was still buying the majority of its parts from the UK. Austin Rover, for example, still purchased 85 per cent of its parts from the UK in 1984, one-third of these coming from the West Midlands.

However, if Austin Rover did increase its rate of imports, the cost in jobs would in high. A report by the WMCC Economic Development Unit (1984*b*) concluded that if the company trebled its imports, as had been suggested, then 12 900 jobs in the West Midlands would be lost. The report also forecast that Austin Rover's output would climb from 400 000 cars in 1984 to 575 000 by 1986, creating a further 13 000 jobs in the components industry. In that case, if the proportion of imported components remained at 15 per cent, the net loss of jobs resulting from the rise in imports would be in excess of 25 000. The report went on to state that far more jobs would be lost in the West Midlands once the proportion of Austin Rover's components which were imported reached 30 per cent. For every additional 1 per cent of components brought in from overseas 850 jobs would be lost. As an article in the *Engineer* (22 Mar. 1984) pointed out, Austin Rover had not ruled out the possibility of obtaining as much as 45 per cent of its components abroad.

British Leyland is not alone in its search for cheaper raw materials and components. As major users of steel, the 'prime movers' in the West Midlands must have contributed to the increasing importation of foreign steel since 1979. Furthermore, elsewhere in the economy, the rise in the import penetration in many intermediate good markets (for example, castings, fasteners, ball bearings) suggests that many companies are purchasing goods from the cheapest possible source, thus weakening the linkage pattern within the West Midlands.

Marketing strategies

Non-price competition The importance of product in an understanding of a company's success or failure has been little discussed. However, in the oligopolistic market structure in which the majority of companies operate the features of the product itself, its design or quality, are of equal if not greater importance than price. Earlier we illustrated how a number of the prime movers, such as TI, had been adapting their range of products in order to move into markets in which they competed on design rather than price. For other prime movers a failure to update the final product that they manufactured underlay their decline. For example, British Ever-Ready (later renamed Berec) saw sales slump when it failed to respond to the challenge posed by the alkaline batteries of Duracell.

Failure to develop marketable models in the late 1960s and 1970s was another of the root causes of BL's decline as the market leader in UK car sales, and a cause of its failure to expand into Europe. The two new models that the company introduced during this period, the Marina and Allegro, failed to capture sales. Furthermore, when these products were sold in BL's limited markets, low-volume production of models was the almost inevitable result (Williams, Williams, and Thomas 1983).

Turner (1971) argues that the failure of BL's models was the result of a corporate planning process which was preoccupied with the design of 'high style' motor cars, cost-engineered so they were cheap to manufacture. In setting these objectives, BL management misread the European car market and misunderstood the significance of cost-engineering which could improve margins in the mass-production business but could not produce profits if individual models did not sell in volume. Hence the profits crisis of the mid-1970s.

If product-led decline contributed to collapse, Michael Edwardes saw the development of new marketable models as one of the keys to future success. Under Edwardes, BL began a complete revision of its product range in 1978. The first fruit of this reassessment was the Metro in 1980, followed by the Maestro in 1983, and the Montego in 1984, followed by the new Rover in the same year. By 1985, BL had a competitive range spanning the complete spectrum. However, the company has been attempting to increase sales at a time when there has been massive overcapacity in the European car industry and all assemblers are competing vigorously to win sales from their rivals. This has been the case for some time (Central Policy Review Staff 1975).

Elsewhere in the economy of the West Midlands the development of new products has been an integral part of companies' survival strategies. At Cadbury-Schweppes the launch of Wispa was a crucial element in the company's attempt to reverse twenty years of declining market share. Like the introduction of the Metro, Cadbury-Schweppes linked the development and manufacture of the new product to the introduction of new automated production lines. The Wispa line is a key part of the £160 million new investment at Bournville.

Thus the marketability of a company's products is crucial to its profitability. The unattractiveness of BL's products, rather than any cost considerations, led to the decline in the company's sales in the 1970s. Its survival depends on the marketability of its new products. Conversely GKN benefited from a rapid increase in demand for a product it was producing, the constant-velocity joint. This was developed originally in the 1950s for the then innovatory front-wheel-drive Mini and has been in constant demand as all European producers have moved to front-wheel-drive cars. GKN patents ensured that it captured more than 90 per cent of the European market. As competitive pressures increase, both within the developed economies and from low-cost economies in the Third World, the differentiation of product by design or technological features will become of increasing importance in the ability to gain market share. Many of the 'prime movers' in the West Midlands are now recognizing this and are taking steps to expand research and development either in-house (for example, GKN) or through joint ventures (for example, the collaboration between Lucas and Smiths Industries). Those that fail to adopt such a strategy will face problems in the future.

The Restructured Economy: Success or Failure?

The economy of the West Midlands County in 1984 was fundamentally different from that of 1964. The growth and prosperity which characterized the local economy in the 1960s had gone, to be replaced by unemployment and decline. Although the character of the manufacturing base of the area remained essentially dominated by the metal-using and engineering industries, many of the traditional activities of the local economy—steel-making, motor cycles, foundries, fasteners, machine tools—had been drastically run down. Furthermore, the decline of the vehicle industry had brought into question its centrality in the industrial nexus of the West Midlands economy.

The general malaise of the local economy in recent years has been popularly viewed as an indication of the failure to invest, improve productivity, or develop new products. The work-force has also been used as an explanation for decline. Militancy and high wages, it has been argued, have discouraged potential investors and added to the cost of indigenous goods, and hence undermined competitiveness. Yet our research has highlighted the complexity of change occurring within the economy of the West Midlands.

To put it simply, this complex process of economic change encompasses both 'prime movers' who have been unsuccessful in the competitive struggle and those who have been successful in diversifying, expanding output, and returning to favourable rates of profit. Success and failure are in fact interdependent. Given the competitive free market, a firm can only increase its market share at the expense of its rivals. Furthermore job loss and plant closure are as much the result of successful adaptation as of failure to adapt. Rationalization of production locally has been inextricably tied to corporate strategies aimed at diversification or the internationalization of production. Although the purging of redundant capacity may have taken place in the absence of these other trends, given widespread over-capacity produced by deep recession, it is difficult to abstract one from the others.

An appreciation of the interaction between investment and disinvestment, or rationalization, is therefore crucial to an understanding of the decline of the West Midlands. Investment in new sectors and markets by the 'prime movers' has been paralleled by disinvestment in those areas in which the relative rate of profit is low. This is a continuous process of change under market conditions in which the pursuit of maximized profit drives the national economy. This process of change, however, has spatial outcomes as local economies win or lose in the search for profit.

Furthermore the means by which firms diversified into new markets and sectors militated against the economy of the West Midlands. Our research has shown that if 'prime movers' wished to increase their involvement in a sector in which they previously had no interest, they did so by purchasing or merging with another company which already had a stake in that sector. As the West Midlands was specialized in the industrial sectors which the 'prime movers' were attempting to shift away from, acquisition by definition had to take place outside the county or region. Even if acquisition did take place within the West Midlands, this did not alter the industrial structure of the local economy but merely concentrated ownership. (For a fuller discussion of this point see Flynn and Taylor 1984, pp. 133–9.)

Between the mid-1960s and mid-1980s the West Midlands economy deteriorated. Disinvestment and rationalization were the dominant features, as key industries and companies were restructured. This is not to argue, however, that production or investment was transfered from the West Midlands, or that other regions benefited at the cost of the West Midlands. We have tried to show that investment in new sectors and markets was necessary to ensure the survival of the 'prime movers' under the economic rules which prevailed. Those companies which failed to diversify markets and products were those hit hardest by recession (for example, Rubery Owen).

As 'prime movers' were diversifying into sectors and markets which gave more favourable rates of return, it is fair to assume that their more traditional activities in the West Midlands would have been most vulnerable at a time of recession. Any programme of rationalization reduces a company's dependence upon those areas which are producing the lowest return on capital or have the lowest expected rate of return in the future. Therefore it was likely that West Midlands plants would bear the brunt of plant closures. While it is difficult to confirm this proposition with empirical evidence, given the unreliability of redundancy data, our work points in this direction. The proposition is confirmed by a CBI survey of its members which estimated that between 1980 and 1983 the number of employees in manufacturing in the West Midlands Region had fallen 33 per cent as a weighted average compared with a fall of approximately 20 per cent in the total number employed in manufacturing in the UK. Thus the post-1979 recession has had a disproportionate effect on employment in the West Midlands, much of which can only be understood in the context of the corporate strategies pursued by the 'prime movers' over the previous two decades.

One final point needs to be made. Although the depth of the recent recession has caused large-scale scrapping of capacity, much of this may have been viable under different economic conditions. Factories and plants which were closed in the post-1979 recession were not all old, obsolete, and inefficient. Indeed the closure of the most modern electric arc furnace in Europe followed the near-bankruptcy of Duport. Although this plant was outside the West Midlands Region, its closure is an indication of the effect on a modern efficient plant of the wave of rationalization forced upon companies during the recession. Within the West Midlands County, Duport re-rolling mills which had recently been modernized were also closed. Investment in modernization had been viewed as advantageous when undertaken only a few years earlier, but the recession drastically altered the economic conditions in which the company operated. In the economic downturn the company was in a very weak competitive position against the subsidized BSC and its more diversified and larger rivals in the private sector GKN and TI.

Elsewhere in the county, rationalization involved the scrapping of relatively modern plant. For example, BL's Rover plant in Solihull was only five years old at the time of its closure in 1981. Thus whatever its cause, rationalization has been a dominant feature of job loss in the West Midlands, as both new and old capacity have been scrapped. When this combined with the other processes of corporate change—intensification, policy towards sources, shift to low-cost locations, and investment in new technology—it is clearly correct to point out, as Massey and Meegan (1982) do, that 'job loss is not one single or simple process'. The aggregate results in employment terms however, are, all too obvious. As Table 5.1 illustrates, the 'prime movers' in the local economy shed an estimated 40 per cent of their work-force between 1977 and 1982. This illustrates well the scale of contraction in the manufacturing base of the local economy and the size of the problem facing policymakers in the West Midlands and nationally.

Is the West Midlands economy in the mid-1980s emerging from the recession smaller and weaker, caught in a spiral of decline, or leaner, fitter, and better equipped to compete in the world? The answer for the 'prime movers' may be different from that for the national economy as a whole, or for the work-force within the local economy. Certainly a majority of the 'prime movers' were reporting improved profits by 1985, as they reaped the benefits of substantial improvements in productivity and management performance. However, in 1985 industry in the West Midlands was operating from a much smaller base than in 1980, even if there are grounds for believing that the new base was sounder. The loss of jobs has been dramatic. The structure of a number of the 'prime movers' has drastically altered. Although the 'prime movers' have largely survived, for those without jobs in the local economy the outlook for the future is not optimistic. Large sections of West

Table 5.1. *Employment Change among the Top Twenty-six Manufacturing Companies in the West Midlands County, 1977–1982*

| | No. employed | | Employment change |
	1977	1982	1977–1982 (% reduction)
Locally controlled[a] companies	105 963	58 368	44.9
National, externally controlled companies	174 243	108 336	37.8
Overseas-controlled companies	26 170	16 076	38.6
Total	306 376	182 780	40.3

Note: [a] Within the West Midlands Region.
Source: WMCC, West Midlands Prime Movers Data Bank.

Midlands industry no longer exist, competitive pressures are still intense, and therefore there is continuing impetus for further improvements in productivity and reductions in costs. Much of West Midlands industry is operating below full capacity. Even if demand increases dramatically, employment seems unlikely to rise. Thus a return to the prosperity of the 1960s and 1970s appears unlikely.

6

Central-government Policy and Economic Change

In Chapter 3 we examined the changes in the West Midlands economy which produced the weakened economy which was confronted by the recession after 1979. In this chapter we look at one of the groups of factors which caused that weakness, that is, the policies of successive governments. Not all policies have been designed to revive the national economy or to rescue sectors and companies represented in the West Midlands. This chapter will examine those policies, or interventions in the economy, which have been designed to contribute towards the revival of the West Midlands.

Discussion of the effects of government policy on the economy of the West Midlands has tended to concentrate on the collection of actions which have been included in regional policy. At various times since 1934 there have been policies designed to reduce the differences between the unemployment rates of Development Areas (whose definition has also changed over the years) and those of the more prosperous areas of the UK. These policies have been of two types: incentives for investment in the Development Areas (grants, loans, tax concessions, subsidies on costs such as the costs of premises or labour) and regulation of factory, office, and warehouse building in the more prosperous areas. Until the 1980s the West Midlands has been defined as a more prosperous area, where to varying degrees development has been discouraged in favour of the areas of higher unemployment.

However, in addition to these policies there have been various actions by government which have had an impact on the region's economy, but which were designed without account necessarily being taken of their impact on the West Midlands, or indeed on any other region. These actions have mainly resulted from policies which have had as their main objective the interests of the national economy, and specifically the manufacturing sector.

There have been actions which have resulted from policies concerned with the national economy and not necessarily with any particular sector. These policies, which have had profound effects on the development of the companies represented in the West Midlands, include exchange-rate policy, the various measures of demand management which have had a specific impact on manufacturers of consumer durable goods at various times, and trade policy, which has shifted the direction of trade and the scale of trading with the major world trading partners. While none of these policies was designed with the West Midlands in mind, they have all, at various times, had a

113

deleterious effect on the companies operating in the region, as exemplified in Chapter 5.

Since the late 1970s we have seen policies directed towards the reduction of public expenditure. The West Midlands has in most years been a net contributor to the exchequer. In the 1980s recently this has been less frequent as increased unemployment has reduced the tax contribution made by the region and increased the demand on public expenditure for unemployment benefit and social-security payments. However, there has been a reduction in one element of public expenditure in the region, and that is the contribution of central government to local-government spending in the area (see Chapter 2). This reduction has brought with it the multiplier effects which any reduction in demand would have.

To isolate the impact of a particular policy is not a simple matter. Analysis of the impact of regional policies on the levels of employment and unemployment in the regions for which the policies were designed to produce benefits has been beset with the fundamental difficulty of determining what would have happened in those regions had there been no policy. Would companies have been attracted by the availablity of labour and reduced wage rates in those areas if they had not had the incentives provided by regional policy? This problem is at least as difficult in the regions where there has been a policy of reducing development in order to divert it to the Development Areas. Would companies have left the former because of the congestion which was thought to increase costs or because of the shortages of labour which made control of manufacturing processes difficult?

In the case of some of the other policies, the problem may be even more difficult. Companies will always complain of government policy as a contributory factor to their lack of success. Increasing value of the national currency, tariff restrictions in export markets, and restrictions on consumer credit, for example, make more acceptable explanations to shareholders than inadequate management foresight and strategy for reversing the declining fortunes of companies.

However, this chapter attempts to establish the evidence as to the impact of central-government policies on the economy of the West Midlands Region. It will necessarily be tentative in its conclusions for the reasons just stated, but we shall seek to show that policy has generally been more conducive to weakness than to strength in the local economy. We shall also try to establish why those policies have been pursued.

Import Penetration, Exports, and the Value of Sterling

Price competitiveness of UK exports in foreign markets and of producers in the UK market is affected by three factors:

(*a*)   the relative costs of production in the competing economies; these will

be determined by the level of technological development, wage rates paid, working practices, and prices of materials
(b)   the exchange rate of sterling with the currencies of the competing economies
(c)   taxation and tariff policies.

The first two factors can clearly change in opposite directions in any period. It was argued, (for example, by the Bank of England before the 1967 devaluation) that a high value of sterling would force changes in productivity and unit costs in UK manufacturing by making price competition with foreign producers more difficult. A devaluation, it was argued, would protect manufacturers from increased overseas competition (Coakley and Harris 1983, p. 233). The value of sterling and the general level of inflation are not within the control of any company, but in combination inflation and an increase in the value of sterling can have a devastating impact on import penetration, export sales, and sterling profits made from export sales.

Williams, Williams, and Thomas (1983, pp. 12–13) argue that devaluation of sterling after 1967 was sufficient to compensate for UK price increases in excess of those of competitor countries. It was not until the appreciation of sterling from 1979 that UK companies' competitiveness was seriously reduced, thus causing major problems of import penetration and export failure. They argue that competitive factors other than price have been more important than prices in determining trade performance. Dunnett (1980) shows the positive effect of the 1967 devaluation on exports of motor vehicles to Europe, Canada, the USA, and Australia. The upturn of sterling after 1979 was certainly a contributor to the difficulties of the West Midlands. Edwardes (1983, p. 136) reported that the increased value of the pound in 1980 negated efforts to improve BL's productivity:

I told [the Governor of the Bank of England] that if the government persisted in these policies, 50 000 of our people would lose their jobs . . . it was infuriating. Just as we got the business into a semblance of shape and order there would be another surge in the pound which yet again threw us off course.

This concern about the high value of sterling was also voiced by many other leading companies in the West Midlands. Outlining the adverse effect of high interest rates and a strong pound Sir Brian Kellett, Chairman of TI, argued that

[the] exchange rate . . . has reduced export margins and increased import competitiveness far more than is compensated by import costs of raw materials . . . Government must recognise the danger that some sectors of manufacturing industry may not survive in sufficient strength to play their part in national recovery in due course. (TI 1979; p. 4.)

James F. Insch, Chairman of Birmid Qualcast, stated:

It is disturbing that, although our efficiency factors and manning levels are comparable with the best European competitors, imported castings pose a major threat due to the strength of sterling. (Birmid Qualcast 1980, p. 2)

And Lord Caldecote, Chairman of the Delta Metal Company, reported:

the strong pound has stimulated competition from imports and is adding to our difficulties of meeting competition from less developed countries in export markets. (Delta Metal Company 1978, p. 7.)

However, the increasing value of sterling only partially explains the deterioration in the competitiveness of UK exports after 1977. Between 1977 and 1982 the national increase in relative unit labour costs was 45 per cent (OECD 1983). In the early years of this rise increased prices produced an increase in the value of exports: later increased prices produced a reduction in the volume of exports. Between 1971 and 1982 the reduction in export market shares by product volume in manufactures was 25 per cent. OECD (1983, p. 21) estimated that 'The effective appreciation of sterling contributed about 5 percentage points to the 45 per cent rise in relative unit labour costs over this period and excessive pay rises coupled with low productivity contributed the additional 40 percentage points'.

Trade policy

The other influence on price competitiveness is the trade tariffs payable on exports and imports. Morgan (1978) has estimated that tariff reductions over the period 1959–72 accounted for more than one-third of the total increase in UK imports of semi-manufactures and more than a quarter of the increase in imports of finished goods (see also Morgan and Martin 1975). In January 1960 the average tariffs on semi-manufactured goods and finished goods were 12.1 per cent and 18 per cent respectively. By 1972, after the Dillon and Kennedy rounds of tariff reductions and the European Free Tax Association (EFTA) negotiations, the average tariffs had been reduced to 5.8 per cent and 8.5 per cent. Although tariff reductions do not explain the whole of the increase in imports during the 1960s, Morgan (1978, pp. 561–2) concludes: 'by its influence on imports of manufactures, commercial policy has reinforced the swing in the origin of imports away from the Commonwealth and towards Western Europe'.

The UK's entry to the EEC in 1973 gradually changed its tariff structure so that by July 1977 customs duties on imports from the EEC had been removed and UK tariffs replaced by the Common External Tariff of the EEC. However, the system of Commonwealth preference had already been eroded through the creation of EFTA and the previous negotiations about entry to the EEC. Both Commonwealth preference and sterling area arrangements acted to the advantage of UK manufacturers. The holding of sterling balances in non-convertible form in London banks ensured that members of the sterling area bought imports with sterling. Commonwealth preference encouraged exports to the UK and thus the building of sterling balances.

The switch in trade patterns, encouraged by commercial policy, had an impact on the manufacturing sectors in the West Midlands. In 1950 more than two-thirds of UK car exports went to Commonwealth countries. In 1955/6 Australia and New Zealand took more than 31 per cent of BMC exports (Williams, Williams, and Thomas 1983, p. 236).

The relative protection of Commonwealth markets was to the advantage of UK manufacturers. The loss of Commonwealth markets had adverse consequences in several sectors. In the motor-car sector, Dunnett (1980, p. 33) shows that the sterling area offered protection for UK manufacturers in the immediate post-war period while there was a shortage of dollars in the world: 'Given the state of the European industry, the British motor industry held a virtual monopoly over the many would-be buyers who held sterling'. However he cites the temporary convertibility of sterling in 1947 as evidence that these markets were safe only when protected: 'Demand for British cars decreased immediately. One million pounds worth of export orders for Nuffield alone were cancelled [in Australia]'. (Dunnett 1980, p. 34.) As the sterling areas slowly collapsed, these advantages were removed and protection was lost.

Massey (1979) reports similar effects of changing trade patterns in electrical engineering. In the case of heavy electrical machinery, market decline was primarily due to loss of markets in the Commonwealth with the ending of Commonwealth preference.

The adverse effect which the dominance of Commonwealth markets had on the prosperity of industry in the West Midlands was compounded by the latter's failure to develop alternative openings in Europe and North America. BL, for example, failed to develop an efficient distribution network in Europe. This failing was particularly apparent in France and Germany, two of the big three national markets on mainland Europe, where throughout the 1970s BL, like its predecessor BMC, had no dealer network. Consequently, in 1975, when three and a half million new cars were sold in France and Germany, BL managed to sell just 7204 cars in these two markets (Williams, Williams, and Thomas 1983, p. 238).

GEC also failed to diversify its overseas markets and to make inroads into Europe or North America. GEC has, until the 1980s, continued to do best in a number of Commonwealth countries and former British zones of influence, which were protected territories for British firms in the inter-war years of the internal cartel of the electrical-engineering industry (Jones and Marriot 1970). The early 1980s did see a growth in export sales to non-Commonwealth Asia, the Middle East, and Latin America, but the company has apparently made no significant breakthroughs in either of the two major markets of Europe or the United States (Williams, Williams, and Thomas 1983, p. 150).

Other companies operating in the West Midlands did, however, recognize the importance of the European and North American markets, although somewhat belatedly, in the early 1970s. Unfortunately, this shift in market effort coincided with the end of the post-war boom and added to the intensification of competition among the developed economies (Armstrong, Glyn, and Harrison 1984). This made the push into Europe more difficult, although it was clearly seen as a possible market for increased sales and profits especially after the UK's entry to the EEC.

Some West-Midlands-based companies were major participants in the shift in the pattern of trade away from the old Empire markets in recognition of the need to exploit better returns in Europe and North America. This move away from the Commonwealth was not, however, entirely due to strategic decisions by the companies, but in many cases was forced upon them by the breakdown of Commonwealth preference and by national legislation to sustain a high degree of local contact in products in countries such as India and Australia. The UK's entry to the EEC gave an added spur.

Domestic demand management

While companies in the West Midlands were affected by changing patterns of trade, which were in turn influenced by changing trade policies, they were also affected by demand-management policies at home. Consumer-credit regulations have been changed very frequently during the post-war period of Keynesian economic regulation. The control of consumer credit particularly affects producers of consumer durables, including electrical goods, motor cycles, and motor cars. Construction, especially construction of housing in the public sector, has also been a frequent tool of governments wishing to control aggregate demand in the economy. Policy-induced fluctuations in building have an adverse effect on those industries supplying building materials and architectual hardware. More generally, counter-cyclical measures to affect investment have an impact on the capital-goods sectors of the economy. Had all these policy measures successfully regulated demand in such a way that there was a consistent level of demand, they would have been beneficial to these capital-goods sectors. In fact the policies resulted in periods of acute changes in demand, both up and down, and had a harmful effect on manufacturing industry.

Credit controls on hire-purchase have been used as economic regulators from the beginning of 'stop–go' policy in 1953. The instruments used were restriction on the maximum repayment period allowed and restriction on the minimum deposit required. Purchase tax has also been used for short-term demand management and has particularly affected demand for consumer durables. In the case of cars and motor cycles, excise-duty rates on vehicles and car tax have also been used as regulators of demand.

Examples of the use of these controls include the attempt to damp home demand in 1955, following a deterioration in the performance of car exports. The minimum hire-purchase deposit was reintroduced at 15 per cent in February 1955 and raised to $33\frac{1}{3}$ per cent in July, while purchase tax was raised from 50 per cent to 60 per cent. The Suez crisis in the following year produced a further reduction in demand. The recovery in demand began in 1957, and was sustained by the removal of hire-purchase controls in 1958. However, balance-of-payments problems in 1960 led to the reintroduction of hire-purchase restrictions, and by 1961 the output of the UK motor industry had been reduced to 40 per cent of capacity. The next balance-of-payments crisis produced similar restrictions on consumer credit (as alternatives to devaluation) in 1965.

These changes in demand induced by alterations to credit availability have had important consequences for industry: the frequency of the changes has made sales unpredictable and has disrupted cash flow; the cutting off of demand at times of growth has inhibited the development of capacity and therefore contributed to the increase in imports at times of high domestic demand. The Crowther Committee on consumer credit in 1971 accepted that the use of credit controls was detrimental to industry: 'the industries affected . . . have the right to enquire whether the net benefit to the community is commensurate with the undoubted damage done to them' (quoted in Blackaby 1978, p. 227).

On the car industry the impact of changes in credit controls was dramatic. The easing of credit restrictions in 1971 produced an increase in domestic demand for cars of 43 per cent which generated a large increase in imports (see, for example, Dunnett 1980, p. 128) which was maintained through the deflation of 1974. The frequent changes in the credit rules, combined with the lifting of tariffs and other international changes over the period, reduced the ability of the UK car industry to re-equip and invest.

Similarly stop–go policy adversely affected the white-goods (for example, fridges, washing-machines) and motor-cycle industries. Smith (1981, p. 41) argues that in the case of motor cycles economic policy adversely affected sales and prevented forward planning. In particular, the coincidence of the Budget and the start of the motor-cycle selling season in April meant that adjustments to production were difficult to implement. Thus removal of taxes could leave markets unmet, while their introduction on another occasion could leave a company loaded down with unwanted stocks. By way of illustration, BSA considered that tighter higher-purchase regulations had cut its sales by one-third in 1959/60 and noted that these changes were the tenth such change in eight years.

In addition frequent changes in demand induced by the alteration of credit availability had important knock-on consequences for the machine-tool industry. Through their impact on investment decisions, demand-management policies served to compound the cyclical nature of demand for machine tools. It was these cyclical fluctuations, it was argued in the House of

Commons, Trade and Industry Committee's inquiry into the industry, in 1983, that weakened the UK machine tool-industry and led to increased import penetration. Machine-tool companies could not affort to maintain capacity to supply the peaks in demand, and therefore have chosen to produce for an average level of supply. The consequence of this is two-fold:

(*a*) in recession deliveries are very short and some companies build for stock
(*b*) in periods of high demand, delivery dates are long and excessive demand is met by importers who can offer shorter deliveries and better terms.

It is thus claimed that successive cycles of activity enable importers to establish a 'bridgehead' of sales, service, and spares, such that in the next upturn they are in a stronger position to achieve more orders against indigenous industry, which has been further weakened by the loss of orders at the peak of the previous cycle. (WMCC 1983*b*, p. 27).

However, a note of caution is needed. Although commentators such as Dow (1964, p. 176) have argued that fiscal policy has served to heighten fluctuations in demand and hence produced an adverse environment for UK industry, others have argued that changes in fiscal policy have usually been relatively small (see Williams, Williams, and Thomas 1983, p. 97). Furthermore, the economic fluctuations experienced by the UK were, in the 1960s and 1970s, worse than those experienced by other countries. There were problems with periodic collapses of demand in the consumer-durable sectors, but in the case of vehicles, other national economies coped successfully with equally severe fluctuations (Jones and Prais 1978). Thus even if the difficulties produced by stop–go policies had been removed, other problems would have remained.

Government Policy towards Particular Sectors

Under the Industry Act, 1972 and the Industrial Development Act, 1982, various payments have been made in the West Midlands, adding up to £57.1 million at the end of March 1983 (Bentley and Mawson 1984). Offers of assistance totalling £92.95 million were made by the same date. The money spent was mainly directed towards the ferrous foundry sector (£13.8 million), non-ferrous foundries (£12.1 million), machine tools (£10.7 million), and drop-forging (£4.1 million) (these figures are to March 1981). The Small Engineering Firms Investment Scheme contributed £6.2 million by March 1983.

The predominant share received by these sectors of the assistance granted to the region reflects the mix of industries in the region. Payments to other sectors were small. Under the Electronic Components Industry Scheme the West Midlands had only one successful application for assistance. The region received only 2.9 per cent of the cash available under the Instrumentation and Automation Industry Scheme, while it received £243 000 of the total of £33 million spent under the Mirco-Electronics Industry Support Programme. Since these schemes are essentially demand-led (that is, companies make applications for assistance) the lack of expenditure reflects the general low level of investment in these sectors in the region.

Concern for the low level of take-up of these schemes caused some concern in the Department of Trade and Industry (DTI) and led to efforts to increase awareness of, and applications for, assistance. A 'Team for Innovation' was established in 1982 to promote the 'Support for Innovation Programme' which had been introduced in May 1982. This programme was not new, being an amalgamation of various schemes of assistance already on offer. Linked to the setting up of the promotion team was the declaration that John Butcher, a junior minister at the DTI, was to be given responsibility for the West Midlands, a role which was maintained until late 1984.

Apart from these general schemes of assistance, central government also gave aid to particular companies, for example, Chrysler and Norton-Villiers Triumph, or was involved in a more direct way, principally by the intervention of the Industrial Reorganization Corporation and the National Enterprise Board (Bentley and Mawson 1984; Flynn and Taylor 1984).

By far the greatest involvement of central government in West Midlands industry was its intervention in BL. The formation of the company, through the acquisition of BMH by Leyland in 1968, was sponsored by the British government through the Industrial Reorganization Corporation. However, although the government helped Leyland management in many ways (it provided an informal assurance that any merger would not be referred to the Monopolies Commission, and Harold Wilson hosted a dinner party at Chequers for the chairmen of BMH and Leyland), the government did not provide large-scale financial assistance for the new British Leyland Motor Corporation (Williams, Williams, and Thomas 1983, p. 225). Nevertheless, the initial £25m loan, with the addition of a further £10 million later, did constitute the Corporation's biggest advance of money to any company (Hague and Wilkinson 1980).

The collapse of BL in 1975 brought government into closer contact with the company. The rescue of BL was a test for the newly elected Labour government's interventionist policy towards the economy. The rescue plan included a 95 per cent government stake in the company and a call for an inquiry into the future strategy for success. The resultant Ryder Plan called for a 'massive programme to modernize plant and equipment at BL' whereby £2000 million, mainly government money, was to be invested over eight years.

However, by 1977 Ryder had failed and Edwardes was brought in to head the company. The Ryder Plan was abandoned in favour of a more modest corporate plan of February 1978 which was to be supported by the issue of £450 million by government equity. The new management's strategy was partly defensive, in that it relied upon a programme of plant closures. At the same time, state financing allowed the new management to make offensive plans for a 'product-led recovery'.

So what was the role of government in the affairs of BL? Certainly, the State has provided the company with a great deal of financial support. Between 1977/8 and 1983/4 BL Ltd. received some £1979 million (HMSO 1983 and 1984). A number of reports were commissioned on the future of BL and the UK car industry, notably by Ryder, and by the Central Policy Review Staff (Central Policy Review Staff 1975). Yet there was never a distinctive government strategy for the firm or the industry (Williams, Williams, and Thomas 1983). The management of BL was left to decide how the money was spent, the government's role was to oversee the general strategy without providing any real input into the running of the company. Nevertheless, government has played an important role in legitimizing management's plans to restore profitability (Taylor 1980). This was of particular importance during the early years of the Edwardes era, when the Labour government backed his plant-closure plans. Government acceptance of the plant-closure strategy became clear when James Callaghan, then Prime Minister, said that he would not try to stop the closure of plants, adding that he did not wish to 'pull Michael Edwardes coat tails' (quoted in Benyon 1978, p. 13). Thus the government's role was one of overseeing the restructuring of BL while freeing the company from the need to make profits by giving it substantial aid. However, it is argued, much of this aid, rather than being used for the strategic development of the company in the form of long-term equity finance, was used to service and repay short-term debt (Williams, Williams, and Thomas 1983).

Although State intervention in BL was the largest of its kind in a West Midlands company, other companies received aid as part of government industrial strategy. Alfred Herbert was a partner in the ill-fated Herbert-Ingersoll machine-tool company set up by the Industrial Reorganization Corporation in 1967 (Hague and Wilkinson 1983). Later, following its collapse, the State became further involved in the company, when the National Enterprise Board took a 100 per cent stake in it.

The corporation was also involved in the merger between Associated Electrical Industries (AEI) and GEC, which had an impact on a number of plants in the West Midlands (see Massey and Meegan 1978). Government was also involved through the corporation in the rescue of Rolls Royce and Cammell Laird, the parent company of the bus and carriage makers Metro-Cammell.

In the 1970s the West Midlands was particularly affected by central government's policy towards the steel industry (Bentley and Mawson 1984; Flynn and Taylor 1984). Local steel producers were hit by nationalization in 1967, although many steel-rolling and finishing plants in the region remained in private hands. Through the 1970s the local economy was affected by plans by British Steel to rationalize steel production by reducing capacity and concentrating production in the five main integrated plants. This led to the closure of the Bilston steelworks in 1975.

With the collapse of demand after 1979 further rationalization occurred. In engineering steels the Phoenix plan has resulted in a number of plant closures. Between 1979 and 1982 six steel plants were closed in the West Midlands, resulting in the loss of 6886 jobs in the county (WMCC, EDU 1982*a*, p. 9), after a period of contraction in employment in steel-making in the county from 44 496 in 1971 to 38 365 in 1978. By 1981 only 23 848 were employed in the steel industry.

Finally, to many companies operating in the West Midlands government purchasing policy is as important as any policy aimed directly at their industry. For example, the Coventry plants of GEC manufacturing telephone and telecommunications equipment, are heavily dependent upon the purchasing programme of British Telecom and will be affected by the liberalization of equipment supply which has followed privatization. Defence spending is crucial to companies such as Lucas Aerospace and to parts of GKN.

Thus before the West Midlands was designated a Development Area, government industrial policy was active, and affected the operating environment, in the local economy. The involvement of government in the affairs of the West Midlands economy is a reflection of the latter's decline; central government has responded to the collapse of key companies or sectors in the region. Intervention has also been part of government's wider national strategy for the steel industry. As such it was not based on any analytical perception of the region's malaise but, was rather, in response to problems as they arose on a piecemeal and partial basis.

Regional policy

Locational decisions have also been influenced by government regional policy (Bentley and Mawson 1985*a*). IDC control, and regional development grants and other incentives, have altered the calculations of companies and encouraged the development of production facilities outside the region. Dunnett (1980) cites the case of BMC which was instructed to spend £20 million of its £50m expansion in 1961/2 in the Development Areas. Other companies have diverted or cancelled development plans at particular periods when regional policy has been actively pursued: 'The relocation of the motor industry's expansion had negative effects on their costs. This was reflected in that the government's considerable financial incentives were alone inadequate to induce relocation' (Dunnett 1980, p. 79).

Many authors (for example, Mawson and Smith 1980; Wood 1976) have argued that regional policy has had a detrimental effect on the economy of the West Midlands Region by encouraging the movement of growth-oriented firms away from the West Midlands while discouraging new industries from setting up in the region. IDCs, it has been argued, blocked expansion and investment in industry in the West Midlands and thus reduced its efficiency and competitive position. In addition, the movement of plants to the other regions disrupted local linkage patterns and added to the costs of companies operating in the West Midlands. While it has been estimated that a minimum of 39 000 jobs were diverted from the West Midlands in policy-induced moves betwen 1960 and 1974, there is disagreement over the effect this had on the local economy.

Between 1945 and 1971, 336 West-Midlands-based firms either set up a new manufacturing plant in another region or completely transferred business from the West Midlands or another part of the UK. Department of Industry information suggests that a further fifty-one firms moved out between 1972 and 1975; 63 per cent of the moves between 1945 and 1975 were to the Development Areas, with Wales accounting for 31 per cent and the North-west of England for 16 per cent (see Table 6.1). When we look at the employment levels involved in these moves, we see 44 400 jobs transferring between 1945 and 1951, 15 800 between 1952 and 1959, 34 500 between 1960 and 1965, and 17 000 between 1966 and 1971.

It is not possible to isolate the different impacts of the various causes of these moves. During periods of labour shortage in the West Midlands, companies which wished to expand may have been willing to move to Wales and the other Development Areas even without regional incentives and IDC controls. However, it is noticeable that the number of moves was higher between 1945 and 1951 (when the refusal rate of IDCs was high) than between 1952 and 1959, a period which is generally recognized as one when the policy was relaxed.

Refusal of an IDC did not necessarily cause a company to move or to develop new plants in an assisted area. Companies had the option of remaining in their existing premises, putting up a building within the floor-space limits, or indeed acquiring an existing building of appropriate size. Many companies followed these courses of action (see Smith 1972), and between 1958 and 1963 only 14 per cent of refusals of IDCs resulted in moves to Development Areas (see Table 6.2).

Even companies operating in the West Midlands disagreed about the effect of regional policy on operating environment. Thus in evidence to the House of Commons Expenditure Committee's review of regional development policy in 1973, GKN argued that regional policy did not have a decisive influence on investment decisions, adding that the company had never invested in a Development Area merely because an IDC had been refused. IDC policy was inconvenient rather than detrimental (*Financial Times*, 22 Feb. 1973). Chrysler, however, in its evidence to the same committee, said of its decision to set up a new plant in Linwood in 1963:

were there no IDC's or were there no constraint, we would undoubtedly have devel-

Table 6.1. *Destination of Moves by Firms from the West Midlands to Other UK Regions, 1945–1975*

Destination	No. of firms moved from West Midlands					Total	% of moves to all regions
	1945–1951	1952–1959	1960–1965	1966–1971	1971–1975		
Scotland	5	4	17	8	8	42	10.5
Wales	34	4	21	49	17	125	31.1
North	2	2	6	12	3	25	6.2
North-west	11	7	17	17	11	63	15.7
South-west	7	9	19	12	1	48	11.9
Yorkshire and Humberside	4	3	3	0	3	13	3.2
East Midlands	5	3	6	10	6	30	7.5
East Anglia	0	0	2	2	1	5	1.2
South-east	3	5	5	18	7	38	9.5
Northern Ireland	5	4	2	2	0	13	3.2
Total	76	41	98	130	57	402	100.0

Source: Law (1980).

Table 6.2. *Summary of the Results of Refusals of Industrial Development Certificates to Firms in the West Midlands Region, July 1958–June 1963*

Results of refusals	Refusals		Area refused	
	No.	% of total examined	sq. ft.	% of total examined
Steered to preferred areas	27	18.9	1 751 715	28.7
Steered to assisted areas:[a]				
refusals wholly sustained	10	7.0	838 090	13.7
package deals	10	7.0	649 380	10.7
Steered to other referred areas:				
to West Midlands overspill areas	6	4.2	238 745	3.9
to Forest of Dean	1	0.7	25 500	0.4
Other solutions in UK	85	59.4	3 202 926	52.4
Entered vacated premises in non-preferred areas	42	29.3	2 188 899	35.8
Built up to 5000 sq. ft. of industrial floor space	21	14.7	391 100	6.4
Built storage premises	6	4.2	219 220	3.6
Internal transfer within the group	7	4.9	188 682	3.1
Solved space problems by other unspecified means	9	6.3	215 025	3.5
No solution in UK	15	10.5	656 668	10.7
Still looking for space in the Midlands	4	2.8	143 920	2.3
Project abandoned	8	5.6	385 748	6.3
Firm closed	2	1.4	120 000	2.0
Work done in Germany	1	0.7	7 000	0.1
No further information	16	11.2	498 072	8.2
Total examined	143	100.0	6 109 381	100.0
Speculative development	1		150 000	
Total of returns	144		6 259 381	

Notes: [a] Development Area or Designated District.
Source: Bentley and Mawson (1985, p. 18).

oped in Coventry as one major complex. We have plenty of space . . . The refusal of
IDC's meant we expanded at Linwood which necessitated the purchase of land leaving the land at Coventry unutilised. (Quoted in Healey and Clark 1984.)

On the question of IDC's, the DTI argued that refusal had not encouraged
the movement out of the West Midlands (DTI 1975). The department also
referred to the low rate of refusal of IDC's in the West Midlands, amounting
to 8–10 per cent of applications, involving 15–20 per cent of floor space in the
1960s. These rates fell further in the 1970s. However the DTI's analysis does
not include those who did not apply for an IDC locally and either moved out
of the region to expand or continued production in cramped and obsolete
premises.

Certainly regional policy has been blamed for the poor performance and
financial collapse of a number of West-Midlands-based companies. For
example, it was argued at the time of the near-bankruptcy of Duport at the
end of 1980 that regional policy had had a detrimental effect on the company's performance. In particular, Duport's failure in 1961 and 1971 to
obtain an IDC to build a new steel plant next to its existing rolling mills in
Warley was thought to have added substantially to its costs and hence to
have been a factor underlying its collapse (*Birmingham Post*, 19 Dec. 1980).
The refusal of an IDC led the company to develop a new steel plant in
Llanelli, South Wales. Its 'integrated' steel operation then involved the
transportation of scrap from the West Midlands to be smelted at Llanelli into
steel billets. These were then returned to Warley to be rerolled and formed
into metal components.

However, such analysis may give undue weight to the importance of the
disruption of linkages in the company in an understanding of its financial difficulties. Of probably greater importance were the depth of the recession, the
strength of sterling, the high cost of energy, and rising interest rates. This last
point was of particular significance given Duport's late 1970s investment in
two new electric arc furnaces in its South Wales plant. The impact of increasing debt payments on cash flow was the primary reason for loss of confidence
in the company. Paradoxically this investment, which gave Duport the most
modern facilities in Europe, almost bankrupted the firm, and in the rescue
plan for the company it was scrapped before ever being used to full capacity
(*Financial Times*, 24 Feb. 1981).

Thus although it would be wrong to dismiss regional policy as a factor
influencing change in the economy of the West Midlands, its effect upon
industry and employment in the region has often been overstated (Bentley
and Mawson 1985*a*). Clearly during the period of growth and expansion in
the 1960s regional policy may have constrained the process of industrial
adaptation, but in the longer term it was only one of many features of the
regional environment which influenced enterprise calculations and economic
outcomes in the West Midlands conurbation.

Policy Processes and Impact

What we have seen is a collection of policies which have had an impact on the economy of the West Midlands Region, but no coherent view of the impact of policy. Ministries operate individual policies, each of what has its own objectives and instruments. Local authorities pursue policies which may be contrary to those of central government in intent and approach. Within local government the different tiers may, and do, pursue different policies on the same issue.

It could be argued that when the policies in question concern intervention in the economy, diversity of approach and types of scheme is appropriate. Nobody knows what are the best policy responses to problems, and so experimentation is positive. However, inconsistency can lead to contradictions between policies, even within central government. For example the D.o.E. operates the Urban Development Grant (UDG) scheme which subsidizes job-creating development on sites which would not be developed without the grant. The DTI does not fund projects on job-creation grounds (unless they are worth £500 000 or more). Hence two regional offices were applying different criteria for the allocation of very similar grants to companies.

The approach to policy issues is that new initiatives grow by accretion. A new problem (such as the low level of technology in engineering companies) is met by a new initiative. When that initiative is taken it becomes part of the routine of the responsible government department. There has never been an analysis by government of the problems of the economy of the West Midlands Region as a whole, or of the possible relevant interventions government might make. Indeed when John Butcher was appointed Minister for the West Midlands it was only to oversee DTI matters which were relevant to the region.

To explain why this should be the case is difficult. The first reason is that the regional offices of the ministries are conceived as implementation arms of central departments. Policies are made centrally and implemented at regional level. In these circumstances the scope for policy analysis or strategic thought at local level is limited. The local authorities have geographical coverage which is smaller than the relevant area for coherent economic analysis. Only the WMCC has a boundary widely enough drawn to enable an economic analysis of its territory which reflects the linkages within the economic system. Even this boundary, though, excludes many connected industrial areas.

Without strategic analysis of the economic changes which are occurring in the West Midlands Region, there can be no coherent policy formulation or establishment of priorities. For example, the D.o.E. was planning to spend more in 1984 on canals in the region than the DTI was planning to spend as a result of the Team for Innovation's efforts to promote take-up of schemes. This, and other, distributions of resources are the outcome of a series of unconnected budget allocations by individual ministries in London. Regional strategies would at least imply regional budgets for the central-government money which is spent. How these budgets should be drawn up and spent is a question whose answer is beyond the scope of this book, but the principle on which such budgets should be produced is that competing claims for cash should be susceptible to comparative scrutiny, so that the relationship between the money spent and the benefits derived can be established. Only in such a way could effective use be made of available resources.

So much for spending programmes in the region. What about the unintended or unforeseen consequences of central government's general economic and trade policies? Should there be a regional dimension of all central-government policies? The answer to this question depends on the view taken about what central-government economic policies are designed to achieve. In the days of counter-cyclical policy it made little sense to deflate the economy in those regions where there were spare capacity and underused resources. However, such policies were pursued in the name of the *national* economic interest. When we look at the detrimental effects of some central-government policies on the manufacturing sectors, and by implication on the regions which depend on manufacturing industry, we need to ask in whose interests those policies have been pursued. We have seen that counter-cyclical measures taken on consumer credit affected the competitive position of UK manufacturers by creating fluctuations in effective demand which operated in favour of overseas competitors at crucial times. These measures were not *designed* to have this effect but were intended to keep the rate of inflation (and particularly wage inflation) under control.

In the case of trade policy, the switch in tariff structures and the reorientation of trading patterns away from the old Empire and towards Europe were partly forced on governments by the UK's loss of control over these territories first through independence and then through the development of indigenous industries. However, the changes operated in the interests of companies which had Europe-wide operations and needed the free flow of goods across national boundaries in order to pursue their production and sales policies.

When we turn to exchange-rate policy we see periods when the pound was defended against downward pressure by the Bank of England at times when manufacturers would have benefited from a lower exchange rate. Manufacturing companies lobbied for devaluations, especially in the mid 1960s and early 1980s, because of the impact of a highly valued pound on sales and sterling profits in overseas markets. The beneficiaries of the highly valued pound have been holders of sterling, especially companies in the banking sector in the city.

We may conclude, then, that the main beneficiaries of the policies we have examined—policies designed to produce benefits for particular sectors of the economy while their detrimental effects on other sectors were ignored or considered less important—were the banking sector and manufacturers with international bases. The beneficiaries from wide fluctuations in consumer demand are more difficult to identify.

7

Local Economic-development Initiatives

This chapter considers the emergence of local-authority economic initiatives within the West Midlands Metropolitan County following the reorganization of local government in 1974. We focus attention on the manner in which local government responded to the deepening economic crisis and the problem of rising unemployment through case-studies of the evolution of the policies of the seven metropolitan districts authorities and the metropolitan county authority. While reference is made to the economic-development policies of the metropolitan district councils, there can be little doubt that it was the county council (which was abolished on 1 April 1986) which proved to be the most active and innovative authority in the period under consideration and is therefore worthy of particular attention.

The Origins of Local Economic-development Initiatives in the West Midlands

Local-government intervention in local economies has a long tradition stretching back well before the emergence of central government's regional policy in the 1930s (Ward 1983). This tradition reflected the view that there was a legitimate role for local government to play in fostering business development and, in certain cases, helping the unemployed directly. By the early 1930s there had emerged in the West Midlands a comprehensive multi-functional local-government system which had developed a tradition of municipal enterprise embracing the major public utilities of water, gas, electricity, and public transport and gave local government officials direct experience of business and commerce. In Birmingham a municipal bank was established, and several county boroughs had begun to tackle the problem of derelict industrial land through the provision of new serviced industrial sites as well as engaging in trunk-road construction, in part, as a social objective to relieve the problems of unemployment brought about by the Depression.

In the immediate post-war years the tradition of municipal enterprise receded as national government took responsibility for full employment, a national regional policy, and the nationalization of a range of industries previously run by local government. In the post-war boom the role of local authorities was to be one of providing social infrastructure such as education and housing which was a crucial adjunct to industrial development. Local-authority involvement in the local economy was generally limited to land-use

131

planning. Within the West Midlands conurbation clearance of slums and construction of new public housing estates resulted in the removal or closure of many small and medium-sized businesses. It was standard practice to clear virtually all property in Redevelopment Areas and to zone all land and segregate residential and industrial uses. A consequence was the elimination of employment providing premises by all kinds of demolition, blight, and change of use. The IDC reinforced this effect (Smith 1977). Frequently, alternative accommodation was not made available or, if it was, it was provided at a high standard conforming to modern building and health and safety regulations, thus presenting the firm with a substantial increase in its accommodation costs (Thomas 1976). Local authorities in the West Midlands were also involved in industrial relocation through the process of regional planning which involved the development of new towns and the negotiation of population-overspill agreements between the conurbation authorities and expanded towns. This relocation included the construction of advanced factories and the laying out of industrial estates (Smith 1972).

The relationship between local government and the private sector in the 1950s and 1960s can be characterized as an 'arm's-length' activity. Local government directly or indirectly affected the costs of location of industry largely in the context of planning policies rather than in the pursuit of direct economic objectives. This approach was conditioned to a considerable extent by the powers available under the post-war local-government statutes which did not explicitly identify economic development as a mainstream activity. However, during the 1960s and early 1970s a number of measures were introduced in relation to infrastructure provision which did provide an opportunity for limited financial involvement—for example, the Local Authorities (Land) Act, 1963, the Local Government (Financial Provisions) Act, 1963, and the Local Government Act, 1972 (Camina 1974). The Land Act permitted local authorities to acquire land by agreement, authorized the development of such land, and allowed loans and mortgages to be made to developers for the erection of buildings on land let or sold to them by an authority. The Act also gave local authorities powers to reclaim land, powers which were extended in the Local Government Act, 1966 and the Town and Country Planning Act, 1971. In a broader context the Local Government Act, 1963 permitted local authorities to spend up to the equivalent of a penny rate (raised in the 1972 Act, Section 137, to a twopenny rate) on anything considered to be in the interests of the area and its inhabitants. However, this wide enabling power was little utilized during this period because of the cautious attitude adopted by local-authority legal officers and the absence of any significance political pressure to develop local employment policies where unemployment levels rarely exceed 4 per cent. Those authorities which did pursue a more active approach preferred the device of securing a private Act of Parliament to widen their capacity to provide financial support to private firms, for example, the Coventry Corporation Act, 1977.

The End of the Post-war Boom, and Local Government Reform

The reorganization of local government in 1974 resulted in a managerial revolution following the Bains Report, with an emphasis on a more corporate approach in the management of local affairs (Greenwood and Stewart 1974). The creation of larger metropolitan district councils, replacing the former county boroughs, and the establishment of a strategic second-tier metropolitan county meant that there were the staff and resources to devote to research and policy formulation. Taking stock of the situation they inherited following reorganization, many West Midlands authorities began to recognize the local economy and labour market as a key policy issue and there was much to be concerned about. The reorganization of local government took place at a time when the problems brought about by the oil crisis of the early 1970s, inflation, rising unemployment, and cutbacks in public expenditure following the International Monetary Fund (IMF) loan of the mid 1970s were beginning to have an impact on the national and local economies. As we have discussed in previous chapters, during the latter part of the 1960s increasing international competition together with declining profitability forced UK industry to reorganize. Such pressures were reflected in the West Midlands in a spate of company mergers and a process of capital-intensification through the introduction of new plants, machinery, and production methods.

In this context, the WMCC produced a number of detailed studies of the local economy, highlighting the problems faced by the UK's leading industrial region. *Time for Action*, produced in 1975, and the *Annual Economic Reviews*, produced in 1976 and 1977, set out trends in investment, productivity and employment and highlighted the relative decline of the West Midlands in comparison with other UK regions in the previous decade (WMCC, 1975, 1976, and 1977). These macro-economic trends had their geographical counterpart within the West Midlands. The wider geographical horizons of the multi-plant company resulted in the run-down and closure of plants in the older urban industrial areas, namely Birmingham and the Black Country (Birmingham Community Development Project 1977). The rates of formation of new firms and industrial diversification in the West Midlands conurbation were insufficient to compensate for contraction and closure of indigenous firms and the wholesale loss of traditional industries (Smith 1978a). There developments paralleled demographic trends of falling population and selective outward migration and resulted in increasing pressure on the services of local government while their rateable base was contracting.

It was against this background that the appointment of Peter Shore as Secretary of State for the Environment in 1976 heralded a significant shift in post-war planning policies. Within the space of two years the strategy of urban development and dispersal allied to the building of new towns had been replaced with a policy of urban regeneration, exemplified in the Urban Programme first established in the late 1960s and the Inner Urban Areas

Act, 1978. Monies were made available to local authorities for construction projects, including advanced factory units, and the 1978 Act gave designated authorities additional economic-development powers including the right to declare Industrial Improvement Areas, prepare industrial sites, refurbish industrial buildings, and make available loans and grants to firms, including co-operatives. Wolverhampton was given Programme Authority status, Sandwell was to be a Designated District and Birmingham became an Inner City Partnership (see also Chapter 8). The complex partnership machinery between central government, the city council, and the county was designed to oversee the preparation of annual rolling programmes of public expenditure (£16 million in 1978/9 rising to £24 million in 1985/6) to achieve economic and social regeneration of the Birmingham inner-city areas. Initially 25 per cent of this expenditure was committed to economic schemes; the proportion subsequently rose to 35 per cent.

Over time more authorities achived higher Urban Programme status (in 1982 Coventry and Sandwell became Programme Authorities, and Walsall a Designated District). Partnership authorities receive the largest grant, followed by Programme Authorities, with Designated Districts receiving the lowest grant of these three levels of Urban Programme status. Increased emphasis was given to economic and employment measures as a result of the Urban Programme, which acted as an important stimulant to the development of local-authority economic and employment initiatives. Since the latter part of the 1970s other major programmes designed to tackle problems of rising unemployment have also had an important effect, most notably the training, work-experience, and community projects of the Manpower Services Commission (MSC) and to a lesser extent the European Social Fund (ESF).

Having set the broad extent within which local economic initiatives evolved in the West Midlands, we may usefully consider in more detail the manner in which the district councils set about developing their policies. Historically, as we have already suggested, local-authority involvement in the economy had been of an indirect kind, largely concerned with locational matters, including zoning, relocation, clearance of derelict land, and provision of sites, the latter two initiatives being undertaken on a rather limited basis.

Towards the end of the 1970s the combination of rising unemployment, closures of well known local companies, and inner-city problems forced the question of economic decline on to the political agenda of local councils for the first time. Initially there was a somewhat *ad hoc* and limited response as individual committees and departments, mainly those concerned with planning, estates, education, and expenditure, began to feel their way towards the development of local economic initiatives. In organization terms this presented a number of problems, not the least of which was the fact that there was no single committee or department which could be easily identified as playing the lead role.

In Walsall, for example, the first impetus came in 1977 following the availability of funds from the government's Construction Package (resources made available for inner-city construction programmes) which led to. the building of a number of small factory units. Preparation of lobbying documents for designation under the Inner Urban Areas Act resulted in analysis for the first time of the problems of the local economy. An economic-development group was established to draw together the work of the various departments and to put together proposals for Urban Programme support. This group was responsible for the preparation of a series of annual economic reviews and for taking stock of the authorities' various economic initatives. The work of the group was given added impetus by the rapid increase in unemployment, the closure of plants of well-known companies such as GKN, and the need to continue to press for designation under the Urban Programme. The group reported to the land and property committee of the district council, but the situation was complicated by the fact that other committees also had responsibilities in this area.

In Sandwell a similar pattern was apparent. Plant closures by major employers such as Patent Shaft and Birmid Qualcast, and the problem of clearing derelict factories to provide land for new industrial units, prompted the authority to prepare a lobbying document in 1979 highlighting the need for more government support in regard to derelict land. (Sandwell Metropolitan Borough Council 1978). As a comparatively small metropolitan authority in rateable terms, Sandwell actively sought government aid (for example, Urban Development Grants, Enterprise Zone status). In the process the authority received a number of ministerial visits and eventually secured Programme status in 1982 together with the establishment in Smethwick of a 'task force' of civil servants and representatives of the private sector to co-ordinate Urban Programme activities. In 1982 a policy statement on economic development was prepared mainly with the intention of securing greater departmental co-ordination, but this objective was frustrated by the spread of responsibility across departments and committees. While Sandwell did have an officer for employment and an industrial promotion group for co-ordination purposes, the group met fairly infrequently and its activites were largely subsumed within the work of the inner-areas team which reported to the inner-areas sub-committee.

In the case of Wolverhampton, a similar pattern of organizational development was apparent, with economic-development activity being carried out by a number of departments but with a large technical services directorate playing a particularly important role encompassing planning, estates and industrial promotion. The education department was responsible for training and unemployment issues. Wolverhampton had both an inner-areas and an economic-development sub-committee. The latter becoming a full committee in 1982, but its term of reference were somewhat circumscribed, reflecting a confused and overlapping pattern of committee responsibilities in this policy area. The one significant organization innovation which the council launched was WELD, a small business-advice centre, in 1982 in partnership with the private sector and the WMCC.

Dudley, unlike the other Black Country boroughs, did not secure Urban Programme support in the late 1970s. Nevertheless it had responded to the issue of economic decline. The corporate planning system established following the reorganization of local government had resulted in early consideration of the long-term structural problems of the local economy. By the late 1970s the annual budgeting system of corporate teams reporting to committees on key issues had broken down but the economic programme area team representing the various relevant departments in this policy area continued to meet to deal with specific projects and issues. Despite its apparently formalized corporate approach to economic problems, in practice the borough's response had developed in a somewhat *ad hoc* and uncoordinated manner. Within the directorate of finance, for example, an economist was employed to undertake research, organize business seminars, and so on. The estates section within planning was to oversee a three-year programme with a budget of £750 000 focusing on reclamation of derelict land, acquisition of sites and the building of nursery units in partnership with local developers. Towards the end of the 1970s the individual strands began to merge, and working relationships developed as schemes, primarily infrastructural, grew in size and complexity, but the work remained project-orientated and, in the absence of an overview, important areas of work remained neglected. It was against this background that in 1980 it was decided to establish a semi-autonomous industrial development unit, headed by an economist within the directorate of finance and initially comprising six staff, to deal with research, estates, industrial promotion, advice, financial support, and, latterly, the management of the enterprise zone. While the consolidation of activities proved successful and led to the preparation of policy statements, there nevertheless remained organizational difficulties due to the unit's obligation to report to several committees, insufficient staff resources, and education functions relevant to unemployment and training outside its scope.

In the case of Coventry, the early introduction of a corporate planning system prior to local-government organization resulted in the preparation of a number of reports on the state of the local economy. The commerce and industry programme area team was responsible for the economic input into the annual budget cycle and was serviced by an economic development group of middle-tier officers from building and properties, treasurer's, and planning departments. In 1976 a small economic unit was established in the treasurer's department to monitor trends in the local economy and prepare advocacy documents. The closure of a number of key local firms in the engineering and motor-vehicle sectors provided an impetus to this policy area. As a substantial landowner in the city, the council's estates and planning departments became increasingly involved in site-preparation and construction of small units (by the late 1970s the council owned 230 acres of industrial land and 72 units on three main sites). In 1977 financial incentives were introduced under the Coventry Corporation Act in the form of loans and grants for the erection or improvement of buildings or development of sites, as well as rent guarantees and rent-free periods (Smith 1978a, p. 77). The education department was responsible for developing a twelve–fifteen week training, recruitment, and assessment scheme known as STAR in local colleges which was funded by the national Training Services Agency and involved 1 000 young people per annum. A youth opportunities unit was set up to enhance take-up of MSC funds and develop Youth Training Schemes. The designation of Coventry as Programme Authority in 1982 released additional funds for economic development and facilitated the expansion of a number of initiatives: business advice; new enterprise workshops; and reclamation of derelict sites and construction of new units on sites not attractive to the private sector.

Coventry district council had no single major committee responsible for economic development. In 1975 it set up a special sub-committee on employment, which included local trade-unionists and businessmen, but this proved to be ineffective and outside membership was subsequently restricted to MPs. As for co-ordination of activities within the authority, working relationships between the three key departments of planning, building properties, and treasurer's in regard to infrastructure issues and educational matters were good. However, there was little co-ordination on training issues or economic promotion which was handled by the chief executive. Overall, Coventry's activites in this policy area could be described as low-budget and low-profile, with an emphasis on infrastructural measures.

Solihull, lying as it does in the rural and suburban belt between Coventry and Birmingham, was the only district within the West Midlands County to experience unemployment consistently below the national average in the first half of the 1980s. It was also the only district to be consistently under Conservative control. Following the reorganization of local government, the council had no economic-development initiatives as such save to minimize the rate burden on local firms. The consequences of recession did not have a serious impact on the district until the late 1970s when unemployment levels began to exceed 20 per cent in the former Birmingham overspill estates of Kingshurst and Chelmsley Wood to the north. However, neither in committee or departmental terms was there a response to the situation.

Birmingham, also under Conservative control in the late 1970s, was, in contrast, engaged in an active economic-development programme. It was at the beginning of the decade that the county borough formally renounced the policy of industrial overspill which had prevailed throughout the post-war period. In October 1971 the city council resolved to deliberately encourage the retention and expansion of existing industry within the city boundary and to back this up with land-allocation policies and a campaign publicizing the city as an industrial location (City of Birmingham 1973, p. 33). At this stage economic development was seen primarily in terms of land use and infrastructure, a not unreasonable view given the city's substantial holdings of land and property, though the city's original reason for such provision had been largely related to the relocation of business affected by planning action.

Immediately following local-government reorganization in 1974 the Labour-controlled city council sought to introduce a new corporate system, but the traditional bureaucratic structure of powerful service departments and committees reaserted itself, and with the return of the Conservatives in 1977 the new system was abandoned. In terms of economic development, policy initiatives evolved in an *ad hoc* manner reflecting the roles of individual departments. Thus the city treasurer's department developed a business and employment scheme to provide loans, loan guarantees, interest- and rent-relief grants, and grants for adapting or improving industrial buildings. The business bureau in the treasurer's department also provided advice services. The city estates department, in addition to managing city properties, pre-pared a registry of vacant premises and was involved with the planning department in the clearance of sites and the construction of advanced factory units. Under the auspices of the chief executive, a promotion campaign was launched around a brochure entitled *Birmingham Means Business* (*Birmingham Post*, 22 Sept. 1976). In the case of the planning department, an industrial development group was established in 1978 as a project team to deal with the Construction Package and subsequent opportunities arising from the founda-tion of the BICP. (Additional funding through the Urban Programe pre-sented the group with the opportunity to experiment with new initiatives such as enterprise workshops and industrial improvement areas.)

In the absence of an overall policy framework the group prepared a policy statement entitled *Industry and Employment: the Birmingham Approach* (City of Birmingham, 1978). Its aims were: the stabilization of job losses; the creation of new jobs and wealth; the diversification of the economic base (to be achieved by attracting outside firms); alleviation of the problems faced by indigenous firms; and the development of high technology firms via measures such as the development of the Science Park at Aston University. Because of the hostility of both Conservative and Labour council members to the prep-aration of this type of document, *The Birmingham Approach* fell far short of a comprehensive economic strategy; nevertheless, it served as an important referrence document, reflecting preoccupations with a temporary cyclical crisis and an approach which was based primarily on industry rather than people.

An economic development group of senior officers was established to co-ordinate the work of the various departments; however, in the absence of a clear organization focus and with rivalries persisting between departments, the incoming Labour administration in 1979 decided to establish an econ-omic development committee with its own budget and control over the work

of the relevant economic activities with the exception of education and training matters. By the early 1980s the economic development committee had its
own budget of £5 million per annum and a similar funding from the BICP.
The majority of the main programme expenditure was on land purchases,
site development, and clearance of derelict land, along with support of the
business and employment bureau. Expenditure on BICP schemes was more
wide-ranging, covering infrastructure works, industrial improvement areas,
enterprise workshops, business advice, training schemes, and support for
voluntary employment projects.

The return of the Conservatives to power in May 1982 and the appointment of a new chief executive heralded further changes in the organization of
the city's economic policies. Despite the creation of an economic development committee, it was felt that there was a need to draw together some of
the key functions under one administrative focus, so a development and promotion unit was established under the chief executive. The unit, with a staff
of sixteen, was to deal with inquiries concerning grants and assistance, commercial property, and planning, and to oversee the convention and visitors'
bureau (set up to boost Birmingham's share of the conference business), the
National Exhibition Centre, and the special company designed to run the
Aston University Science Park. In addition £10 million was made available
for a rolling programme to buy up and demolish old factories and prepare
sites for redevelopment and £1.5 million to change the image of the city
through publicity—five times the funding previously available. A scheme
was announced to construct a £120 million international convention centre
which, it was claimed, would create 2000 jobs and bring £40 million into the
local economy (*Financial Times*, 21 Oct. 1983).

The Period of Transition 1979–1985

In our summary of the position which the metropolitan district councils had
reached in their economic policies by the early 1980s it is clear that despite
certain obvious differences there were nevertheless a number of significant
common themes. On the basis of a summary carried out by WMCC in 1981
(see Table 7.1) and the research undertaken for this project, it is probable to
conclude that in policy terms the primary focus was on the preparation of
sites, clearance of derelict land, and construction of small units. This was
paralleled by industrial promotion and advice services and some relaxation
of planning controls in respect of industrial development. The Urban Programme had provided an additional impetus, but at this stage the emphasis
was also on infrastructure schemes, for example, industrial improvement
areas, reflecting in part the inherent capital bias of the BICP. Excluding the
BICP, the level of expenditure on industrial aid in the county was minimal in
relation to the scale of the problem, rarely exceeding £1 million per annum
(capital and revenue) per authority.

Table 7.1. *Aid to Industry Available from the West Midlands District Authorities, 1981*

Authority	Industrial promotion	Loans and grants to industry	IIAs[a]	Refurbished factory units	New factory units	New enterprise workshops	Business advice centres for small firms
Birmingham	Advice, Advertising brochure	Loans to firms, Loan and rent guarantees, Interest-relief and rent-relief grants, Installation grants, Grants to firms in IIAs Grants to worker co-ops (£266 000 capital, £30 000 revenue)	Declared 3	4 buildings providing 187 units	141 small units built	2 workshops open providing 28 units, 1 workshop planned to open in 1982	
Coventry	Advice, Advertising brochure	Loans to manufacturing industry (£150 000 capital)			150 units built	Plans being developed for a workshop	1 planned to open in Autumn 1981
Dudley	Advice, Advertising brochure on borough and Enterprise Zone	Loans to purchasers of land for industrial development		1 building		One workshop open and two more being considered	Developing an Enterprise Zone Advice Centre with Dudley Technical College
Sandwell	Advice				32 small units built, 13 under construction		

Solihull						
Walsall	Advice Advertising brochure, Advice		Declared an Industrial Priority Area		34 small units built	1 recently established
Wolverhampton	Advertising brochure, Advice	Grants to firms in IIA	Declared 1	3 buildings	101 small units built	1 may be established in the near future

Note: [a] Industrial Improvement Areas.
Source: WMCC, EDC (1981).

The swings of political control within the districts do not appear to have significant impact on the direction of policy; indeed, differences between authorities of similar political persuasion appear to have been as great if not greater than those between authorities of opposite persuasions. The statement made by a leader of Birmingham council that if public money will lead to more development of private industry and more jobs, it is well spent (*Financial Times*, 21 Oct. 1983) is in marked contrast to the position adopted by Solihull's political leaders. Conservatives controlled both authorities.

Because of the disparate nature of the activity and the absence of a clear organizational focus, there were few attempts to develop a coherent and explict economic and employment strategy. The authorities were still feeling their way forward in rapidly changing circumstances. Underlying the approaches there were a number of implicit assumptions about the temporary cyclical nature of the unemployment problem and an uncritical view of the value of site-clearance and unit-construction as the most effective and relevant local-authority strategy for generating jobs and creating wealth.

However, the period between 1979 and 1985 was a particularly traumatic one in the West Midlands which led to a serious questioning of what had gone before and further significant changes in the approaches of the district authorities. Before returning to this issue and the manner in which WMCC responded to the crisis between 1981 and 1985, we shall briefly consider this changing context.

The Changing Economic Background

More than one-third of the manufacturing jobs which existed in the West Midlands County in 1978 had disappeared by 1983, a loss of some 225 000 jobs which trebled the unemployment rate in the county to 16 per cent. There were some 48 000 acres of derelict land in 1982, an increase of more than 1000 acres over the previous eight years, much of which reflected the closure of major industrial installations in the late 1970s (WMFCC 1984, p. 13). Estimates suggested that the amount of empty industrial property had grown threefold between 1981 and 1984 to around 30 million sq. ft. (30 per cent of which was constructed before 1960).

In social terms the consequences of industrial decline were reflected in high levels of unemployment throughout the county affecting suburban estates in the outer county as well as the inner-urban areas. As Chapter 2 has shown, by 1984 more than three-quarters of the county's unemployed had been out of work for more than six months and nearly 50 per cent for more than a year. Almost one in three households were living at or below the official poverty line with the number of persons claiming supplementary benefit in the county 50 per cent higher than in 1980. Among those in work, wage rates had been seriously depressed as the threat of unemployment forced workers to accept falling real wages and take low-paid work. Certain groups in the labour market had suffered the consequences of these trends more severely than others—for example, the young, ethnic minorities, and women. Significantly manual workers in the West Midlands Region had fallen from top of the regional pay hierarchy to nearly the bottom by 1983 (see Chapter 2).

Although comparative regional figures on investment, productivity, and output had shown the rapid deterioration of the local economy over a decade (see Chapter 3), it was not until the late 1970s and early 1980s that local authorities began to consider them in detail and consider their implications. By 1984 investment per employee in manufacturing in the West Midlands Region was only 76 per cent of the UK average for manufacturing, the lowest of all regions (see Chapter 3). A survey of the country's thirty-one largest pension funds found that they considered the West Midlands a poor investment prospect and that many were considering withdrawing from the region altogether (Debenham, Tewson and Chinnocks 1983). Regional figures for public expenditure showed that the West Midlands had the highest deficit on government expenditure and transfers (defined as public consumption and fixed investment plus grants and social benefits less direct and indirect taxes) of all UK regions (*Cambridge Economic Policy Review* 1980). Between 1973 and 1982 the West Midlands Region was awarded only 1.5 per cent of the total grants and loans made available to the English regions from EEC sources (Mawson, Gibney, and Miller 1983). Excluding assistance to a single company, BL, firms and industries in the West Midlands received a mere £57 million of government industrial aid, just over 1 per cent of total expenditure under the 1972 Industry Act and subsequent Acts between 1974 and 1983 (Bentley and Mawson 1984).

Central-government intervention in the motor-vehicle industry through BL and major direct consequences for employment in the region, as well as indirect effects through a reduction in purchasing of component basic materials (Mawson, Jepson and Marshall 1984, p. 64). It has been estimated that in 1984 about 4000 firms were dependent on BL, equivalent to more than 30 per cent of total employment in the region. It is clear that the wider context of the regional economy, the multiplier impact on sectors and individual firms, and an overall perspective in the motor-vehicle industry were not considered when government intervention was undertaken. As previous chapters have shown, the effect was to create a restructured and efficient assembly sector but to leave the interlinked components, metal-manufacturing, and foundry sectors to 'sink or swim'. Many small and medium-sized locally owned firms saw their regular customers disappear overnight. Years of dependence on a reliable single market for their products left them vulnerable and lacking in managerial capacity to diversify. The reluctance of family-owned firms to take in outside equity and the difficulty of gaining unsecured loans meant that such companies were starved of development capital and forced to borrow short-term at a time of high interest rates.

Towards an Economic-development Strategy for the West Midlands: the Role of the County Council

It was against the background of the dramatic collapse of the local economy and the inadequacy of existing central and local government policies that the WMCC launched its economic-regeneration strategy in 1981 (Mawson 1983c, pp. 4–7). This was predicated on the assumption that it was necessary to establish a strategic county-wide approach based on in-depth knowledge of the local economy and with financial and staff resources on a sufficient scale to be capable of providing an integrated programme of economic and social initiatives. The proposals represented a significant shift from the county authority's previous programme in terms of both scale and nature of policies. Specifically there was a commitment to make use of the county's Section 137 twopenny rate, totalling some £8 million per annum, and to move away from an approach characterized by limited main-programme support (less than £500 000 per annum) for small firms through grants, a rent and rates subsidy scheme, infrastructural measures, and industrial promotion and advocacy.

To give a clear political and organization thrust to the programme the WMCC immediately established an economic-development committee (EDC) and an economic development unit (EDU), the latter reporting directly to the chairman of the committee. In November 1981 the chairman presented a statement to the committeee which set out the principles upon which the new programme would operate (Edge 1981). The principles were reaffirmed in 1984 (WMCC 1984a). They were:

1.   The future prosperity of the West Midlands would depend on the survival and strengthening of its traditional industries.

This principle was based on the view that although there might be new firms and industries moving to the West Midlands or emerging in the county, these would only have a limited role to play in providing future jobs compared with companies which already existed. Thus the council was to give priority to increasing investment in established companies and encouraging local firms to improve business planning and take advantage of technological developments.

2.   There was an urgent need to increase the flow of investment funds into the West Midlands.

In this context the view of the committee was that although there were a range of different agencies providing investment finance to companies, these were often unwilling to enter into risk-sharing equity investments; they far too often provided short-term loans and were too much preoccupied with investment in land and property as opposed to productive industry. Concern

that there were few regionally based financial institutions available to provide long-term development capital and other financial services to local firms
provided the rationale to set up an enterprise board.

3.   There was a need to ensure public accountability where public funds
     were used to support private industrial and commercial activity.

In terms of investment policies the committee replaced the practice of giving
grants by one of making loans and equity (share) investments. Companies in
which the enterprise board invested have been required to enter into planning and investment agreements ensuring, among other things: good
employment practices, future business plans, and that the investment and
any associated jobs are retained in the area for a specified period of time.

4.   There was a need to invest in human skills as well as buildings and
     plant.

The committee was concerned about the collapse of skill training in the
county brought about by the reduction in apprenticeships offered by companies in the recession, as well as the run-down and closure of skill–training
centres and industry training boards. It therefore decided to develop a major
training programme with two objectives:

(*a*)   to try to anticipate future need for skills and ensure that local people
          had the skills to take jobs created by new investment
(*b*)   to improve training opportunities for women, the handicapped, and
          members of the black and Asian communities, groups for whom it
          had proved particularly difficult to gain the training necessary to
          secure employment.

5.   It was recognized that there was within the community a whole series of
     energies and talents which could be bought together to create employ-
     ment opportunities—jobs which could not always be provided by tra-
     ditional forms of business.

For this reason the committee gave special emphasis to the establishment of
co-operative and community business which would provide a way for local
people to create their own jobs and at the same time the opportunity for full
worker-participation in the decisions of the enterprise.

In order to implement the wide range of policies set out in the 1981 mani-
festo, several staff were brought into the authority on short-term contracts
and a number of staff were transferred from the planning and treasurer's
department to set up the EDU. Between 1981 and 1985 the establishment of
the unit grew from an initial six posts to 85. After a management review in
1984 the unit was organized around four teams of officers: economic intelligence and strategy, community strategy, inner areas and capital projects,
and co-operative development. In 1984/5 the unit had a total budget of £19
million which represented 3 per cent of the WMCC's overall budget. As well

as receiving support from the council's main programme, including Section 137, the EDU also secured funding from a number of other sources, for example, the MSC, the ESF and the European Regional Development Fund (ERDF). The Urban Programme provided an important source of funds for economic development in the older industrial areas of the county. The county shares of Urban Programme resources in 1984/5 were: BICP £4.5 million; Wolverhampton Programme £600 000; Coventry Programme £600 000; Sandwell Programme £250 000; and Walsall (Designated District) £42 000 (1983/4 figures).

In view of the scale and innovative nature of the initiatives taken by the WMCC it is worthwhile considering them in more detail. Taking first of all the issue of business development, undoubtedly the most significant initiative was the enterprise board.

West Midlands Enterprise Board (WMEB) was established in February 1982 as a company limited by guarantee and controlled by a board of directors, the majority of whom were county councillors, with others selected for their industrial or commercial expertise (Mawson 1983a). The purpose of the board was to provide a source of equity and long-term-loan finance for medium-sized and large local firms. The county council itself was not considered to be the most appropriate body to undertake this work for legal and organizational reasons; its departmental and committee procedures were regarded as incompatible with the need for speedy decision-making in a commercial environment. The board therefore had its own staff of investment executives and premises separate from those of the Council located in the financial area of Birmingham. The initial funding of WMEB came from the EDC in the form of an annual grant which by the autumn of 1984 totalled £12.4 million.

In order to be considered for assistance firms must primarily be engaged in the manufacturing sector and employ fifty or more persons, or have realistic prospects of growing to that size. WMEB has been flexible in its approach to investment including subscription for ordinary and preference shares and the provision of loan and equipment-leasing facilities. By 1985 capital was provided in the range of £100 000–£750 000, although the board did engage in larger-scale exercises in syndicates with other financial institutions. Typical investments by WMEB have been in: expansion, where expansion has outstripped the capacity of existing shareholders, retained earnings, or bank borrowing; financial restructuring, where a company's borrowings have become high in relation to its equity; management buy-outs as a result of, for example, changes in the parent group's corporate strategy or the parent group going into receivership; and mergers and takeovers leading to increased efficiency.

Investment decisions by WMEB have been based on an appraisal by investment executives of a business plan prepared by the applicant, which is set within the context of a sector statement by officers of the EDU regarding wider economic trends within the industry and the strategic significance of the investment for the local economy. Companies are expected to enter into a planning and investment agreement covering employment, business practices, industrial relations, and commitment to remain in the county for a specified period. In the spring of 1985 two key decisions were taken to secure the future of the board: firstly, the memorandum and articles of the board were altered to allow the district councils to nominate members to the board; secondly, in conjunction with a leading London merchant bank, a West Midlands Regional Unit Trust was launched to attract public- and private-sector pension funds which initially raised £4 million.

The role played by WMEB in the local economy in its first three years of operation is revealed by the following figures: it had approved thirty-eight investments, totalling £9 million, in twenty-six companies; total finance raised through the investments was £54 million. The WMEB had been able to lever £4 from the private sector for each £1 it had invested. The board had experienced losses through the closure of three companies, but this rate was well within the limits of failure accepted by equivalent development-capital organizations in the private sector. Recorded profits at the end of the 1984/5 financial year were £300 000, a figure forecast to rise to £500 000 per annum. The twenty-six companies employed 4500 persons at a cost to WMEB of £1900 per job. In the absence of WMEB involvement, the activities of all these companies would have been constrained and some would have failed, a fact recognized by Sir George Young, Under-secretary at the D.o.E. who, in announcing government approval for the 1985/6 WMCC grant to the board, stated: 'It seems that the WMEB has concentrated on the job in hand and has attracted the full support of all District Councils in the area, which will take control of the Board when the County Council is abolished. At a cost of £12.5 million, to the County Council and its ratepayers, the WMEB has created over 4000 jobs' (*Hansard*, 26 July 1985, p. 492).

In terms of investment and business development, WMEB was not the only initiative launched by the EDC. An interest-relief scheme was introduced in 1982 in conjunction with the Industrial and Commercial Finance Corporation (ICFC) to reduce the burden of high interest rates on companies considering further development within the county. Under the scheme a company which borrowed money for investment from the ICFC received interest relief to the value of the capital borrowed for a period of five years from the start of a loan. To be eligible for support under the scheme the proposed development had to create employment, and before assistance was approved the company had to sign a planning and investment agreement. By the summer of 1985, thirty-eight loans in thirty-six companies had been made, involving a total of £1.3 million invested with £14 million associated investment, preserving 2497 jobs, and leading to an additional 725 jobs at an average cost of £1900 per job.

Another important role played by the WMCC was in the provision of business advice. Through an active 'hands-on' approach to investments WMEB, in its monthly monitoring reports and insistence on the preparation of a business plan, became more directly involved with companies. An investment study commissioned by the EDU in 1983 to identify investment prospects for WMEB in traditional metal-based industries in the Black Country indicated the need for the introduction of modern management techniques (Tym & Partners and Arthur Mclelland Moores & Co. 1983). Consequently, in December 1984 a business development team, of staff seconded from a leading management consultancy was established to help small and medium-sized firms in the traditional metal-based and engineering sectors to introduce broader management techniques and business planning and to secure development capital, and financial support from the public sector. In an eighteen-month period the team provided twenty days of free consulting advice to some thirty firms.

A second business-advice initiative was targeted on the ethnic-minority population. Research has shown that members of ethnic minorities experience difficulty in obtaining finance, suitable premises, and relevant advice and training when starting or expanding businesses. A five-person business-advice team was employed by the EDU to provide comprehensive advice and training from locations within the inner-city of Birmingham. In October 1985 the government announced its own programme of assistance to ethnic-minority businesses. The EDU also supported, through the Urban Programme, a number of voluntary community organizations—Handsworth Employment Scheme, Community Roots, and Ashram—fulfilling similar functions. A community-enterprise and business-development centre was also established in the inner-city which was designed to assist disadvantaged groups to explore opportunities for self-employment. It provided flexible work-space, with equipment to assist product development, and a wide range of support facilities. In a similar vein, new enterprise workshops in Wolverhampton, Wednesbury, and Smethwick provided start-up units, equipment, and business advice. The EDU also developed a clothing resource centre to provide a computer-aided design facility for clothing firms within the county. Research on the local clothing industry has revealed a thriving sub-sector of small Asian-owned firms, often employing sweated female labour in poor working conditions and on very low wages (Leigh and North 1983). A major challenge facing the industry is the introduction of computerized technology, which is beyond the means of smaller firms. By providing this facility on a commercial basis together with management advice and training the EDU's intention was to improve productivity and thereby help to improve pay and working conditions.

In seeking to raise the demand for local industrial products the WMCC initiated an export-marketing scheme to provide financial and technical assistance to groups of companies hoping to trade overseas. Three successful joint marketing initatives were launched. The council itself was responsible for purchasing more than £50 million-worth of goods and services anually, so an exhibition, Purchex 84, was held to build closer links between purchasing officers and local firms (1500 businesses attended and 150 local firms were added to the list of suppliers). In an attempt to encourage other public-sector agencies to adopt similar policies a seminar was held in June 1984 in which district councils, health authorities, and other public utilities were represented.

Turning to the question of infrastructure, the WMCC since its inception pursued a programme of providing industrial units and freehold sites which included the clearance and redevelopment of derelict or vacant land and buildings. In March 1984, however, a new land-and-premises scheme was launched to tailor infrastructure measures to the needs of specific companies. Under this scheme the council could purchase and lease back a company's premises and lease its surplus property on the open market. Property could be purchased to allow companies to expand or relocate and new premises provided where investment institutions were unwilling to invest. The following two conditions were attached:

(*a*) any capital released by, for example, the acquisition of surplus property, would be reinvested in the company on the basis of an agreed business plan which would include a commitment to stay in the inner city
(*b*) the company must comply with a 'good employer code' which included the recognition of trade-unions and legislation covering equal opportunities and low pay. (Burgess and Ham 1985.)

By the summer of 1985 six companies had been assisted at a total cost of nearly £2 million involving some 1350 jobs.

The main problem associated with company-related schemes is that they are opportunistic, with a high drop-out rate, so that it is difficult to programme in advance and can lead to underspending on capital allocation. In order to offset these risks a second-priority rolling programme of area-based initiatives was undertaken by the council which was based on industrial priority areas in which efforts were concentrated with regard to land assembly, clearance, road improvements, and so on.

To assist local companies to introduce new technology the EDU launched two major initiatives. In 1983, in collaboration with Coventry and Wolverhampton councils, and Warwick University, it became a joint founder of Warwick Science Park with the objective of facilitating technology transfer and information exchange between university research departments and those involved in commercial exploitation of high-technology products and processes. In addition to an initial £620 000 contribution for infrastructure costs, the county council funded the construction of an advanced-technology building for larger firms. The park has achieved the fastest start-up rate of all science parks and is characterized by a close relationship between university departments and firms as well as by a range of size of units to allow companies to expand on site. To foster the introduction of new products, processes, and materials into existing firms in the West Midlands, the EDU set up, in the summer of 1985, a Technology Transfer Company based at Aston University. Its aim was that, within the context of the council's sector strategy, technical consultants would work with client firms to assess their technological needs and, where appropriate, help them to gain access to research and development capital.

One of the most comprehensive aspects of the WMCC's business-development strategy was the encouragement of worker co-operatives—commercially viable businesses owned and controlled by their members (Mawson 1983*b*). In 1982 three co-operative development agencies were established, serving Birmingham, the Black Country, and Coventry. The agencies, which employed fifteen development workers in total, assisted potential co-operatives in preparing their business plans and provided business advice to new and existing co-operatives. Training courses were provided for existing and potential co-operatives. Product development by co-operative and community enterprises was assisted by the Unit for the Development of Alternative Products (UDAP) established at Lanchester Polytechnic following the initative of shop stewards of Lucas Aerospace. Co-operative centres, providing a range of accommodation and shared facilities, were set up in Coventry and on the site of the former Bilston steelworks in Wolverhampton. The EDU provided support to the co-operative development agencies and evaluated funding proposals, which were submitted to West Midlands Cooperative Finance Ltd., a company established by the WMCC in 1984 with an initial grant of £700 000. Finance was normally provided to co-operatives in the proportion 70 per cent grant to 30 per cent loan, while it was usual for co-operatives simultaneously to submit funding applications to Industrial Common Ownership Finance Ltd., who operated a £500 000 revolving loan fund on behalf of the county council. Between 1981 and the summer of 1985 the number of co-operatives in the county grew from six to seventy, employing some 400 people at a cost of £2500 per job. There were nine failures between 1981 and 1985 of which five occurred prior to the establishment of the agencies.

Training was a critical element in the development of the WMCC's economic strategy. Firstly, the development of craft, technical and managerial skills was regarded as being important to industrial regeneration as financial investment in modern plant. Secondly, the acquisition of such skills was considered to be a vital factor determining an individual's chances in life; consequently the promotion of training facilities was seen as a crucial part of an economic and employment strategy designed to benefit the community in general and disadvantaged social groups in particular (42 per cent of training places were filled by members of ethnic minorities between 1981 and 1985).

The EDU provided support on an annual basis to more than 3000 training places through various initiatives in conjunction with training boards, local colleges, voluntary groups, and the WMCC's own task force. More than forty schemes covered a wide range of training activities, for example, high-technology training for young people in the inner cities, training in a range of construction and design skills for women returning to work, training in new technological methods for older unemployed engineering craftsmen, and industrial-language training for ethnic minorities. Every training scheme was scrutinized to ensure that it provided training of a high quality in areas which provided significant employment potential. Their success was reflected in the fact that 80 per cent of trainees subsequently found employment.

From 1984 high unemployment in the county led to its being designated as a 'priority area' in terms of the ESF, and hence the majority of EDC training initatives becoming eligible for grant aid. Between 1983 and 1985 the number of successful bids for aid rose from two to twenty-five, with the net grant rising from £150 000 to £1.2 million. The EDU was also responsible for establishing a number of training centres, the most significant being at Tyseley, in the inner-area of Birmingham, which included four elements:

(a) an information technology centre (Itec) jointly funded by the MSC, DI and BICP
(b) training facilities for the WMCC's community-programme task force
(c) community workshops, linked to the training facilities, to assist in the generation of new enterprises
(d) a substantial adult training facility based on previous proposals for a YTS training workshop for which funding had been withdrawn by the MSC.

The complex was designed to offer training of a high quality to both adults and young people with an emphasis on new techology and its application in manufacturing and service industries. The Itec became fully operational in May 1985 and was designed to provide disadvantaged young people in the inner cities with an introduction to training in new technology.

Following the withdrawl of MSC resources for the training workshop, and a protracted and inconclusive dispute between the MSC and D.o.E. over which should fund provision in this part of the centre, the WMCC took the initiative and established a training company, West Midlands Training (Tyseley) Ltd. Funded through an initial grant of £400 000, the company was to provide approximately 300 training places per annum for unemployed adults. The training centre at Tyseley was unique in being designed to demonstrate, in the face of trends to close skill centres and reduce training opportunities for the most disadvantaged, that given the right opportunities the long-term unemployed could be retrained to prevent future shortages of skills in areas critical to the development of local industry.

The scale of unemployment and poverty in the West Midlands led the EDU to launch publicity and advice campaigns aimed at improving the take-up of welfare benefits and thereby achieving an immediate increase in the incomes of those suffering greatest hardship. The EDU in 1984 estimated that as many 126 000 people in the county were eligible for supplementary benefit but were not claiming it—frequently because of the complexity of the social security system and the stigma attached to being a claimant. The inadequacy of many aspects of the social-security system, with particular reference to its operation in the West Midlands, was highlighted through a series of representations to government and the social-security reviews.

Starting in 1983 a series of take-up campaigns was run in conjunction with district councils and the Citizens Advice Bureau (CAB). The success of the campaigns, which brought an additional £3.5 million to claimants in benefits for an outlay of £20 000, led to the establishment of a welfare-rights team which increased take-up to £8 million per annum by 1985. The campaign organizers issued households with postcards which provided information on welfare rights and included a claim form returnable to the DHSS by freepost. They met some of the special difficulties faced by ethnic minorities when claiming benefits by translating leaflets into Asian languages and arranging local advice sessions with campaign workers fluent in Asian languages. To avoid leaving claimants without support at the end of the campaigns, the EDC funded staff to represent clients who had unsuccessfully claimed benefits as a result of the campaigns and wished to appeal at a tribunal.

Early in 1983 the EDC launched a campaign, supervised by the London-based Low Pay Unit to publicize low wage rates and their effect on the economy. A West Midlands low pay unit funded by the WMCC was established whose role included: increasing the awareness of workers in industry of their legal rights; responding to inquiries (this included providing an information sheet explaining the rates of pay in the industry it covered and advising on claiming welfare benefits); providing training sessions for advice workers and engaging in campaigning research.

The WMCC also developed a number of initiatives to help trade-unionists respond to the economic crisis, both at plant level—particularly when faced with closure or contraction—and by putting their case about the decline of the West Midlands to government and other relevant bodies. Grants were given to Coventry Workshop, an independent resource centre for the local trade-union, labour and community movement, and to Birmingham Trades Council to establish the Birmingham Trades Union Resource Centre to fulfil a similar role. The council also supported a health-and-safety advice centre providing advice and information to workers on a wide range of industry, health, and safety issues. In January 1984 a 'Jobs at Risk' information pack was prepared to help workers whose jobs were at risk; it contained information sheets on warning signs of plant closure, redundancy rights, low pay, worker co-operatives, and so on.

In 1982 the TUC launched an 'action programme' to open centres for the unemployed throughout the UK and subsequently requested the WMCC to support such centres. Seven centres were established, each functioning according to the particular character and problems of its own area. In general terms they provided information and advice on matters such as welfare rights, training schemes, and employment initiatives. They also existed to develop contacts between the unemployed, the employed, and trade unions. Their function extended to encouraging social activity and leisure pursuits; campaigning on issues such as the prevention of unemployment and the problems faced by the unemployed; and helping unemployed people to develop their own ability to respond to problems.

In summarizing the experience of the WMCC it is important for us to stress that the EDC did not start from the premiss that it was going to resolve on its own the severe economic crisis faced by the county; rather, it believed that, within the limits imposed by constraints on resources, it could demonstrate a number of effective economic-development initiatives which, if introduced in an integrated manner at national, regional, and local levels within the context of a planned reflation, could present a solution to the problems of the West Midlands.

By carrying out economic development at a county-wide level, the EDU had found it possible to build up teams with specialist expertise. Thus it was possible to tailor assistance to the specific needs of projects, whether for investment, training, new technology, business advice, property, or some other purpose. It was recognized that effective implementation depended on detailed knowledge of the local economy, and this led to the preparation of studies covering the majority of local industrial sectors.

The EDU's economic-intelligence team of twelve officers was the only group of economists working full-time on the West Midlands economy. Consequently in the preparation of a revised regional-strategy document, for example, the WMCC drew almost entirely on EDU expertise. The work carried out by the team operated in a two-way process: the experience of investment and project implementation informed the sector studies, while the research carried out resulted directly in a number of initiatives, for example, the business-advice team, the clothing resource centre, and the export-marketing scheme.

Given the EDU's stress on detailed knowledge, it is perhaps not surprising that its policy documents emphasized the importance of targeting initiatives. It reacted against the view, found among some local authorities, that it was sufficient simply to offer loans and grants to firms without any clear criteria; and that to clear sites, build units, and improve road access, with no particular understanding of the dynamics of the land and property market, or of the investment and other business needs of companies, would somehow lead to economic regeneration, the benefits of which would in turn 'trickle down' to the most disadvantaged in the labour market. Rather, the EDU held the view that for economic effectiveness it was necessary to target initiatives on specific companies and types of commercial problem; to have a 'people-based' approach to economic initiatives which ensured that measures adopted reached those in greatest need; and emphasize not just numbers of jobs but also the quality of jobs in terms of worker involvement in management decisions, incomes, access to opportunities, trade-union recognition, working conditions, and so on.

In organizational terms, the WMCC's economic-development initiatives had a clear focus through one committee and a single major department covering all critical functions with the exception of estates and valuation. In contrast to many local authorities, which have a 'policy vacuum' in this field and whose activity in this field is therefore officer-led and reflects the perspective of the particular profession or professions by which it is dominated, the council had a clear economic policy framework emanating from elected members. It proved possible to implement an innovative economic-development programme because of the substantial resources which the council could mobilize, particularly through the Section 137 power, which yielded considerable flexibility in the development of new initiatives.

While much thought had been given by the elected members to the nature of their economic-development programme prior to the 1981 local authority election, less attention had been given to the organizational questions concerning the means by which it could be implemented. Initially, for example, the departments which had previously been responsible for various economic-development functions resented losing their role. Throughout the four-year development of the programme, the innovative nature of the initiatives continually presented problems of legal interpretation, as well as questions about the proper use of local-authority finance and assets. Although the Local Government (Miscellaneous Provisions) Act, 1982 clarified the the use of Section 137 funds for economic-development purposes, there remained ambiguity surrounding the nature and extent of the use of powers and resources, and there were inevitable inter-departmental conflicts, as EDC schemes pushed the WMCC service departments into new areas of professional experience which challenged traditional practices. These problems were compounded by the fact that it was not until the autumn of 1984 that the head of the EDU became a chief officer and member of the management team of the WMCC.

Economic Development in the Districts 1979–1985

By the early 1980s the persistence of high levels of unemployment within the county led to a recognition among the district councils that the West Midlands was not suffering a temporary cyclical problem and hence that more needed to be done, particularly in regard to helping the long-term unemployed. In 1982 joint lobbying resulted in greater support through the Urban Programme, and Dudley was successful in securing an Enterprise Zone. In the context of the government's review of regional policy, all the West Midlands local authorities lobbied hard to secure regional aid, and early in 1984 the county was designated as an Intermediate Area, which gave local companies access to regional selective assistance and public bodies access to infrastruture support from the ERDF. Increased support also became available through the establishment of a national Youth Training Scheme (YTS) by the MSC and an expansion of training provision for the long-term unemployed. During this period the D.o.E. established an Enterprise Unit to oversee its increasing role in local economic development, particularly through the Urban Programme, and the DTI set up its Team for Innovation to encourage increased take-up by local companies of DTI aid for development of new technology.

While these developments were welcomed by the local authorities, they were nevertheless regarded as inadequate to the scale of the problem. Furthermore much of this additional support was based on the concept of matching finance from local government. Given the continuing reduction in support given by central government to local-authoirty finances, and controls on capital expenditure, there was naturally scepticism about the value of the new measures for local economic development. In terms of national regional aid received, the West Midlands remained in a disadvantageous position relative to the upper-tier Development Areas which had access to automatic regional development grants as well as selective regional assistance. Support from the ERDF for infrastructure projects counted against capital allocations to local authorities, so no 'additional' schemes were possible on receipt of support.

Since the Intermediate Area stretched beyond the county into the comparatively prosperous fringe areas of the West Midlands, there remained a danger that demand-led applications for selective assistance and the inherent bias within the ERDF towards green-field sites would deflect aid away from the hard-pressed inner-urban areas (WMCC 1985a). Moreover the reduction in real terms in Urban Programme support from 1982/3 onwards was regarded with cynicism, particularly in the light of the inadequacy of the funds available to the task in hand. Local authorities were also critical of the excessive emphasis placed on joint public–private-sector financing when Derelict Land Grants, UDG's and Urban Programme moneys were being allocated, at a time when private investment was being withdrawn from the county.

A further problem which the local authorities faced in securing support from the central government and the EEC was the pressure which project applications and project management put on staff resources. Increased contact with both the private sector and voluntary organizations was required in order to bring forward projects, involving lengthy discussions with no guarantee of success. The complexity of regulations, particularly with respect to EEC financial instruments, required the development of staff expertise and contact with relevant officials. Budgetary planning was made more difficult by increased uncertainty as to the success of bids, particularly in the context of the ESF, whose calender-year allocations did not synchronize with the local-authority financial year. By the mid-1980s the West Midlands district councils, particularly the smaller ones were still grappling with the organizational problems which outside funding posed. It was clear that central government had little understanding of their problems of organizational capacity. It is worthwhile considering this question in greater detail.

A survey undertaken for the financial year 1983/4 revealed that since 1981 there had been a rapid expansion in the scale and range of local economic initiatives (Mawson and Naylor 1985). Excluding assistance from the Urban Programme, Solihull, Walsall, Sandwell, and Wolverhampton were spending between £250 000 and £1 million per annum, Dudley and Coventry £1.5 million per annum, and Birmingham £15 million per annum (capital and revenue). Total expenditure on economic schemes across the districts under the Urban Programme was £15 million, with additional expenditure in the BICP of £9 million.

Undoubtedly the biggest element in expenditure was still the provision of sites and premises, with Birmingham City Council, by far the biggest investor, committed to recycling industrial land at a rate of 130 acres per annum and bringing forward 125 acres of new land on large sites. Birmingham had also built 400 small units since 1978, Coventry 80 units since 1975, and Wolverhampton 100, Dudley 62, Walsall 37, and Sandwell 11 since 1979. Small nursery units with managerial and technical assistance had been constructed in Solihull, Wolverhampton, and Coventry. By 1983/4 all districts with the exception of Solihull had established programmes of financial assistance on a limited scale in relation to the provision of loans, grants, and rent relief, and five Industrial Improvement Areas had been declared in Birmingham, three in Wolverhampton and one in Sandwell. In addition to providing business-advice services directly, a number of authorities had established separate centres, in partnership with local industry, polytechnics or Chambers of Commerce—for example, WELD, Coventry Business Centre—and had joined with the WMCC in funding the Co-operative Development Agencies. A particularly interesting development was the establishment of centres focusing specifically on new technology and product development. Birmingham had set up four such centres: the Innovation and Development Centre Unit in association with the National Westminster Bank, the Industrial Research Institute in association with Birmingham University, and the Metrology Club and the Micro System Centre with Birmingham Polytechnic; Coventry had set up the Coventry Innovation Centre and Walsall the Walsall Innovation Service with their local Chambers of Commerce; while Walsall and Dudley had established similar ventures with local colleges. On a more significant scale, Coventry was involved with the county and Wolverhampton in the 25-acre Science Park at Warwick University, and Birmingham was in partnership with Aston

University and Lloyds Bank in Birmingham Technology Ltd., which was responsible for the development of a 22-acre site and the provision of a development-capital fund.

The rapid expansion of economic-development activity summarized above presented major organizational problems for the authorities concerned. In only one authority, Birmingham, was there an economic-development committee, with an explicit economic-development budget. In other cases responsibility was spread across policy and resources, finance, planning, estates, and inner-area committees, and thus was reflected in the distribution of staff resources. Staff levels were clearly inadequate to, the scale of the task in hand: Birmingham could identify seventeen officers working full-time, and three part-time; Wolverhampton seven full-time; Dudley eight full-time; and Coventry five full-time; while in Sandwell, Walsall, and Solihull there were no posts which could be identified as being responsible solely for economic development (Mawson and Naylor 1985). As the scale of activity continued to increase there were increasing pressures to undertake a reorganization of functions.

In February 1983 Solihull undertook its first review of local economic development, which suggested a limited programme of support to small units and the marketing of sites for high-technology industry (Solihull Metropolitan Borough Council 1983), but no proposals for organizational changes were forthcoming. In Coventry, following the appointment of a new chief executive with some background in economic development and a change in the leadership of the city council, a series of reviews were set in train during 1983. They showed that there was no single committee with effective control of economic development and that administrative and budgeting mechanisms were split. It was argued that this meant that inadequate political consideration was given to the subject and hence it failed to secure a fair share of resources. It was pointed out that the officers who serviced the interdepartmental economic-development group only did so on a part-time basis. Although the group worked well on an informal day-to-day basis, it nevertheless experienced problems of conflicting priorities. Although proposals were presented to streamline these arrangements, no action was taken. At a time of increasing financial pressure on the authority, the traditional service departments education, housing, and social services, and their committees saw the proposals as a potential threat in budget terms, and there remained general uncertainty about the way forward.

In Birmingham, following a change of control in May 1984, the new Labour chairman of the economic-development committee tabled a chairman's statement which reflected very similar policy directions to those developed at the WMCC (Bore 1984). It emphasized that the city was likely to experience high levels of unemployment for a considerable time and that this would have a differential impact on certain social groups and areas. As regards the various initiatives to be undertaken, assistance to industry was to focus not only on small and new firms but also on existing medium-sized and large companies, and was to be achieved through equity and loans, and the signing of investment agreements. Local self-help was to be promoted through co-operatives, community businesses fostered and high-quality training schemes were to be pursued, targeted at disadvantaged groups. Lower priority was to be given to efforts to attract industry from other areas through costly advertising. As regards organization, it was pointed out that

> There is a multiplicity of uncoordinated initiatives under different spending programmes, inadequate resources and an unsystematic approach to economic planning . . . There is a lack of systematic processes for identifying costing and prioritising potential schemes and inadequate evaluation of past/current activities and resource use (Bore 1984, p. 4).

Immediately before the elections, the leading officer responsible for economic development in the city, the chief planning officer, had commissioned a study by a consultant to provide a basis for an economic-development strategy which could be interpreted as taking the authority in a somewhat different direction; the study focused on questions about the 'image' of the city and attracting mobile industry through promotion.

In a follow-up report on the city's organizational arrangements, the chief executive confirmed the weakness highlighted in the committee chairman's Statement (City of Birmingham 1984a). Despite the establishment of a development and production unit in 1983, implementation and budgetary responsibilities remained scattered across four key departments: planning, estates, treasurer's, and education. It was therefore decided to transfer staff and functions to a new unit under an economic-development officer responsible to the city planning officer. The economic-development unit which was established at the end of 1984 comprised twenty four posts and was divided into four sections: business development, land and property, training, and community-enterprise development. Unfortunately the new unit contained some inherent tensions, as the estates and education officers were seconded to it, the treasurer's staff remained accountable to their chief officer in respect of financial matters, and responsibility for economic research and policy development was given to the assistant chief planning officer. In the spring of 1985 when the city published its first *Economic Strategy and Development Programme for Birmingham*, it contained an interesting mixture of Birmingham's traditional preoccupations with industrial promotion and infrastructure, and elements of the 1984 statement by the chairman of the economic-development committee (City of Birmingham 1985).

The four Black Country local authorities—Walsall, Wolverhampton, Sandwell, and Dudley—recognized in the early 1980s that they needed to work together and present a united voice in order to secure additional resources from central government under the annual block-grant settlement, Urban Programme, regional aid scheme, and so on. In September 1982 it was agreed that the chief executives and leaders of the councils should meet on a regular basis to consider a number of matters, including economic development. Given the councils' lack of experience in this policy area, it was felt that it would be advantageous to work together, sharing research and lobbying, and launching joint initiatives. As the scale of their work expanded and the problems of economic decline continued unbated, there were pressures within the individual councils to reorganize.

In Walsall, for example, an internal document on the council's economic-development objectives was prepared in the summer of 1983, and in the autumn discussions took place about a reorganization, in view of the fragmented nature of the council's efforts (Walsall Metropolitan Borough Council 1983). Shifts in control of what was effectively a hung council did not lead to any firm decisions being taken until December 1984, when the chief executive presented proposals to consolidate activities by creating a small estates and economic-development unit under his control (Walsall Metropolitan Borough Council 1984). In July 1985, for the first time, a framework for a 'Borough Economic development and Employment Strategy' was presented to the council to be subject to annual review related to the budgetary cycle (Walsall Metropolitan Borough Council 1985).

In Wolverhampton, following the appointment of a new chief executive formerly head of the WMCC's EDU, a similar exercise took place with the establishment of a small team operating within a newly established chief official's secretariat in the spring of 1985. In Sandwell, in anticipation of the abolition of the county council, two new posts were established to work on economic schemes in the summer of 1985. In Dudley the problems of shifts in control of another hung council delayed decisions on reorganization. Perhaps the most significant characteristics of these developments, beyond a common recognition of the need to tackle organizational problems, were the very small numbers of additional staff and insignificant additional resources committed to economic development.

In this context, it is worth noting that one of the most significant initiatives launched as a result of co-operation between the Black Country authorities was the commissioning of a major study by a team of consultants entitled 'The Promotion of Newer Industry in the Black Country' (Dudley, Sandwell, Walsall, and Wolverhampton Metropolitan Councils 1984). Specifically the consultants were asked to identify growth sectors with prospects of introducing new or adapted technology, materials, or products; to advise the district authorities on ways of assisting existing industries to introduce technological change; and to identify newer types of industry that could be attracted to the Black Country. Without any prompting from the authorities concerned, the consultants concluded that the best solution was to establish a Black Country development agency controlled by a board of elected members with divisions concerned with finance and grants, innovation and linked productivity centres, export marketing, promotion, and strategic site planning.

The arguments in favour of such an economic-development function for the four authorities were: economies of scale, particularly in relation to staff; the need to co-ordinate a diverse and potentially confusing range of initiatives through a single point of reference; enhanced capacity to mobilize private-sector finance and lobby for central-government and EEC funds; speed of action in the business environment; ensuring that at the WMCC's abolition the Black Country's interests would not be overshadowed by those of Birmingham. The consultants argued that over a five-year-period the programme would cost about £3.5 million per annum—an equivalent of 1.9 pence on the rates. The four district councils adopted a cautious line towards the proposals and specifically felt unable to meet the sum mentioned although they did approach the D.o.E. about possible support under the Urban Programme for the various proposals in the consultants report.

The WMCC, in responding to the document, pointed out that in the light of impending abolition of the county council it was interesting that the consultants had to rely on it for information and analysis on the Black Country economy; that its EDC was already carrying out the functions identified in the proposals; and that it had allocated £4.3 million in 1984/5 to environmental-improvement schemes and a similar sum for economic-development initiative (WMCC 1984*b*).

Conclusions: the Future of Local Economic Development

By the summer of 1985 all the local authorities in the West Midlands County were actively involved in economic development. Over the previous five years the scale and range of activities had expanded rapidly, reflecting the growing economic and social crises. For the majority of the authorites concerned this was a new policy field, and the pace of the development raised major political, organizational, and implementational questions.

As regards the future, a number of general observations can be made. Firstly, given that local authorities are now clearly committed to introducing their own measures to develop the economy and generate employment, consideration needs to be given to the powers and resources available. On the basis of the experience of the West Midlands authorities, there is evidence to suggest that much can be achieved at the local level which is both cost-effective and yields results in terms of job creation, business development, training, and anti-poverty initiatives. There is a strong case for a more formal recognition of the importance of such local-authority activities in national industrial, employment, and regional-aid programmes. However, there is a danger that in return for additional resources such activities would be subject to excessive regulation and control. One of the key lessons to be learned from the experience of the West Midlands authorities is that only at local level are there the knowledge, experience, and commitment to enable many of the tasks of economic and social regeneration to be undertaken.

It is worth bearing in mind that while the Urban Programme has provided a stimulus to economic-development initiatives, it nevertheless remains heavily circumscribed by central-government regulations. The annual budget cycle, the capital bias in the programme, the restrictions on the development of community businesses, excessive detailed monitoring, for example, all work against a long-term and innovative programme. The manner in which other central-government and European aid programmes operate indicates lack of understanding of the problems of implementation on the ground. It is perhaps not surprising that it has been through the general enabling power of Section 137 that some of the most innovative and effective initiatives have been developed. A trebling of the present twopenny rate which would bring the rate back to its 1973 value in real terms, together with subsequent linking to inflation, would probably do more than anything else to free local authorities from present constraints and allow them to become economic-development agents.

In organizational terms, the experience of the West Midlands authorities has shown that present structures in local government are ill-equipped to deal with this important new area of local-government activity. In this regard, a single committee responsible for economic development is important, allied to a management focus bringing together the key functions—investment, advice, infrastructure, training, and community-employment initiatives—in such a way that projects can be developed and policies formulated, unhindered by professional or departmental conflicts. Experience suggests that this is best achieved under the remit of a single chief officer, although in the case of smaller authorities it could be secured through the location of related blocks of activity within a department or departments or under the control of the chief executive. Given, however, that economic and employment matters impinge on the work of virtually every department in a local authority, there would still be a need to establish a corporate and budgetary process which considered the implications of the work of all committees on the economy and the labour market. Experience in the West Midlands indicates that the typical fragmented, committee-based, and incremental annual budget cycle militates against the development of a coherent economic and employment strategy. Moreover, the emergence of economic development as a major local-authority service has clearly presented a challenge to some of the traditional practices of the key local-authority professional disciplines and a somewhat cautious interpretation of what is legally possible, a challenge which they have yet to come fully to terms with.

One of the most important lessons to be learnt from the activities of the WMCC concerns the advantages to be derived from undertaking economic development on a strategic county-wide basis. Clearly the demand for major public-investment projects cannot always be generated within the confines of a single local boundary; furthermore economic problems and processes in the metropolitan areas spill over local boundaries. The economic problems of the major urban centres are so complex, large-scale, and interrelated that there is a need for a matching response in terms of resources and specialists skills. However, as this chapter has shown, the district councils, with the exception of Birmingham, have still committed comparatively little finance and few staff to economic development. While they are increasingly aware of the need to undertake local initiatives, they are handicapped by a staff skill shortages. Moreover, given the increasing financial pressures on local governemnt, it is unlikely that they will be able to expand this area of work in the near future.

In functional terms, the abolition of the WMCC in 1986 has resulted in the loss of a central source of intelligence on the county's economy and made it more difficult to organize an effective lobby. Should the district councils take on the research role individually, this would involve duplication of data banks and professional staff, and greater difficulty in sustaining major research programmes. The abolition of the WMCC has meant the loss of an agency capable of completing large-scale land assembly and undertaking major investment projects. In respect of the Urban Programme, the WMCC's team of twenty-three officers has been responsible for the development with others of some of the most innovative economic schemes. These could only be taken on by the district councils if they were to recruit substantial additional staff and even then might well not be effectively replaced because of the expertise built up within the county council and the economics of scale which it has been possible to exploit. Similar arguments apply to the county's training programmes, co-operative-development programmes, voluntary-employment schemes, and welfare and low-pay campaigns.

The Government's position was clearly stated in the White Paper *Streamlining the Cities*, which in its single reference to economic development stated:

Borough and District councils already have powers to assist industry in their areas. The Government consider, therefore, that no specific arrangements are required to replace the role of the GLC and the Metropolitan Councils in assisting local industry and in drawing on the Urban Programme or Urban Development Grants. (D.o.E. 1983).

While the Government was correct in its statement concerning the question of powers, nevertheless, there remains a serious problem arising from its decision not to allow the district councils to retain the product of the county council's twopenny rate under Section 137 after abolition (Knowles 1985). As has already been argued, Section 137 has proved a most valuable and flexible source of monies for economic development, yet the removal of a tier of government in the metropolitan areas results in the amount of monies potentially available for economic initiatives being halved while the surrounding fringe local authorities, with their two-tier system, will retain the combined potential to raise a fourpenny rate under Section 137. The problem is well exemplified in the West Midlands, where between 1981/2 and 1984/5 the county council raised its full rate under Section 137 of more than £8 mil-

Table 7.2. *Section 137* ª *Expenditure in the West Midlands County, 1983–1985*

Local authority	Actual spending (£m) 1983/1984	Anticipated spending (£m) 1984/1985	Product of 2p rate (£m) 1984/1985
WMCC	8.234	8.500	8.500
Birmingham	1.230	1.400	3.300
Coventry	0.022	0.050	1.070
Dudley	0	0.200	0.850
Sandwell	0.842	0.700	0.944
Solihull	0.020	0.091	0.614
Walsall	0	0	0.738
Wolverhampton	0.578	0.843	0.851
Total	10.926	11.784	16.867

Note: ª Local Government Act, 1972.
Source: WMCC (1985*a*).

lion and spent the majority on economic development. In contrast in the 1984/5 financial year the seven district councils expected to raise a total of around £3.2 million (39 per cent) out of a possible £8 or so million (see Table 7.2). The district councils in aggregate, even if they raised and spent all their Section 137 entitlement on economic projects, would still only be able to undertake the equivalent of the county council's Section 137 economic programme before its abolition in 1986. In certain districts, for example, Wolverhampton and Sandwell, where the full twopenny rate is currently raised and spent, the situation is particularly serious.

Thus in both organizational and resource terms the future potential beyond 1986 for local-authority economic initiatives in the West Midlands has been reduced. To end on an optimistic note, however, by the summer of 1985 the district councils had all become members of WMEB and discussions were proceeding to widen its role, so that it would cease to be purely an investment agency and would take on a range of economic functions and thereby become a strategic and democratically controlled development agency for the West Midlands controlled by all the district councils in the former WMCC.

8

Policy Assessment

Chapters 6 and 7, in concentrating upon central-government policy and local economic-development initiatives respectively, have already touched upon policy impacts. Unintended as well as intended consequences of policy are important. This chapter selects a number of policies for further investigation, all of which, whether major or minor, new or old, have been designed to have an ameliorative impact on the problems of economic decline, including in the inner cities. The policy areas which are explored further in this chapter are regional planning; the MSC and youth unemployment; the Dudley Enterprise Zone; the UDG scheme; and, finally, inner-city policy. However, before discussing these policy areas it is necessary to say something about our approach to policy assessment.

The ESRC inner-city research initiative placed specific emphasis, among a wide range of other issues, on the monitoring and assessment of policy interventions, especially those in the public sector. One of our roles has, therefore, been to 'monitor the impact and effectiveness of public policy responses—not merely specifically "urban" spatial policies but also aspatial ones—on the health and welfare of the particular cities concerned' (Hall 1981, p. 148). Given the wide range of interventions by the public, private, and voluntary sectors, which also include forms of joint intervention, the implication is that such studies would be exploratory, descriptive, and analytical, but not rigorously scientific. Given the extremely large number of initiatives in the West Midlands (reflecting an experimental State approach), a strong degree of selectivity has been inevitable. At the same time we have concentrated on the effects arising from the practice related to those interventions (Spencer 1984).

Effectively much of our work takes the shape of informed judgement rather than scientific evaluation. Different perceptions, analysis, hunch, feeling for policy relevance, gaps in opportunity, mapping of interests, are all relevant to our formation of judgements (Stewart 1982). Indeed, 'in the real world in which most action research operates, a detailed description of the processes is as important as the (often illusory) search for statistical rigour', hence what is needed is 'as careful a balance as is possible between precise measurement and a more qualitative case-history' (Willmott 1975). This is similar in concept to Rein's policy stories (Rein 1976, p. 136).

We have also to recognize that attempts to assess the effects of public policy interventions have to take account of conflicts of values in the political decision-making process. Our derived knowledge presupposes a framework to interpret it, yet in pluralistic systems there are competing frameworks. As a result, social-science findings are seldom so conclusive that they permit a firm choice amongst competing perspectives (Rein 1973). We also need to bear in mind that assessment of programmes may be resisted by various actors in the situation, especially those concerned more with the launching of initiatives than with judgements about effects.

House (1980, p. 23) provides a useful taxonomy of evaluation methods. The approach adopted by the West Midlands research team has been oriented to House's 'goal-free' and 'case-study' models. In these the distinction between intended and unintended consequences becomes less important, as indeed do the stated objectives of the policy-makers, assuming, of course, that they are clearly articulated and do not change over time (assumptions which are both questionable). It has already been shown, from evidence in the USA and Europe, that in programme evaluation some officials 'placed their hopes for the future specifically on "quantitative evaluation" of such projects and their "cost effectiveness" . . . such an approach to evaluation is bedevilled by the looseness with which the objectives of these projects tend typically to be stated and by the reorientation of their activities as they learn by doing' (Room 1983, p. 160). Learning by doing, and changing objectives accordingly, is a flexible approach adopted by many organizations responsible for new policy initiatives (Spencer 1982). The necessary wide scope of the inner cities research programme does not enable detailed in-depth economic analyses of public policy interventions. However, our work does draw on such detailed studies as exist.

We start by looking at regional planning in the West Midlands, an example of a policy-formulation process designed to provide a regional framework which has had to adapt to new, different, economic pressures and circumstances. We then concentrate on a major group of ameliorative policies to reduce the impact of the scale of unemployment among young people (especially school-leavers). Two recent initiatives with the object of drawing in private-sector resources in conjunction with public-sector resources are exemplified in Enterprise Zones and Urban Development Grants. Finally we turn to consider some of the issues arising from the operation and evolution of inner-city policy, a policy designed to alleviate conditions in the inner city and to enable central government, local authorities, and other agencies to collaborate in tackling the very real problems found in the inner city. We concentrate on the Birmingham Inner City Partnership.

Regional Planning

Regional planning, as it applies to the West Midlands, concerns policy choices about the spatial distribution of population and economic activity mainly within the region. Originally, the purpose of regional planning was to facilitate growth and improve standards, as well as to negotiate the location of additional population and economic activity spilled over from the congested conurbation. Currently its objectives are rather to cope with economic decline and to assist regeneration.

This is an enormous subject (see Martins 1982, summarized by Bentley and Mawson 1985*b*; Saunders 1977). Only a few issues can be highlighted here, against a background in which there have been frequent changes in the composition of, and degree of participation of central government in, local authorities and regional-planning bodies. Several regional-planning issues are highlighted below.

First, a balancing of interests has been necessary especially between the West Midlands County and its surrounding shire counties, where environmental, agricultural, and often middle-class commuter interests are strong and contrast with those in the county. The shire counties have provided competition in attracting population and industry, with the urban–rural shift indicating the tipping of preference towards the shire counties and the changing balance of interests, if not power, in regional planning.

Second, 'principles' of town and country planning have influenced regional planning (containment; overspill; new and expanded towns for population and industry; Green Belts; and, inside the urban areas, the separation of uses and raising of densities, one result of which was the building of high-rise flats). These shaped regional planning and outcomes into the 1970s with the Green Belt lobby, at least, still powerful in the mid-1980s. They required overspill population and industry to move across the Green Belt, complicating the operation for all and preventing, except as a succession of one-off concessions, the extension of the urban development on the edge of the built-up area. Each close-in development, except for Aldridge-Brownhills and Wombourne, has been hard fought at protracted inquiries at which the conservation lobbies have defended their holdings in the Green Belt (Cadbury and Wise 1968). These principles worked to disperse and polarize industry and population, taking from the county assets needed later when its traditional industries flagged. They confined inhabitants of the conurbation to poorer housing and reduced their green areas, which had to be built on (Hulse 1976).

Third, overspill has been a problem for shire-county interests, while planning principles for the county have positively needed shire counties to receive overspill population. Planning principles have merely influenced the location of this overspill and the speed and shape that it has taken. But there have been many disputes—over lack of progress in designation, house-building, and provision of industrial sites, and mismatches between houses and jobs, and because of the reluctance of people and firms to move so far in the days before the urban–rural shift. There have been disputes about industrial sites beyond the conurbation, although these have changed emphasis as fear of loss of industry among authorities within the conurbation has become mixed with the need for attractive green-field sites.

Fourth, growth of population and of the economy were taken as given, rather than needing to be engineered by helpful regional and local planning, until after 1971 (WMPAC 1971). The sober view of the economy taken in *The West Midlands, an Economic Appraisal* (WMEPC 1971) was followed by the county council's *A Time for Action* (WMCC 1975). Regional-planning documents that set out the serious implications of economic and population decline appeared in 1979, when the downturn was clear, and 1985, when further and far more serious de-industrialization had taken place (WMPAC 1979; WMFCC 1985*a*). These two documents contained new elements. They were disagreement with central-government's view and an advocacy drive to persuade the government of the need for urgent remedial economic and industrial policies. This reflected the county's and the region's ongoing problem of persuading central government that the economic decline in the region was novel, profound, and structural and would not merely dissipate with cyclical upturn, were it to come.

Fifth, conflicts have been endemic within regional planning. Those over policies have included the three-way conflict between overspill and regional and inner-area policy, with manufacturing jobs and firms unable to satisfy the job needs of all three. Overspill ceased first; regional-policy differentiation was reduced next (1979–84); but the inner areas have yet to counter the competition of more attractive areas. There have been the conflict between inner-urban areas and new towns, and the view that new towns have robbed inner-urban areas of economic and human resources. (Fothergill, Kitson, and Monk 1983). There has been constant debate about narrow physical land-use versus wider essential social and economic planning. The problem here has been the apparent practical need to limit planning to policy areas controlled by the D.o.E., a reflection of the lack of inter-departmental collaboration in central government. This issue came to the fore in the first county structure plans in 1971 as elements not controlled by the D.o.E. were gradually eliminated by central-government fiat and the inspectors at the public inquiries. It became crucial when the case for economic and social policies was pressed by the local authorities and the West Midlands Economic Planning Council (WMEPC) but had to be relegated to a companion volume on the economy which was refused endorsement by central government as part of the structure planning process.

Conflicts also occurred between parties to regional planning: between the D.o.E. and DTI; between the West Midlands Planning Authorities Conference (WMPAC) and WMEPC, and, through these, between local and central government; and between industry and planners. The regional-planning system has operated rather to highlight problems and conflict than their resolution.

When the WMEPC was set up in 1965, the local authorities took exception

168 *The Industrial Heartland*

to a non-elected invader of their planning role, though little planning at a conurbation or regional level was taking place. They established the WMPAC. After disagreements about the overspill figures in the WMEPC's *The West Midlands, Patterns of Growth* (WMEPC 1967), the WMPAC decided to make its own regional study. Central government decided to co-operate in order to have some control and the tripartite regional-planning system was established, involving the WMEPC, central government, and the WMPAC, often in uneasy co-operation.

Since 1974 the WMCC in particular had been drawing attention to the implications of economic decline and insensitive government policy. The WMPAC restricted its membership to the counties and re-emerged as the West Midlands Forum of County Councils (WMFCC).

Sixth, the lack of a unified and strong regional voice has been one consequence of these conflicts. The West Midlands Region has lacked the political ability to pull regional and local interests together to constitute a lobby for the region in dealings with central government or the EEC. This has been detrimental to the region and county in obtaining sympathetic and sensitive government action. One of the objects of the WMFCC was to foster this united voice. However, the abolition of the WMCC in 1986 has required a reconstitution of this body. Some results have been evident too from the temporary Butcher initiative (see Chapter 6), in the winning of selective regional-aid assistance in 1984—although from a much reduced total budget—and in the formation, with the private sector, of the West Midlands Industrial Development Association.

In conclusion, regional planning has served to constrain industrial development in the West Midlands County and on its periphery and to disperse it across the Green Belt beyond travel-to-work distance. IDC's supported overspill as well as regional policy. Unlike regional policy, however, regional planning involved the migration outwards of both population and jobs. In both cases, it is likely to have been the most dynamic firms that moved and the least dynamic that remained *in situ*. Thus, regional planning has been a factor in social and economic polarization and has weakened the conurbation's powers of regeneration. However, regional planning may only have given official support to a dispersal that was developing under the impetus of market forces and corporate strategies in the late 1960s and 1970s. It boosted rather than created the urban–rural shift in the West Midlands, with direct transfer limited at peak to about 1000 jobs per year. By far the more serious problems economically were closures and decline within the West Midlands County.

The MSC and Youth Unemployment

Table 8.1 shows the estimated number of school-leavers in the West Midland Region in 1982/3 and 1983/4. There are about 50 000 school-leavers per

year, of whom about 29 000 are in the West Midlands County. The table also
shows the provision of places on the MSC schemes, that is the Youth Opportunities Programme (YOP) and the YTS. The Young Workers Scheme
(YWS) is administered by the DE and the table shows places approved
under this scheme. Although the sets of figures are not exactly comparable
because they refer to slightly different age-groups, they do show that the
overwhelming majority of school-leavers are catered for by some form of
government scheme. The YTS, which caters for 16-year-olds, accounted for
40 880 people in December 1983, three months after an estimated 50 500
people had left school. There were almost 15 000 approved places under the
YWS (not all of which would have been filled) which catered for 16- and 17-
year-olds during January to December 1983.

The schemes

There were antecedents of the YTS, going back to 1976. The Work Experience Programme ran from September 1976 until 1978 and was designed to
give unemployed school-leavers a chance to work on employers' premises.
No training was involved. The scheme was relatively small-scale, accounting
for 60 000 people nationally, at a gross cost of £15 million (*Employment
Gazette*, Mar. 1978, 294–7; Aug. 1978, 901–7). This scheme was absorbed
into the Work Experience on Employers Premises scheme, part of the YOP.

YOP replaced not only the Work Experience Programme but also the
youth part of the Job Creation Programme, and the Youth Employment Subsidy (see later). YOP started on 1 April 1978. The government made an
undertaking, known as the 'Easter Undertaking', that no one who left school
at Easter or in the Summer of 1978 and remained unemployed by Easter
1979 should be without the offer of a suitable place on the programme. The
undertaking was repeated for 1979/80.

There were two elements of YOP, work experience and work preparation.
Work experience consisted of:

1. Work experience on employers' premises (WEEP).
2. Community service.
3. Project-based work experience.
4. Training workshops.

While work preparation consisted of:

1. Employment induction course.
2. Short training courses and other work-preparation courses.

Nationally the total number of entrants to YOP were: 1978/9, 162 000;
1979/80, 216 000; 1980/1, 360 000; 1981/2, 553 000; 1982/3, 543 000 (MSC
1983). In the West Midlands Region the numbers on YOP were 25 211 at

Table 8.1. Youth Unemployment, YOP, YTS, and YWS in the West Midlands Region, 1981–1983

	No. of unemployed school-leavers aged under 18 Sept. 1981	No. of unemployed school-leavers aged under 18 Sept. 1982	No. of people on YOP Sept. 1981	No. of people on YOP Sept. 1982	Estimated no. of school-leavers 1982/83	Estimated no. of school-leavers 1983/84	YTS places filled end Dec. 1983	No. approved for YWS Jan.–Dec. 1982	No. approved for YWS Jan.–Dec. 1983
Birmingham	8 058	9 177	4 332	4 818	11 250	11 200	8 737	3 294	3 089
Solihull	988	1 680	743	921	2 050	2 000	1 509	365	347
Dudley	1 460	744	997	1 474	3 200	2 975	2 144	691	868
Sandwell	2 419	2 602	2 135	2 334	3 700	3 750	2 102	1 063	1 094
Walsall	1 754	1 892	1 631	1 767	2 600	3 050	2 523	1 000	1 079
Wolverhampton	1 992	1 870	1 939	2 540	2 850	2 800	2 900	899	974
Coventry	745	508	2 569	2 684	2 950	3 000	2 524	921	798
County total	17 416	18 473	14 346	16 538	28 600	28 775	22 439	8 233	8 249
Warwickshire	2 568	2 439	1 835	2 080	3 700	3 750	2 679	988	781
Hereford and Worcs.	2 843	2 934	1 832	2 116	5 200	4 650	3 436	1 536	1 852
Shropshire	1 580	1 522	2 708	2 897	3 100	3 200	2 726	1 186	1 315
Staffordshire	5 609	5 407	4 490	5 625	9 950	10 000	9 600	2 611	2 643
Regional total	30 016	30 775	25 211	29 256	50 550	50 375	40 880	14 554	14 840

Source: MSC (1983 and 1984).

September 1981 and 29 256 at September 1982. The distribution within the region is shown in Table 8.1.

During 1982–3 there were a series of trial schemes to replace YOP by the YTS. This was to become the main destination for school-leavers and was designed to provide training for everybody not continuing in education after school, including those who were employed. The YTS was established for a first intake in September 1983. It was originally planned to provide 460 000 places nationally and to cost about £1 billion.

The scheme was implemented by the MSC, although training was to be provided by managing agents who might be employers or training agencies. The scheme design had eight elements:

1. Induction to the scheme.
2. Occupationally based training.
3. Off-the-job training and education.
4. Work experience.
5. Core skills which are relevant to any occupation.
6. Guidance and support for each trainee.
7. An assessment process.
8. A record of achievement.

The scheme design was finished in April 1983 and the places had to be provided by September 1983. There are two 'modes' of YTS. Under Mode A schemes an employer, local authority, or other body agrees with the MSC to act as managing agent for the YTS, and provides a scheme of training, work experience, and education for the trainees. Under Mode B schemes the MSC acts as managing agent, and arranges a sponsor (usually a training workshop or a community project) to provide a programme (Mode B1), or the MSC contracts out some of the management (Mode B2).

In the Midland Region as a whole (including the East Midlands) it was planned to provide 85 000 places for 1983/4. In the event 93 000 places were approved and there were 68 000 entrants. Because of the over-provision of places the guarantee of a place was virtually met. By Christmas 1983 there were only 900 applicants who had not been offered a place on the programme. In the West Midlands planning region 40 880 places were filled by Christmas.

Targets were set for the distribution of places among Mode A and Mode B schemes. A target of 70 per cent Mode A was set. Table 8.2 shows that, whereas this target was not met by all the area offices in the West Midlands, the overall proportion was 71 per cent Mode A. The Government announced during 1984 that it would like to see a reduction in the proportion of Mode A places provided.

How was the target for Mode A places met? Details of the proportion of Mode A places provided by different types of managing agent for one Area Manpower Board, which covered some 9452 Mode A places, while Mode B

Table 8.2. *Entrants to the Youth Training Scheme in the West Midlands (Provisional Figures), January–December 1983.*

MSC area office	Mode A		Mode B1		Mode B2		Total
	No. of entrants	% of total in area	No. of entrants	% of total in area	No. of entrants	% of total in area	No. of entrants
Birmingham (including Birmingham and Solihull)	8 235	80	1 866	18	145	1	10 246
Telford (including Hereford and Worcs., and Shropshire)	4 711	77	1 291	21	150	2	6 152
Coventry (including Coventry and Warwickshire)	3 673	68	1 384	26	363	7	5 420
Dudley (including Dudley and Sandwell)	2 616	62	903	21	728	17	4 247
Wolverhampton (including Wolverhampton and Walsall)	3 101	57	1 997	37	325	6	5 423
Total % of entrants by mode		71		24		5	31 488

Source: MSC, Midlands Regional Office, Planning and Budgeting Section.

Table 8.3. *Types of Managing Agents for Approved places on Youth Training Schemes, Mode A, Birmingham and Solihull Area Manpower Board, 1983/1984*

Managing agents	No. of approved places	% of total approved places
Employers	1 518	16
Further education (college-led)	1 619	17
Voluntary agencies	135	1.5
Private training agencies	5 325	56.5
Others	855	9
Total	9 452	100

Source: Birmingham and Solihull MSC Area Manpower Board.

places numbered 3098, are given in Table 8.3. Although we have no data for other Area Manpower Boards we were told by an area programme manager in one of the other areas in the region that a problem was had finding employers willing to act as managing agents for 'genuinely employer-led schemes'. Many employers wished to be sent YTS trainees for their work experience but few were willing to undertake the task of organizing a training programme.

This rush to fulfil the quota of Mode A places caused certain problems. First, it was difficult for the MSC to monitor the schemes which were run by the private training agencies, especially their work-experience element, because the trainees would be spread over a wide area and a large number of premises. A senior MSC official in 1984 said: 'We are not able to visit 100 per cent of placements or anything like it but we are visiting a significant number of placements on each scheme.' Second, integration of the elements (on- and off-the-job training and education, and work experience) was difficult to control. We were told; 'We [the MSC] are at one remove from the placement. The crunch point is the relationship between the managing agent and the placement provider. In the beginning they went for volume rather than quality of placements.'

Take-up and drop-out rates

It was a surprise both locally and nationally that the take-up of places on the YTS was so low. In the Midlands the 68 000 entrants represented only 73 per cent of the places approved. What were the reasons for this low take-up? One MSC officer felt that the scheme was new and that young people may have felt that it was similar to YOP. We were also told that there was a mismatch between the types of places demanded and the types of places offered: 'there has been a massive rejection of engineering by young people'. The consequence was an over-provision of places in the engineering fields and an under-provision in the 'caring' occupations.

By an accident of policy the YWS was operating for 16- and 17-year-olds during the first year of the YTS. This scheme, which was managed by the DE, independently of the YTS, was designed to encourage employers both to employ workers aged under 18 and to depress the wages of these workers. The scheme was introduced in January 1982 and made payable to employers a subsidy of £15 per week in respect of any employee under 18 who was paid less than £40 per week gross and £7.50 per week for any employee under 18 paid less than £45 but more than £40 per week. The wage rates below which the subsidy was payable were raised to £42 and £47 on 1 August 1983 and to £45 and £50 from 1 April 1984. Table 8.4 shows the number of YWS places approved in the Midlands Region (including the East Midlands) between January and December 1982 and between January and December 1983. Although the numbers approved are not necessarily the same as the numbers of places filled, and although the scheme applied to all under-18-year-olds, the number of places is roughly the same as the difference between the number of school-leavers and the number of entrants to the YTS. (The DE officer responsible for the scheme estimated that 50–75 per cent of YWS entrants were 16 years of age). This anomaly in a policy which was supposed to be designed to provide some form of training for all school-leavers was removed on 1 April 1984, when the Secretary of State for Employment announced that in 1984/5 the YWS should no longer be available for those who left school at 16 until they had been out of school for a year. This change would apply to those who took up jobs on or after 1 April 1984. Young people staying on in education and leaving at 17 would continue to be eligible for the YWS immediately upon leaving education. The industrial breakdown of approvals for YWS is also shown in Table 8.4. Ignoring the miscellaneous category, the Midlands Region had far more entrants to distributive occupations. Other larger groups went into textiles, construction, and mechanical engineering.

Some MSC officers we interviewed were surprised at the drop-out rates from the YTS. We received figures for 'premature terminations' for Dudley and Sandwell between April 1983 and March 1984 (including drop-outs from the YOP up to September 1983). In the case of Sandwell there were 470 drop-outs from YTS between September 1983 and March 1984. In December 1983 there were 3102 filled places, so the drop-out rate was about 15 per cent. In Dudley there were 370 drop-outs in that period, and 2144 filled places in December 1983, which indicates a drop-out rate of 17 per cent.

Why had such rates occurred? In both cases the predominant recorded reason for leaving was 'found employment' (174 in Sandwell and 138 in Dudley). These will have included people who found permanent employment with their placement employer. The second-largest category was 'left voluntarily', which says nothing about the actual reason for leaving.

These MSC and DE schemes represent a transformation of the job market

Table 8.4. *Distribution by Employment Sector of Approved Applications to the Young Workers Scheme in the Midlands Region (including East Midlands), January 1982–December 1983*

SIC order no.	Order	No. of applications approved		
		Jan.–Dec. 1982	Jan.–Dec. 1983	Jan. 1982–Dec. 1983
1	Agriculture	624	557	1 181
2	Mining	29	16	45
3	Food, drink	480	568	1 048
4	Coal and petrol	2	6	8
5	Chemicals	286	166	452
6	Metal manufacturing	369	572	941
7	Mechanical engineering	1 808	1 599	3 407
8	Instrument engineering	120	60	180
9	Electrical engineering	1 017	760	1 777
10	Shipbuilding	17	20	37
11	Vehicles	374	311	685
12	Other metals	1 226	899	2 125
13	Textiles	2 875	1 864	4 739
14	Leather	150	219	369
15	Clothing	1 590	1 180	2 770
16	Bricks, pottery	429	461	890
17	Timber	786	951	1 737
18	Printing and publishing	654	623	1 277
19	Other manufacturing	650	1 022	1 672
20	Construction	2 285	2 017	4 302
21	Gas, electricity, water	0	0	0
22	Transport	567	501	1 068
23	Distribution	6 156	5 331	11 487
24	Banks	753	745	1 498
25	Professional/scientific	1 152	1 068	2 220
26	Miscellaneous services	3 787	4 140	7 927
	Total	28 186	25 656	53 842

Source: Data supplied by DE.

for young people. Although we do not have a complete picture of school-leavers, the figures in Table 8.1 indicate that there was in 1983 a very high probability that a school-leaver in the West Midlands would have as a first destination either a YTS place or a job under the YWS. MSC and DE are not so much intervening in the market-place for school-leavers as dominating it. The other traditional route into skills training, the apprenticeship, which used to be available to a small proportion of school-leavers is apparently already much restricted. Between 1979 and 1981 in Birmingham there was a significant decline in apprenticeships: in metal and machinery (including motor services and machinery) craft apprenticeships fell by 79 per cent to 229, and technical apprenticeships fell by 66 per cent to 86; in construction occupations the decline was more marked, with a fall in craft apprenticeships of 78 per cent to 63, and a fall in technical apprenticeships of 89 per cent to 4 (City of Birmingham 1982).

There is no planning of the types of skills training to be offered on the various MSC and DE schemes, and no attempt is made to match the skills produced by the scheme to the demands of local employers. An almost random collection of training is offered. The justification offered is that the schemes produce transferable skills of numeracy, decision-making and computer literacy, but this does not represent the sort of training which is offered to adults. The use of private training agencies seems to offer no obvious advantages over college-led training schemes provided by local authorities. They are difficult to monitor and the profit motive may not be the best incentive to running schemes of a high quality.

The changed employment market has affected the motivation of some of those near the end of their schooldays. At the same time there are questions about whether existing education is preparing people for life in the late 1980s and 1990s. The danger is that the skills needed for industry and commerce will not be there if and when required.

The Dudley Enterprise Zone

The objective of Dudley's Enterprise Zone is 'to encourage development within the Enterprise Zone by reducing the cost of development by way of tax concessions' (Dudley District Council 1983).

The analysis which follows is based on our work on local economic-development initiatives (Mawson and Naylor 1985). The Enterprise Zone is an experimental initiative by central government. It is administered by the D.o.E. and is designed to last for ten years, from July 1981 to July 1991. The concept is to create as much freedom as possible for private enterprise to make profits and create jobs. This freedom was to be created by the lifting of town-planning regulations and the reduction of taxes which were assumed to stifle enterprise. The 'de-planning' aim was gradually watered down as it was realised that sub-standard, unregulated industrial development was unlikely to be helpful in regenerating the inner-city areas. Some control and influence over the zone has remained with the local authority. The aim now is to see how far industrial and commercial activity can be stimulated by the removal of taxes and the streamlining of legal and administrative controls (Smith 1982).

Dudley Enterprise Zone is an area of 538 acres in the Blackbrook Valley, one and a half miles to the south-west of Dudley town centre. Unlike any of the other Enterprise Zones in the UK it is entirely owned by a large number of private developers. At the time it was opened part of the land in the zone was being farmed (19 per cent of the total area) and part was unused (34 per cent of the total area). Very little of the land was occupied by vacant buildings, so the agricultural and unused land represented the main opportunity for development. Of the developed area approximately 60 per cent was in manufacturing use. Metal-processing industries accounted for 41 per cent of 127 firms in the zone and 70 per cent of employment, with transport and distribution the next most important sector in terms of employment and establishments (Tym & Partners 1982).

The incentives available within the Enterprise Zone are:

1. *Exemption from Development Land Tax.* This tax (60 per cent in 1981) is levied on the difference between land values before and after development. Developers are exempt for the ten-year-period of the scheme on all sales of developed land normally subject to the tax.

2. *Exemption from rates levied by the local authority.* Retail, commercial, and industrial property within the zone are exempt from rates for ten years. Occupiers are notified of their rates and of any revaluation for record purposes only. Domestic rates (even on partly business property) and water rates still have to be paid. Dudley receives a grant from the government to compensate for the loss of revenue resulting from rates exemption. The rates payable in 1981 would have been about £900 000 (Tym & Partners 1983*b*).

3. *Exemption from Industrial Training Board levies.* Employers within the zone are not required to pay a levy to the appropriate Industrial Training Board and are no longer required to provide the boards with information about training arrangements.

4. *Easement from planning procedures.* Applications for planning permission for building development are dealt with speedily and sympathetically by the local authority. This is made possible by the planning scheme drawn up for the zone which indicates acceptable land-use conditions. Developments conforming to this receive permission automatically. Building, and environmental health and safety regulations have not been waived, though procedures have been speeded up.

5. *Easement from statistical and other returns to government.* Government requirements for information from firms in the Zone are kept to a minimum.

6. *Easement from Customs regulations.* Priority is given to firms in the zone in dealing with Customs over warehousing and other facilities for goods imported for processing under 'inward processing relief' without requirement of subsequent re-export.

7. *Provision of 100 per cent capital allowances.* A special allowance of 100 per cent is given on capital expenditure on industrial and commercial buildings for the purpose of reducing income and corporation tax payments. The allowance is available for construction, improvement, and extension work on buildings. If the building is sold within twenty-five years there is a clawback of the allowance. The scheme is modelled on industrial-building allowances (Smith 1982).

Dudley Borough Council are co-operating with the government in the operation of the Enterprise Zone. Until a marketing organization is established by the major landowners, the council is acting as the focal point for Enterprise Zone inquiries and promotion (Tym & Partners 1982).

In order to ensure that development of the Enterprise Zone takes place, the government, uniquely in the case of Dudley, has insisted the landowners provide proof of their intent to develop their properties. The major landowners have been required to sign an agreement to develop. Should they break this agreement in the future the local authority will have the power to acquire the land under a compulsory-purchase order. The land agreements are timetabled to ensure that development takes place in a phased period throughout the ten-year experiment (Rodrigues and Brinvels 1982).

The council has also been involved in derelict-land-clearance schemes in co-operation with private-sector firms and has sold a small plot of land (1.6 hectares) on which firms have built premises for their own occupation (Tym & Partners 1983*b*). During the ten-year life of the Enterprise Zone experiment approximately 290 acres of land are to be developed. It is hoped that this will eventually produce between 7000 and 10 000 extra jobs in Dudley (Rodrigues and Brinvels 1982).

In the year up to June 1982 Dudley Enterprise Zone attracted twenty-six firms, employing 193 people. Nine of these firms were completely new. Eight had moved in from other parts of Dudley, and six had transferred from elsewhere in the West Midlands County. Most were small independent firms, with twenty-one employing fewer than ten people. The majority were engaged in transport and distribution. At the same time established companies within the zone continued to close or to shed labour. During 1981–2 nine firms closed or left the area, resulting in a loss of 142 jobs. In total the zone contained 2675 jobs in June 1982, a net increase of four jobs over the year (WMCC EDU 1983).

During 1982–3 forty-four firms and 360 jobs moved into the Enterprise Zone, half these being new firms. No large employers moved into the zone, the largest firm having thirty-nine employees, and thirty-seven of the firms having between one and ten employees. Five of the firms which moved into the zone in the previous year ceased trading during 1982–3; the other twenty had increased their employment from 156 to 163 jobs. The number of jobs lost due to closures or labour reductions among firms established before the opening of the Enterprise Zone has not been recorded (Tym & Partners 1984), but a net gain of about fifty jobs has been estimated. The zone has failed to avoid company closures in the area, has distorted land and rental values, and is the least successful of all the Enterprise Zones in the country (Tym & Partners 1984).

Since the opening of the Dudley Enterprise Zone the area in beneficial use has actually declined by 17 hectares, mainly because of the extension of the zone to include 29 hectares of land previously owned by Round Oak steel-works. The area of vacant land has shown a corresponding increase to 121 hectares, 61 per cent of the total Enterprise Zone area. In all 9.9 hectares of land were developed in the period 1981–3 at a cost of £7.894 million to the private sector and £0.12 million to the public sector. Off-site investment in land acquisition, site preparation, and servicing has amounted to £1.941 million. The costs are high; the achievement in regenerating the local economy is extremely low. However, the zone has still to operate for the rest of its ten-year span. Its main impact so far has been to move a few small firms into the area and create a few jobs. Outside the zone, firms competing in the same local products and markets as those within the zone feel they have to bear much heavier costs and are facing unfair competition (*Birmingham Evening Mail* editorial, 3 Apr. 1984).

Urban Development Grants

Another initiative to tackle the problems of the inner cities was launched in April 1982 in the UDG scheme. (This section is contributed by Wilde (1985).) The scheme, which was recommended by the Financial Institutions Group of private-sector advisers and modelled on the Urban Development Action Grants in the USA (Alderton 1984; Greene 1980; Webman 1981), is seen by many as a radical approach to urban development. It is designed to enable private companies to undertake socially beneficial developments in the inner cities by providing the minimum grant necessary to persuade them to proceed with otherwise unprofitable projects. Any project for industrial, commercial, housing, or leisure development of any size is eligible and rules for administering the grant are largely replaced by subjecting each proposal independently to evaluation by a small team of appraisers seconded from the private sector. The UDG scheme also requires the close co-operation of local authorities and developers—often unlikely and even hostile partners (Spring 1983)—since proposals are submitted to the D.o.E. by local authorities, which as well as vetting and endorsing them are required to pay 25 per cent of the grant eventually determined.

The UDG scheme neatly symbolizes many aspects of the present Conservative Government's approach in general—that grandiose public-sector schemes exacerbate, rather than solve, problems and that the way forward is by the involvement of the private sector, preferably through joint working of the public and private sectors within individual communities. The major role of central government is to make such enterprise profitable. In promoting the scheme, the D.o.E. thus tries to allay any doubts among private-sector participants by emphasizing the limited involvement of government, except in providing the grant, and by contrasting the scheme with the practices of some of the local-authority enterprise boards which, in return for assistance, may impose conditions on hiring practices or union involvement, or require equity or decision-making involvement in assisted firms.

Not surprisingly, the UDG scheme has evolved in ways not necessarily intended or envisaged by its initiators. While any local authority is formally entitled to bid for UDGs and to demonstrate a social need addressed by a project, in practice only the sixty or so local authorities formally invited to apply, by virtue of being designated as Partnership or Programme Authorities, or Designated Districts, under the Inner Urban Areas Act of 1978 or containing an Enterprise Zone, have been significantly involved. Many of these local authorities see UDG as a means of increasing their capital allowance from Whitehall and furthering their objectives in land-use planning, particularly in developing derelict and difficult sites. Despite the political reservations of some local authorities, most of them actively prepared applications and sought private sector involvement.

Although the scheme received limited notice—the deadline for applications was September 1982, subsequently extended to January 1983—the D.o.E. was overwhelmed by more than 300 applications, with all but one of the sixty-one invited local authorities making at least one application. With the criteria for success unclear to the local authorities, or indeed to the D.o.E., which was still developing the ground rules, many of these early applications were submitted on a trial basis. Many were incomplete, especially as regarded financial details from the private firms involved, and some were inappropriate for UDGs—for example, where schemes were clearly viable without a grant, where sites were judged to be capable of supporting alternative developments without support, or where schemes were virtually entirely funded by the public sector. Many of these initial applications were consequently refused or withdrawn.

Subsequently, the D.o.E. and its private-sector appraisers have given advice during the preparation of applications and, while the application rate has slowed down, particularly since February 1984 when fixed application dates were abandoned, the success rate among applications has increased. Precise figures and a breakdown for different periods are not available, but Table 8.5 gives an indication of the situation in November 1984, after the scheme had been in operation for two years. In all, more than 40 per cent of

Table 8.5. *Results by November 1984 of Urban Development Grant Applications in England, September 1982–November 1984 (Approximate Figures)*

	No. of applications
September 1982–January 1983	312
July 1983–January 1984	115
February–November 1984	43
Total September 1982–November 1984	470
Decision pending	50
Refused or withdrawn	240
Offer made	180
Offer made but grant declined	48
Live[a] projects	132
Projects completed	21
On-site activity	50
Projects in preparatory stages	61

Note: [a] Live schemes are ones on which the offer of a grant was outstanding or had been accepted (including completed schemes).

Source: Data supplied by D.O.E.

applications had not been offered a grant and more than 25 per cent of projects offered grants had failed to proceed, often because private-sector participants were not fully committed, financially or organizationally, to schemes which were essentially promoted by local authorities. The private sector lacked the organizational capacity to respond in some instances, even where resources were made available. Thus by October 1984 only thirty-five of the sixty-five invited authorities had live schemes (that is, schemes with offers accepted or outstanding). The D.o.E. has since been much more careful to ensure a firm commitment by the private-sector participants before an offer is made, though some local authorities believe that the public sector should be prepared to risk committing UDG funds to specific schemes as a way of attracting potential private-sector participants.

The capacity of a project to address specific social needs, and especially to create jobs, is given prominence in UDG literature, and indeed is necessary to satisfy the Local Government Grants (Social Needs) Act, 1969, under which payment is made. While some attempt at social assessment is made, this criterion appears to be satisfied primarily by the location of projects within the invited authorities, after which financial assessment, judgement of viability, and a satisfactory ratio between public and private funds (usually around 1 : 4) appear to be determining factors in successful UDG applications. Despite the emphasis on job creation, very few offers have been made for business-development schemes, and there appear to be tensions between the DTI, to whom most industrial schemes are referred, with its concern for nationally significant and viable industry, and the D.o.E. with its mandate and organizational structure to consider local issues and revitalize the inner cities. Most UDG projects fit the accustomed role of the D.o.E. and local authorities to be involved in construction and the provision of infrastructure. Thus typical schemes are the provision of small industrial units, either purpose-built or by conversion of redundant industrial premises, the refurbishment and privatization of council housing which is hard to let, and the preparation of derelict or difficult sites for housing (Munday and Mallinson 1983; Mallinson and Gilbert 1983). However, the provision of facilities for shopping, offices, and leisure in places judged commercially viable has given rise to some of the biggest projects, including half of those receiving a UDG of more than £1 million, and such projects accounted for a large share of total UDGs (see Table 8.6).

UDG projects in the West Midlands

The West Midlands has been successful in initiating UDG projects to a markedly greater extent than any other region, despite the relatively low number of authorities in the region invited to apply (see Table 8.7). While the six invited local authorities within the West Midlands County have all made some effort to encourage private-sector participation in the scheme, there have been marked differences between local authorities in both the number of applications made and the projects successfully implemented (see Table 8.8).

Birmingham City Council has been by far the most active authority in submitting projects, many of which were initiated by the council to further its land-use-planning objectives. Despite many failures, often because of insufficient private-sector commitment, Birmingham by November 1984 accounted for more than 70 per cent of the value of the region's UDGs and had obtained the two largest grants in England—one of almost £6 million towards a £22-million project for infrastructure improvements and the construction of industrial and warehouse units on the Imperial Metal Industries (IMI) site at Halford Park, and one of more than £4.5 million to which the council added more than £5 million for its own project in a £34-million project to complete the comprehensive development of Paradise Circus, a scheme left in abeyance for many years. Dudley district council has also made a major commitment of time and effort to securing UDGs, and has achieved a high success rate for a limited number of applications for a range of different projects. However, the remaining authorities had by late 1984 acquired only ten UDGs, worth scarcely 10 per cent of the region's total grant, despite having submitted half the applications.

Birmingham City Council in particular appears to have been successful because of a strong commitment at political and administrative levels to attract to the city as much funding as possible from this source, with the concomitant commitment of considerable staff resources over an extended period. Moreover, planning officers have seen an opportunity to implement

Table 8.6. *Live[a] Projects Receiving Urban Development Grants, in England, October 1984*

Project category[b]	No. of projects	Estimated total cost of projects in category		Total UDG contribution to projects in category	
		£	% of total	£	% of total
Industrial development	11	25 227 000	7.8	5 099 000	8.5
Industrial units	35	28 146 000	8.7	7 137 000	12.0
Housing	28	48 832 000	15.1	11 240 000	18.8
Shops	14	29 014 000	9.0	4 139 000	6.9
Office, leisure, and other commercial	41	133 705 000	41.3	27 494 000	46.1
Infrastructure	4	59 136 000	18.2	4 527 000	7.6
Total	134[c]	324 060 000	100.0	59 636 000	100.0

Notes: [a] Projects on which the offer of a grant was outstanding or had been accepted (including completed schemes).
[b] Classified by the author from data supplied.
[c] Including one scheme for which details are unavailable. The total does not tally with that in Table 8.1 as the date is slightly different.

Source: Data supplied by D.O.E.

Table 8.7. *Regional Distribution of Live*[a] *Urban Development Grant Projects, October 1984*

Region	No. of invited local authorities	No. of projects	Estimated total cost of projects in region		Total UDG contribution to projects in region	
			£	% of total	£	% of total
West Midlands	7	30	98 458 000	30.4	16 246 000	27.2
London	15	26[b]	63 181 000	19.5	12 914 000	21.7
North	11	23	71 141 000	22.0	11 303 000	19.0
Yorkshire and Humberside	11	20	35 159 000	10.8	7 542 000	12.6
North-west	8	14	19 970 000	6.2	5 249 000	8.8
Merseyside	7	12	19 360 000	6.0	3 492 000	5.9
East Midlands	4	9	16 791 000	5.2	2 890 000	4.8
Total	63	134[b]	324 060 000	100.0	59 636 000	100.0

Notes: [a] Projects on which an offer of grant was outstanding or had been accepted (including completed schemes).
[b] Including one project for which no details are available.

Source: Data supplied by D.O.E.

Table 8.8. *Results by November 1984 of Urban Development Grant Applications from the West Midlands County and Telford, September 1982–November 1984*

	No. of applications						
	Birmingham	Coventry	Dudley	Walsall	Sandwell	Wolverhampton	West Midlands County[a]
Total	38	10	11	7	12	20	98
Decision pending	1	1	1	0	1	2	6
Withdrawn	12	0	1	1	3	5	22
Refused	10	4	1	5	3	5	28
Offer made	15	5	8	1	5	8	42
Offer made but grant declined[b]	4	1	1	0	1	3	10
Live projects[c]	11	2	7	1	4	3	28[d]
Projects completed	1	0	1	0	3	1	6
On-site activity	5	1	5	0	1	0	12
Projects in preparatory stages	5	1	1	1	0	2	10

Notes: [a] Telford appears to have made no applications during this period.
[b] A number of these were being renegotiated and resubmitted.
[c] Projects on which an offer of grant was outstanding or had been accepted (including completed schemes).
[d] Figure does not tally with that in Table 8.3 as 2 offers were formally declined in the intervening period.

Source: Data supplied by D.O.E. and West Midlands local authorities.

planning strategies by this means and have been very active in approaching the private sector with the UDG scheme as an incentive to develop
particular sites. There has also been close liaison between planning and
finance departments and with the regional office of the D.o.E. Dudley district council shares many of these characteristics, while some other authorities appear to lack the capacity or organizational structure to turn the
UDG scheme to their advantage, or face political resistance, especially
when the sale of council land or housing is involved. Local authorities thus
have different capacities to respond to the UDG initiative. The D.o.E.
regional office also has its views on the merits of particular authorities in
the West Midlands and their capacity to respond. This also influences
UDG decisions.

While the type and size of project supported by UDGs varies quite markedly among the West Midland authorities (Wilde 1985), for the West Midlands as a whole the distribution of grants is fairly similar to the national
pattern (see Table 8.9). Major differences are in the over-representation in
the West Midlands of the industrial-unit category, inflated by the IMI project, and the relative insignificance there of live housing schemes. The relative
insignificance of grants for industrial development despite the lack of
regional-aid assistance available until late 1984 is striking, even though the
West Midlands accounts for more than half the schemes and more than a
quarter of the grants in this category.

In conclusion, any judgement on a scheme which has been in operation for
only two years and which has had less than thirty projects completed must be
partial and couched with qualifications. One of its objectives, of encouraging
closer co-operation between public and private sectors within individual
communities is perhaps being achieved, with undoubted benefits in
increased understanding between the participants. Yet to date the scheme
has been very dependent on local authorities to initiate projects. Moreover,
despite high initial applications and optimism, sufficient appropriate projects
have not yet come forward to reach the funding ceiling. Such is the concern of
government over this issue that a study of UDG and how to encourage
greater use was commissioned in 1985.

Evidence from the West Midlands suggests that the capacity of the UDG
scheme to assist with social problems in the inner city is at best piecemeal
and limited, except perhaps incidentally in the provision in the region of
much needed small industrial units. UDGs are having a negligible impact in
replacing the funding cuts and limitations imposed on other forms of public
expenditure in the inner city. The suspicions and scepticism of much of the
private sector towards UDG, exacerbated by the slow decision-making process and high failure rate of early submissions, have scarcely been overcome,
while many local authorities appear to be reassessing the level of commitment of staff and resources against the rather limited benefits from the
scheme to date. On the other hand, those local authorities with the capacity

Table 8.9. *Urban Development Grant Projects in the West Midlands County, November 1984*

Project category[a]	No. of projects			Value of live schemes		Total UDG contribution to projects in category	
	Applied for	Approved	Live	Total costs of projects in category £	% of total	£	% of total
Industrial development	19	8	6	6 387 000	6.8	1 312 000	8.2
Industrial units	29	14	10	27 832 000	29.6	6 951 000	43.3
Housing	7	5	3	1 334 000	1.4	142 000	0.9
Shops	3	3	2	6 397 000	6.8	839 000	5.2
Office	8	3	2	6 297 000	6.7	317 000	2.0
Leisure	6	1	0	0		0	
Other and mixed commercial	20	4	4	38 852 000	41.3	5 345 000	33.3
Infrastructure	6	2	1	6 907 000	7.3	1 150 000	7.2
Total	98	42	28[c]	94 006[c]	100.0	16 056[c]	100.0

Notes: [a] Classified by author from data supplied.
[b] Projects on which an offer of grant was outstanding or had been accepted (including completed schemes).
[c] Figures do not tally with those in Table 8.3 as 2 offers of grant were formally declined in the intervening period.

Source: Data supplied by D.O.E. and West Midlands local authorities.

to satisfy their own priorities under the UDG scheme will doubtless continue to exploit this additional source of capital funding.

However, the political symbolism of the scheme at a national level remains important, especially its capacity to encourage the partnership of public and private sectors in the rehabilitation of individual communities. In consequence, political commitment to the scheme remains high despite its mixed successes. Thus, while the Government tries to cut and control other aspects of the Urban Programme (*Financial Times* 5 Jan. 1985) the role of the UDG scheme appears, for good or ill, likely to be enhanced.

Inner-city Policy

Before we consider inner-city policy as exemplified by the BICP scheme it is necessary to set the context within which we view it. We have stressed that inner-city problems

cannot be understood in isolation from the rest of the conurbation, nor in isolation from the overall economic and social structure of society. Thus policies for inner cities, of themselves, will not necessarily be the most constructive way of dealing with the wider problems of which inner city area problems are a symptom. To concentrate on the inner city moves away from considerations of incomes and taxation policy, economic policy and the redistribution of income and wealth. (JCRULGS 1977, p. 4).

Moreover, the amelioration of some inner-city problems may simply lead to the transfer of the problem elsewhere, for example, to a peripheral estate or new town. Too simple a focus on the inner city 'without this wider understanding may be detrimental to effective actions' (JCRULGS 1977, p. 4). Any real attempt to grapple with inner-city problems must utilize the mechanisms for allocating resources of main spending programmes. Inner-city policy *per se* concentrates on marginal injections of resources through special programmes which, while not unwelcome, have little significance unless placed within the context of programmes involving wider allocations of resources and wider strategies. The latter ongoing programmes need to be given an inner-city dimension. The major instruments of public policy will need to be deployed, rather than special programmes with limited resources being relied upon, to resolve the problems of the inner cities. The issue of resources is critical. Inner-city decline has reflected the withdrawal of private- and public-sector resources, and without a sustained commitment to increase investment in inner city areas, 'there will be little improvement in the circumstances of those living in relatively deprived areas' (JCRULGS 1977, p. 29). Action in the inner cities 'at the local area level should therefore be seen as a minor part of a strategy for tackling the inner area problems which centres on national and local policy-making and resource allocation processes' (JCRULGS 1977 p. 10), whether resources are in the public, private or voluntary sectors.

This view of inner-city policy as making a relevant but marginal contribution to the resolution of the problems of inner-urban areas and their residents provides an appropriate context in which to judge its effects. Other issues have been raised. It has been argued that inner-city policy itself could improve institutional capacity to analyse and understand the nature of the problems and lead to more successful policy outcomes (Parkinson and Wilks 1983). The low level of resources committed and the impacts of the actions of many central- and local government departments may lead to a view of inner-city policy as a mechanism for contributing to the management of decline rather than as a prime instrument for regenerating the economy or dealing with the social consequences of economic decline.

The objective of inner-city policy, as initiated, was to arrest and reverse the decline of inner-city areas, 'to halt that downward spiral; to strengthen the economic and social structures of the inner cities at the same time as we improve their physical environment; and to create confidence in the future of inner city areas as places to live, work and invest' (Shore 1978). This was too embracing an objective, towards which inner-city policy can be claimed to have made very marginal progress. The recession after 1979 and a change of government did not encourage policy continuity or development.

The national background to inner-city policy is fully reported elsewhere (Lawless 1979 and 1981; McKay and Cox 1978; Higgins, Deakin, Edwards, and Wicks 1983; Spencer 1979) and need not be a focal point here. However a few elements need to be highlighted. The urban-aid budget was transferred from the Home Office to the D.o.E. in June 1977, when it was increased from £30 million to £125 million per annum. Seven areas (some including more than one local authority) were given Inner City Partnership status and receive the lion's share of resources. They include Birmingham. Other inner-city areas were designated as Programme Authorities, while others benefited as Designated Districts under the Inner Urban Areas Act of 1978, designed to assist industry in inner-city areas. This legislation emanated from the D.o.E., reflecting the growing interest in industrial policy for inner cities within that department. The number of Programme Authorities was increased from fifteen to twenty-three in 1983, when the number of Designated Districts was also increased, but no extra Inner City Partnerships were created. In addition to these three special categories of local authority there also exists the traditional Urban Programme under which authorities bid for grant aid to fund projects in urban areas with special social needs. Partnership and Programme Authorities, as well as Designated Districts and bids for traditional Urban Programme projects, are all funded from the national Urban Programme budget.

In the financial year 1983/4 the total resources devoted to the four categories of aid outlined above were £256.6 million. Of this 50 per cent went to the seven Partnerships (individual allocations ranging from £10.4 million to Islington, in north London, to £24.5 million to Manchester–Salford, with

Birmingham and Liverpool each receiving £24.1 million). The twenty-three Programme Authorities received 27 per cent, individual allocations ranging from about £1 million to about £6 million. The sixteen Designated Districts received 3 per cent, and 20 per cent was allocated to some 180 authorities for traditional Urban Programme projects (D.o.E., Inner Cities Directorate, 1983, *b*, p. 17). Grants in all categories are payable to local authorities at the rate of 75 per cent; hence authorities have to raise the other 25 per cent from their own budgets.

Guidelines issued by the Government were that, of Partnership expenditure for 1983/4, 39 per cent should be devoted to social projects, 36 per cent to economy projects and 25 per cent to environmental projects. (D.o.E., Inner Cities Directorate 1983*b*, p. 17) In reality a number of projects crossed these boundaries and could be allocated in several ways.

Since 1979 government has emphasized the role of projects to strengthen inner-city economies, and these have been increasing as a proportion of spending. However, in Birmingham's case there was already an emphasis on such projects, as Partnership resources were used locally to develop sites and premises schemes in the inner city. Partnership resources are divided nationally into broadly two-thirds on capital spending schemes—for example, roads and environmental improvements—and one-third on revenue spending—for example, ongoing social support and many voluntary group schemes. This has created tensions, as many local authorities have argued for a higher proportion of revenue schemes and a higher input of projects of a social nature. Over time the accumulation of ongoing revenue projects has meant that the system has become blocked and, unless ongoing schemes are cut, only a few revenue schemes can be drawn in.

In the West Midlands County three authorities have Programme status, Wolverhampton, Sandwell, and Coventry (the last two added in 1982). In the case of Sandwell a three-person task force was established for the initial period, with the regional office of the D.o.E. playing a key role. The purpose was to develop a strategy for the Smethwick area. This task force was disbanded, partly because of conflicts over priorities between the local authority and the task force. We shall focus on the BICP, the area with the largest local resources and an inner-city problem much greater in scale than those of the Programme Authorities.

In the case of Birmingham the planned resources allocated each year for 1984–7 were £24.5 million. The resources were divided into seven topic-group programmes (see Table 8.10), with the greatest emphasis on industry and employment. The projected annual split of expenditure among topic groups for 1984–7 is set out in Table 8.10.

The BICP Committee meets twice annually. It consists of elected representatives of the collaborating agencies (Birmingham City Council, West Midlands County Council, Birmingham Health Authorities) and is chaired by the Secretary of State for the Department of the Environment. In spring

Table 8.10. *Birmingham Inner City Partnership, Projected Annual Split of Expenditure among Topic Groups, 1984–1987*

Topic group	%
Economy	35
Social and community services	12
Health and personal social services	9
Movement	8
Housing	10
Physical environment	15
Voluntary sector	11

Source: BICP (1984*b*).

the committee considers broad policies, and in the autumn it agrees a list of projects to be funded, over which the government has a veto. The resources are divided between the three local participating agencies. Essentially the Partnership scheme represents a project-bidding scheme rather than a coherent strategy for the inner city, though some attempts were being made in the mid-1980s to develop such a strategy. It has thus failed to trigger, with very few exceptions and these mainly at local level, other main-line government spending programmes, though this was one of its initial aims. The Partnership schemes, like other elements of the Urban Programme, have been reviewed by central government. They have survived, but suffered some budget cuts, though the urban riots in the autumn of 1985 have led to a further appraisal of the policy which may lead to additional funding. Opposition to this programme has been strong from the Treasury and, to a lesser degree, from the DTI.

The geographical area within which the BICP scheme operates is complicated by the existence of three types of area (see Figure 8.1). The overall Partnership area which was defined widely in Birmingham, contains an inner-city core area, which since late 1982 has contained, in turn, a priority ring. This ring has, since its inception, been a clearer targeting zone for resource expenditure on projects. It covers those areas with a high concentration of ethnic-minority groups originating from the New Commonwealth. The purpose of the priority ring was to target resources on a smaller area so that the cumulative effect of expenditure would bring more beneficial results. However, its establishment might be interpreted as reflecting a view that existing resources were inadequate to the task of the Partnership, and being a mechanism for reducing the size of the inner-city area to one more related to the resources available.

Though Partnership brings extra resources, when total resources, including block grant, are compared over time there has been a net loss of government grant to the city. By 1984 the city was in net terms (allowing for inflation) some £40 million a year worse off than when Partnership started in

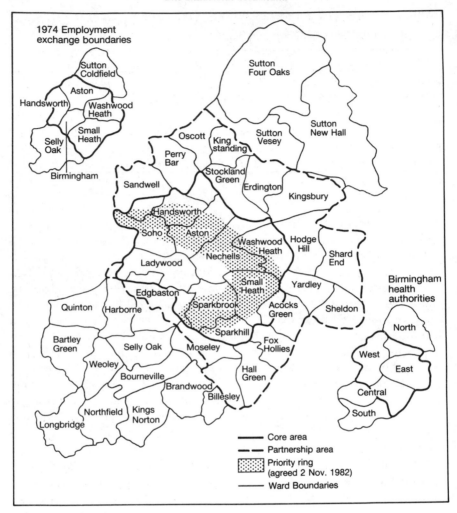

Fig. 8.1. BICP area, core area, and priority ring, November 1982.
Source: BICP (1983).

1978. Resources from central government have been cut and the impact of this felt in the inner city. Partnership projects were not initially supposed to substitute for main service programmes, but there have been political pressures to use Partnership resources to plug gaps in programmes in the inner city when main programme resources (such as housing) have been withdrawn.

Some of the weaknesses and strengths of the scheme were indicated in our interviews with senior officers of Birmingham City Council and WMCC, and central-government officials. They included the view that the resources available were too low to sustain progress against inner-city problems. There was a lack of continuity on the part of central government leading to problems of not knowing what would be funded from year to year. It was felt that central government had no clear view of its purpose or strategic role (reflecting different points of view held by different central-government departments). The scheme was dominated by short-term project-bidding processes.

On the positive side it was felt that ample justification existed to retain Partnership resources as a separate budget and programme and this would be helped by a roll-forward budget over two to three years. Officers felt that without Partnership resources inner-city problems would have been worse; the programme had to some degree slowed down what would have been a faster rate of decline. It had failed, however, to halt the spiral of decline in the inner city.

A 1982 survey of the occupants of new and refurbished small industrial units in the BICP core area, funded by the county council with Partnership resources, showed that in 58 companies only 16.8 per cent of the workforce lived in the inner-city core area. Some 48 per cent lived in the much wider complete Partnership area (WMCC, EDU 1982*b*). Thus though some degree of economic regeneration had been assisted by Partnership, it seemed to have been more for the benefit of others than inner-city core area residents.

It is clear that emphasis of the Partnership scheme lies in identification and stimulation of projects. Little systematic attention, until about 1983 or 1984, was given to what impact the spending had. This lack of monitoring and review is a serious constraint on a policy designed to identify effective ways of helping inner-city communities. In 1984 the D.o.E. commissioned Aston University to review the Partnership scheme in Birmingham. Some of their conclusions are identified later.

Organizationally the existence of the BICP has helped Birmingham City Council to develop skills in local economic development. It has helped to improve organizational capacity, though there have been inter-departmental rivalries over responsibilities for economic development. The Partnership scheme has suffered from insufficient commitment of full-time staff. This is one of the reasons for a lack of strategy (though central-government inter-departmental conflicts have also made this difficult). Partnership has led to a much greater understanding of the issues facing the inner city (BICP 1984*a*), but this remains to be placed in the contexts of formulation and implementation of policy. There is increasing awareness of the need for monitoring and improving the targeting of resources on particular locations and groups of people (BICP 1984*b*).

A review by the University of Aston Public Sector Management Research Unit (1985) of the first five years of the Partnership scheme highlights some key recommendations, among which the following are pertinent to this discussion.

1.   The programme needs to shift back to the original spirit of Partnership, rather than be used to cushion main programmes against cuts.
2.   Targeting of resources should be more systematic, and this will need a systematic monitoring of project effectiveness.
3.   Other central-government departments should contribute much more effectively to Partnership and incorporate an inner-city dimension into their own programmes and spending.
4.   Other bodies such as MSC and the Housing Corporation might usefully report to Partnership on their use of resources and their impact upon the inner cities.

The review is less critical of central government's role than it might have been and fails to address the key issues of the low level of resources available overall in relation to the scale of the problem being faced. Overall resources were withdrawn from Birmingham from 1980 to 1986 at a rate for which marginal extra inner-city resources could not compensate. While the rate-support-grant penalty system of 1985 penalized Birmingham if it spent extra at just *below* its government-determined target spending figure, Birmingham was penalized in 1985/6 most severely of all Partnership authorities if it spent just *above* its target. In effect, if Birmingham spent just above its target, it had to raise £3.36p for every £1 of extra spending (Assciation of Metropolitan Authorities 1984).

City action teams, along the lines of the Merseyside task force, were introduced in 1985 by central government to provide a new route to co-ordination between government departments at the regional level. The proposals have not met with enthusiasm from Partnership authorities. Greater co-ordination is needed, but powers of decision-making at regional level vary considerably between government departments, and inner-city policy is still seen as the responsibility of the D.o.E. Clearly the granting of selective regional-aid assistance to the West Midlands (a DTI role) does need to be related and co-ordinated with inner-city economic development. On past evidence there is likely to be a conflict of views between this form of aid and inner-city policy unless priorities can be agreed.

Inner-city policy has therefore had a useful but very limited ameliorative effect in Birmingham by slowing down what would otherwise have been a slightly more rapid decline in social, environmental, and economic conditions in the inner-city core area. It is important that it continues this role, but action and commitment across a wider range of policy areas and the main spending programmes of local and central government, and other agencies are essential if it is to be anything other than a palliative. We do not have an urban policy in the UK, we have isolated elements, initiated independently of one another, which are generally unco-ordinated and fragmented. Any serious approach to inner-city policy has to confront this much broader policy issue.

Conclusion

Many of the points discussed in this chapter, and elsewhere in this book, raise the general issue of how the institutions involved in dealing with economic problems and the social consequences of decline in the West Midlands can better learn and adapt to a rapidly changing environment. This adaptation will be, in part, related to a capacity to forge new networks of relationships, to seek out resources in a time of constraint, to realign organization to better meet the changing problems being faced (usually with a reduced resource base) and to create a critical mass of support (including a strong political will) to advocate, initiate, and innovate. The host of experimental schemes and new initiatives which proliferate in the West Midlands reflect an experimental state, in which answers are not clear, policy vacuums exist, and a multitude of possible routes to the amelioration of economic decline are being pursued. As indicated, these routes often appear to have only marginal impact on the problems. Some are ameliorative. Others appear to compound existing problems.

The Future of the West Midlands: Possible Policy Responses

This chapter is not a summary of our findings. Earlier chapters have offered an analysis of the processes of economic decline and of the effects of policy. Here we wish to note that whatever, within the bounds of likelihood, happens on the economic front there is a critical need for a renewed concern with social policy to help those who are bearing the brunt of the decline. We have drawn a picture of the West Midlands economy which indicates that the economic future of the region is likely to be faltering. Even with a successful recovery of the national economy, and even if companies operating in the West Midlands share in that recovery, employment in manufacturing is unlikely to grow sufficiently to reabsorb the 270 000 employees in the county who have been 'shaken out' since 1978.

In previous recessions in manufacturing, there have been major increases in the number of people employed in the service sector. There are strong reasons for believing that there will be a much smaller increase in service-sector employment in the future. First, there is unlikely to be a large growth in public-sector employment, because of pressures on public expenditure. Second, the previous periods of growth in service employment have involved the insurance, banking, and finance sectors particularly. Any future growth in activity in these sectors is likely to be achieved through greater use of information technology rather than through extra clerical labour. The same substitution of technology for labour in the 'clerical factories' of the public sector is likely to produce increases in productivity there. The only remaining growth areas in the service sector are the labour-intensive service industries such as hotels, tourism, and other leisure-related industries. It is unlikely that these will absorb the 250 000 who were unemployed in the West Midlands County in 1985, or the 330 000 who were unemployed in the region.

For those remaining in all types of employment there will be an increasing tendency towards part-time work, casual work, and low pay for the unskilled, and highly paid work, albeit with greater flexibility and job changes, for the highly skilled.

A *laissez-faire* policy response to these broad tendencies would allow present trends to continue. Industry would be allowed to locate in its chosen regions on the principle that government interference would increase costs in the long-term and thereby reduce the UK's competitiveness abroad. Wages would be allowed to fall to the market-clearing rate, when the level of employment would reach a new equilibrium. If the requirements of employers for a casual work-force were met, then the consequences would be more employment overall than if the practices of the trade unions, requiring long-term contracts for all employees, were allowed to continue. Equilibrium between regions would be achieved through the market, with low wages in areas of high unemployment making those areas attractive to prospective employers.

A more interventionist strategy might be aimed at reflating the economy, and promoting investment through government assistance to business and direct investment in infrastructure. It might intervene in particular sectors which were important for the economy as a whole, impose controls to protect domestic producers, and deliberately promote public-sector employment in labour-intensive service industries such as health care, education, and other social services. It might also include a policy of incentives and direction for industry to encourage, or force, it to invest in areas of high unemployment.

For the West Midlands, such interventions would need to be on a massive scale if full employment were to be restored. For example, in the county, if the investment required to create one job were say, £30 000, a not unreasonable figure in regional-policy aid terms, then the creation of full employment on the basis of the 1985 figure of 250 000 unemployed would require an investment of £7.5 billion.

This scale of investment is unlikely from either the private or the public sector in the foreseeable future. There is likely, therefore, to be a high level of unemployment in the region which will have a differential impact on different parts of the population. The prospects for school-leavers are particularly bleak, with the main destination for those not entering further or higher education being the YTSs and an uncertain future thereafter. For those who were 'shaken out' of the manufacturing sectors by the recession, employment prospects are remote, and in any case are likely to consist of casual or low-paid work except for the highly skilled in relevant trades. There will also be a growing number of people who are on the margins of the labour market, whose working lives consist of low-paid part-time or temporary jobs interspersed with periods of unemployment. Where a large population is left without access to regular wage-paying employment and depends on low State benefits, there is likely to be a growth in semi-formal and informal economic activity, such as low-wage-paying personal services, street-trading, and crime.

This is a period of increasing polarization not only in the allocation of rewards between the rich and the poor but also between sections of the labour force—between those with appropriate skills and those without, between the employed and unemployed, and between the regularly employed and the irregular and part-time workers. The polarization of the labour market has magnified the significance of the forms of social differentiation which affect entry to and promotion within employment—class, race, sex, religion. Most clearly within the West Midlands, it is the members of ethnic minorities who will suffer disproportionately and for longer periods.

Any foreseeable adjustment of the economy will leave major problems to be addressed by social policy, and these problems are different not only in scale but also in type from those which have hitherto confronted the welfare state. Renewed concern with social policy is vital.

The institutions of the Welfare State were designed to cope with a situation of full employment, in which there were relatively small numbers of poor, handicapped, and temporary unemployed. If the economic prospects are as we prognosticate, these institutions will have to be restructured and will have to adopt different strategies for different sections of the population. The problem of providing social-service and other welfare support for a casual labour force drifting from periods of low-paid work to periods of unemployment is different from that of supporting workers who change from one industry to another via a period of short-term unemployment. School-leavers faced with permanent unemployment are a different proposition for the agencies of government from middle-aged unemployed people suddenly faced with sharply reduced incomes. The problems of social stress and disintegration are different for the young person whose expectation of progress from school to work to family life is blocked by the absence of regular work and affordable housing, and for the mature person whose expectations are shattered by being thrown out of work and becoming dependent on the State for a depressed standard of living.

The massive changes in the labour market have already generated a burgeoning expenditure on what may be described as reactive social policy. Cuts in investment and employment in the public sector are matched by increases in the number of people dependent on social security; cuts in social services are balanced by the increased costs of policing. The present Government, which is committed to cuts in public spending, has been drawn into increased expenditure on income maintenance and measures to control unrest, and is subject to increasing pressures to invest in the urban infrastructure, which underinvestment is allowing to fall into decay.

Much social policy is negative in its impact not only on the groups who are already most vulnerable in the labour market but even on those who are apparently intended to benefit from it. It is the young and unemployed who find themselves subject to the 'short, sharp shock' regime, to attempts to expose them to the discipline of work through youth schemes which often pay wages below those agreed by trade unions, to exclusion from the protection of wages councils, and to inclusion in the meagre social-security 'safety net' only on condition of joining a scheme or of moving their lodgings. It is those at the bottom of the jobs market whose wage levels and security are further threatened by the competition of government-sponsored school-leavers. As they are made marginal to the labour market, so they will be further marginalized by their incapacity to participate in privatized pension schemes. It is the poor owner-occupiers who, having been drawn into home ownership through government programmes, now find themselves facing unemployment and unable to maintain or even keep their homes. They are exposed to the full effects of the decline of the old urban areas as government withdraws from housing repair programmes and expenditure on the urban infrastructure of schools, roads, transport, sewers, and hospitals.

There is an alternative to this reactive and minimalist approach to social expenditure which is to argue that given the likelihood of a long-term employment problem, expanded social expenditure is

(a) necessary on grounds of equity as a means of redistribution of society's resources
(b) part of the solution to the employment problem through the provision of labour-intensive social services and public works.

Allocations of investment in social services, public works, income maintenance, and the private sector need not be seen as in strong competition with each other. There is certainly no shortage of semi- and unskilled labour. Redistribution of resources through public expenditure is a matter not only of equity or common humanity for the unemployed and uncared-for but also of stimulating demand for domestic industry faced by a weak home market.

Our study demonstrates that even if the West Midlands economy were to revive, without positive action by the public sector it would leave a large proportion of the population in the miserable conditions associated with long-term unemployment and partial employment. A minimum programme for these groups requires at least three elements

1. A new concern with equity rather than with merest basic needs in income support, health, housing, and education
2. Investment in public works and the caring services, not only in response to the decay of the physical and social infrastructure of the cities but also as revived sources of employment
3. A focus on the real jobs opportunities so created for the young and long-term unemployed, with particular attention given to the needs of unemployment among the ethnic minorities.

Government has an important role here, so too do other public, private and voluntary institutions.

De-industrialization in the UK has had its greatest regional effect upon economy of the West Midlands. Government and other bodies are slow to react to change, especially where traditional interests are strong and vocal. A vigorous programme designed to tackle the serious problems facing the people of the West Midlands is essential and urgently needed. The alternative is a West Midlands left to continue to suffer economically and socially while a new national geography of production, jobs, and social malaise is fostered in the 'national interest'. Commitment to action by politicians and a radical rethink of present policies are necessary on the part of government and key institutions whose decisions have an impact upon the economic and social problems of the West Midlands.

BIBLIOGRAPHY

Alderton, R., 1984, 'Urban Development Grants—Lessons from America', *The Planner*, 70, 12.

Allen, G. C., 1929, *The Industrial Development of Birmingham and the Black Country, 1860–1927* (London).

Apgar, A., 1975, *Little Green: a Case Study in Urban Renewal* (D. o. E.).

Armstrong, P., Glyn, A., and Harrison, J., 1984, *Capitalism since World War II: the Making and Break-up of the Great Boom* (London).

Association of Metropolitan Authorities, 1984, *Partnership Authorities RSG Settlement 1985–86* (London).

Ball, R. M. 1983, 'Spatial and Structural Characteristics of Recent Unemployment Change: Some Policy Considerations', *Regional Studies*, 17, 2.

BCIC, 1984, *Regional Industrial Development: a Response to the White Paper* (Birmingham).

Beacham, R., 1984, 'Economic Activity: Britain's Workforce 1971–1981', *Population Trends*, 37.

Bentley, G. and Mawson, J., 1984, 'Industrial Policy, 1972–1983: Goverment Expenditure and Assistance to Industry in the West Midlands' (Working Paper 6, ESRC Inner City Project, West Midlands Study, University of Birmingham).

—— 1985a, 'The Industrial Development Certificate and the Decline of the West Midlands: Much Ado about Nothing?' (Working Paper 15, ESRC Inner City Project, West Midlands Study, University of Birmingham).

—— 1985b, 'The Economic Decline of the West Midlands and the Role of Regional Planning—a Lost Opportunity' (Working Paper 17, ESRC Inner City Project, West Midlands Study, University of Birmingham).

Berry, B. J. L. (ed.), 1976, *Urbanisation and Counter-urbanisation* (London).

Beynon, H., 1978, *What Happened at Speke?* (TGWU, Liverpool).

BICP, 1983, *Inner City Partnership Programme 1983–86* (Birmingham).

—— 1984a, *Inner City Profile 1983/4* (Birmingham).

—— 1984b, *Inner City Partnership Programme 1984–87* (Birmingham).

Birmid Qualcast, *Annual Reports and Accounts* (Birmingham).

Birmingham, City of, 1973, *Structure Plan for Birmingham. Written Statement* (Birmingham).

—— 1978, *Industry and Employment: the Birmingham Approach* (Birmingham).

—— 1982, *Careers Service Report* (Birmingham).

—— 1984a, *Economic and Employment Policies in Birmingham: Review of the Supporting Organisation Structure* (Birmingham).

—— 1984b, *Land for Industry at April, 1984* (Birmingham).

—— 1985, *An Economic Strategy and Development Programme for Birmingham* (Birmingham).

Birmingham Community Development Project, 1977, *Workers on the Scrapheap. Final Report No. 2: Employment* (Social Evaluation Unit, University of Oxford).

Blackaby, F. (ed.), 1978, *British Economic Policy 1960–74* (Cambridge University Press).

Bore, A., 1984, 'Priorities for Economic Development in Birmingham' (Statement by Chairman of EDU, City of Birmingham, 8 June).

Broughton, J., 1984, 'Working Class Politics in Birmingham 1918–1931' (mimeograph, University of Warwick).

Brady, T. and Liff, S., 1983, *Monitoring New Technology and Employment* (MSC, Sheffield).

Briggs, A., 1952, *History of Birmingham*, Vol. 2 (Oxford University Press).

Brown, A. J., 1972, *The Framework of Regional Economics in the United Kingdom* (Cambridge University Press).

Burgess, P. and Ham, B., 1985, 'Innovative Approaches to Economic Development within the Urban Programme: a Case Study of the West Midlands County Council' (Planning and Transport Research and Computation Annual Conference, University of Sussex, July).

Cadbury, P. S. and Wise M. J., 1968, *The Expansion of Birmingham into the Green Belt Area* (Birmingham).

Cameron, G. C., 1980, 'The Inner City: New Plant Incubator', in Evans, A. and Eversley, D. (edd.), *The Inner City: Employment and Industry* (London).

Camina, M. M., 1974, 'Local Authorities and the Attraction of Industry', *Progress in Planning*, 3.

Carter, C., 1977, 'The Changing Pattern of Industrial Land Use in the West Midlands Conurbation 1948–1975', in Joyce (1977).

CBI, Special Programmes Unit 1984, *Community Action Programme Report. City of Birmingham July 1984* (Birmingham).

Central Policy Review Staff, 1975, *The Future of the British Car Industry* (London).

Checkland, S. G., 1981, *The Upas Tree: Glasgow 1875–1975* (University of Glasgow Press).

Chisholm, M. and Oeppen, J., 1973, *The Changing Pattern of Employment: Regional Specialisation and Industrial Location in Britain* (London).

City of Birmingham: see Birmingham, City of.

Clark, C., 1966, 'Industrial Location and Economic Potential', *Lloyds Bank Review* (Oct.).

Coakley, J. and Harris, L., 1983, *The City of Capital* (Oxford).

Cochrane, M. F., 1984, 'The Attitudes of Managers and their Wives towards Living and Working in Different Parts of the U.K.' (Ph.D. thesis, CURS, University of Birmingham).

Cousins, J. M., *et al.*, 1974, 'Aspects of Contradiction in Regional Policy', *Regional Studies*, 8.

Crompton, D. and Penketh, L. 1977, 'Industrial and Employment Change', in Joyce (1977).

Croucher, R., 1982, *Engineers at War* (London).

CURS, 1984, 'Pilot Study of Vacant Industrial Sites and Premises in the Metropolitan Districts of Walsall and Wolverhampton. Report to English Estates' (mimeograph, University of Birmingham).

Danson, M. W., Lever, W. F., and Malcolm, J. F., 1980, 'The Inner City Employment Problem in Great Britain, 1952–76: a Shift-share Approach', *Urban Studies*, 17.

DE, 1968, *Labour Costs in 1964* (London).

Debenham, Tewson & Chinnocks, 1983, *Money into Property 1970–1983* (London).

—— 1984, *Industrial Rents and Rates 1973–1984* (London).

Delta Metal Company, *Annual Reports and Accounts*.

Department of Economic Affairs, 1965, *The West Midlands: A Regional Study* (London).

D.o.E., 1975, *Technical Working Group* (West Midlands).

—— 1983, *Streamlining the Cities* (Cmnd. 9063).

D.o.E. Inner Cities Directorate, 1978, *Industry in the Inner City: Case Studies of Mixed Use Development* (London).

—— 1983*a*, *Information Note No. 3. The Comparative Position of Inner City Partnership Areas* (London).

—— 1983*b*, *Urban Programme Fact Sheet* (London).

Dow, J. C. R., 1964, *The Management of the British Economy 1945–60* (Cambridge University Press).

DTI, 1975, *Industrial Movement 1945–1975, with Special Reference to the West Midlands* (Birmingham).

Dudley District Council, 1983, *Economic Policy Initiatives in Dudley* (Dudley).

Dudley, Sandwell, Walsall, and Wolverhampton Metropolitan Borough Councils, 1984, 'The Promotion of Newer Industries in the Black Country' (Final report by C. Buchanan & Partners with Economists Advisory Group, West Midlands).

Dunnett, P., 1980, *The Decline of the British Motor Industry* (London).

Edge, G., 1981, 'Priorities for Economic Development in the West Midlands' (Paper by Chairman of EDC, WMCC, Birmingham, Nov.).

Edwards, M., 1983, *Back from the Brink* (London).

Eversley, D. and Begg, I., 1986, 'Deprivation in the Inner City: Social Indicators from the 1981 Census', in Hausner V. A. (ed.), *Critical Issues in Urban Economic Development*, Vol. 2, (Oxford University Press).

Fagg, J. J., 1980, 'An Examination of the Incubator Hypothesis: a Case Study of Greater Leicester', *Urban Studies*, 17.

Firn, J. R., 1975, 'External Control and Regional Policy', in Brown, G., (ed.), *The Red Paper on Scotland* (Edinburgh).

Firn, J. R. and Swales, J. K., 1978, 'The Formation of New Manufacturing Establishments in the Central Clydeside and West Midlands Conurbations 1963–1972', *Regional Studies*, 12.

Flynn, N., 1983, 'Fiscal Stress in the West Midlands County Area' (Internal research note, ESRC Inner City Project, West Midlands Study, University of Birmingham).

Flynn, N. and Taylor, A., 1984, 'De-industrialisation and Corporate Change in the West Midlands' (Working Paper 8, ESRC Inner City Project, West Midlands Study, University of Birmingham).

Florence, P. Sargant, 1948, *Investment, Location and Size of Plant* (Cambridge University Press).

Fothergill, S. and Gudgin, G., 1979, 'Regional Employment Change: a Sub-regional Explanation', *Progress in Planning*, 12.

—— 1982, *Unequal Growth: Urban and Regional Employment Change in the U. K.* (London).

Fothergill, S., Gudgin, G., Kitson, M., and Monk, S., 1984, 'Differences in the Profitability of the U.K. Manufacturing Sector between Conurbations and Other Areas', *Scottish Journal of Political Economy*, 31.

Fothergill, S., Kitson, M., and Monk, S., 1983, 'The Impact of New and Expanded Towns Programme on Industrial Location in Britain 1960–78', *Regional Studies*, 17.

——— 1985, *Urban Industrial Change: The Causes of the Urban-Rural Contrast in Manufacturing Employment Trends* (D.o.E).

Friedman, A. L., 1977, *Industry and Labour. Class Struggle at Work and Monopoly Capitalism* (London).

Gaffakin, F. and Nickson, A., 1984, *Job Crisis and the Multi-nationals: the Case of the West Midlands* (Trade Union Resource Centre, Birmingham).

Goddard, J. B., and Champion, A. G., 1983, *The Urban and Regional Transformation of Britain* (London).

Green, A. E., 1984, 'Considering Long-term Unemployment as a Criterion for Regional Policy Aid', *Area*, 16, 3.

Greene, A., 1980, 'Urban Development Action Grants: Federal Carrots for Private Economic Revitalization of Depressed Urban Areas', *Urban Law and Policy*, 3.

Greenwood, R. and Stewart, J. D., 1974, *Corporate Planning in English Local Government* (London).

Hague, D. and Wilkinson, G., 1983, *The I.R.C.—an Experiment in Industrial Intervention: a History of the Industrial Reorganisation Corporation* (London).

Hall, P. (ed.), 1981, *The Inner City in Context: the Final Report of the Social Science Research Council Inner Cities Working Party* (London).

Hall, P. and Hay, D., 1980, *Growth Centres in the European Urban System* (London).

Hastings, R. P., 1959, 'The Labour Movement in Birmingham, 1927–1945' (MA thesis, University of Birmingham).

Healey, M. and Clark, D., 1984, 'Industrial Decline and Goverment Response in the West Midlands: the Case of Coventry', *Regional Studies*, 18, 4.

Higgins, J., Deakin, N., Edwards, J., and Wicks, M., 1983, *Government and Urban Poverty* (Oxford).

Hirsch, S., 1967, *Location of Industry and International Competitivenes* (Oxford University Press).

HMSO, 1983, *The Government's Expenditure Plans 1983/4 to 1985/6* (Cmnd. 8789).

——— 1984, *The Government's Expenditure Plans 1984/5 to 1986/7* (Cmnd. 9143).

Hobsbawm, E. J., 1968, *Industry and Empire: the Making of Modern English Society*, Vol. 2 (New York).

Hoover, E. and Vernon, R., 1959, *Anatomy of a Metropolis* (Harvard University Press).

House of Commons Expenditure Committee, Trade and Industry Sub-Committee, 1975, 'The Vehicle Industry in the General Economy of the West Midlands: a Factual Survey' (Memo submitted by West Midlands Economic Planning Board, 14th report, session 1974/5, House of Commons Paper 617–III).

House, E. R., 1980, *Evaluating with Validity* (Beverly Hills, Calif.).

Howells, J. R. L., 1982, 'Location, Technology and Filter-down Theory: and Analysis of the U.K. Pharmaceutical Industry' (Ph.D. thesis, University of Cambridge).

Hulse, K., 1976, 'The Implementation of Containment Policy: a Case Study of Birmingham' (M. Soc. Sc. thesis, CURS, University of Birmingham).

JCRULGS, 1977, *Inner Area Studies: a Contribution to the Debate* (Birmingham).

Johnson, A., 1982, 'Metropolitan Housing Policy and Strategic Planning in the West Midlands', *Town Planning Review*, 53, 2.

Jones, D. T. and Prais, S. J., 1978, 'Plant Size and Productivity in the Motor Industry: Some International Comparisons', *Oxford Bulletin of Economics and Statistics*, 40.

Jones, G. W., 1969, *Borough Politics: a Study of the Wolverhampton Town Council, 1880–1964* (London).

Jones, R. and Marriot, O., 1970, *The Anatomy of a Merger: A History of GEC, AEI and English Electric* (London).

Joyce, F. (ed.), 1977, *Metropolitan Development and Change. The West Midlands: a Policy Review* (Farnborough).

Karn, V. 1983, 'The Dynamics of the Urban Housing Market and its Impact on the Inner City—Processes of Change in the Birmingham Public and Private Housing Markets' (Working Note F, ESRC Inner City Project, West Midlands Study, University of Birmingham).

Keeble, D., 1976, *Industrial Location and Planning in the U.K.* (London).

—— 1978, 'Industrial Decline in the Inner City and Conurbation', *Transactions of the Institute of British Geographers*, 3, 1.

Keeble, D., Owens, P. L., and Thompson, C., 1983, 'The Urban–rural Manufacturing Shift in the European Community', *Urban Studies*, 20.

Knowles, R., 1985, 'Expenditure under Section 137 of the Local Government Act, 1972' (Letter from Leader of Birmingham City Council to Secretary of State for the Environment, 11 July).

Law, C. M., 1980, *British Regional Development since World War I* (Newton Abbott).

Lawless, D., 1979, *Urban Deprivation and Government Initiative* (London).

—— 1981, *Britain's Inner Cities* (London).

Leach, S. and Stewart, J. D., (edd.), 1982, *Approaches in Public Policy* (London).

Leigh, R. and North, D., 1983, *The Clothing Sector in the West Midlands. Problems and Policies* (EDU, WMCC, Birmingham).

Liggins, D., 1977, 'Changing Role of West Midlands Region in the National Economy', in Joyce (1977).

Lloyd, P. and Dicken, P., 1982, *Industrial Change: Local Manufacturing Firms in Manchester and Merseyside* (D.o.E.).

Lloyd, P. and Reave, D., 1982, 'North-west England 1971–77: a Study in Industrial decline and Economic Restructuring', *Regional Studies*, 16, 5.

Lloyd, P. and Shutt, J., 1983, *Recession and Restructuring in the North-west Region—Some Preliminary Thoughts on the Employment Implication of Recent Events* (North West Industry Research Unit, University of Manchester).

McKay, D. H., and Cox, A. W., 1979, *The Politics of Urban Change* (London).

Mallinson, H. and Gilbert, M., 1983, 'The Urban Development Grant Scheme', *Estates Gazette*, (Dec.).

Mandel, E., 1975, *Late capitalism* (London).

Marshall, M, 1985, 'Long Waves of Regional Development' (Ph.D. thesis, CURS, University of Birmingham).

Martins, M. R. de O., 1982, 'Regional Planning in the West Midlands: a Political Organisational Perspective' (Ph.D. thesis, CURS, University of Birmingham).

Massey, D. B., 1978, 'Regionalism: Some Current Issues', *Capital and Class*, 6.

—— 1979, 'A Critical Evaluation of Industrial Location Theory', in Hamilton, F. E. I. and Linge, C. J. E. (edd.), *Spatial Analysis, Industry and the Industrial Environment: Progress in Research and Application*. Vol. 1 (Chichester).

—— 1984, *Spatial Divisions of Labour, Social Structures and the Geography of Production* (London).

Massey, D. B. and Meegan, R. A., 1978, 'Industrial Restructuring versus the Cities', *Urban Studies*, 15, 3.

—— 1982, *The Anatomy of Job Loss* (London).

Mawson, J., 1983*a*, 'The West Midlands Enterprise Board' (Working Note A, ESRC Inner City Project, West Midlands Study, University of Birmingham).

—— 1983*b*, 'Co-operative Development Agencies: the West Midlands Experience' (Working Note B, ESRC Inner City Project, West Midlands Study, University of Birmingham).

—— 1983*c*, 'The West Midlands County Council Local Economic Initiatives' (Working Note D, ESRC Inner City Project, West Midlands Study, University of Birmingham).

Mawson, J., Gibney, J., and Miller, D., 1983, 'The West Midlands and the European Economic Community' (Working Paper 4, ESRC Inner City Project, West Midlands Study, University of Birmingham).

Mawson, J., Jepson, D., and Marshall, M., 1984, 'Economic Regeneration in the West Midlands: the Role of the County Council', *Local Government Policy Making*, 11, 2.

Mawson, J. and Naylor, D., 1985, 'A Summary of Local Authority Economic Development in the West Midlands' (Working Paper 16, ESRC Inner City Project, West Midlands Study, University of Birmingham).

Mawson, J. and Smith, B. M. D., 1980, *British Regional and Industrial Policy during the 1970's: a Critical Review with Special Reference to the West Midlands in the 1980's* (CURS, University of Birmingham).

Mawson, J. and Taylor, A., 1983, 'The West Midlands in Crisis: an Economic Profile' (Working Paper 1, ESRC Inner City Project, West Midlands Study, University of Birmingham).

Miller, D., 1981, 'The Role of the Car Industry in the West Midlands Economy' (Regional Studies Association, West Midlands Branch, Conference, Birmingham, Dec.).

Moore, B. C., Rhodes, J., and Tyler, P., 1980, 'New Developments in the Evaluation of Regional Policy' (Social Science Research Council Conference, Birmingham, Apr.).

Morgan, A. D., 1978, 'Commercial Policy', in Blackaby (1978).

Morgan, A. D. and Martin, D., 1975, 'Tariff Reductions and UK Imports of Manufactures: 1955–1971', *National Institute Economic Review*, 72 (May).

MSC, 1983, *Annual Report 1982/3* (Sheffield).

Mulvey, C., 1978, *The Economic Analysis of Trade Unions* (Oxford).

Munday, N. and Mallinson, H., 1983, 'Urban Development Grants in Action', *Public Finance and Accountancy*, (Dec.).

Murgatroyd, L. and Urry, J., 1983, 'The Restructuring of a Local Economy: the Case of Lancaster', in Anderson, J., Duncan, S., and Hudson, R., (edd.), *Redundant Spaces in Cities and Regions* (Orlando, Fla.).

Nicholson, B. M., Brinkley, I., and Evans, A. W., 1981, 'The Role of the Inner City in the Development of Manufacturing Industry', *Urban Studies*, 18.

OECD 1983, *Economic Surveys: The United Kingdom* (Paris).

Olson, M., 1982, *The Rise and Decline of Nations: Economic Growth, Stagflation and Social Rigidities* (Yale University Press).

Parkinson, M. H. and Wilks, S. R. M., 1983, 'Managing Urban Decline: the Case of Inner City Partnership', *Local Government Studies*, 9, 5.

Prest, A. R. (ed.), 1968, *The UK Economy: a Manual of Applied Economics* (London).

Raybould, T. J., 1973, *The Economic Emergence of the Black Country: a Study of the Dudley Estate* (Newton Abbot).

Rein, M., 1973, 'Values, Social Science and Social Policy' (Working Paper 21, Joint Centre for Urban Studies of MIT and University of Harvard).

—— 1976, *Social Science and Public Policy* (Harmondsworth).

Richardson, K., 1972, *Twentieth-century Coventry* (London and Basingstoke).

Roberts, B., 1978, 'Agrarian Organisation and Urban Development', in Wirth, J. D. and Jones, R. L. (edd.), *Manchester and Sao Paulo* (Stanford University Press).

Rodrigues, D. and Brinvels, P., 1982, *Zoning in on Enterprise* (London).

Room, S., 1983, 'The Politics of Evaluation: the European Poverty Programme', *Journal of Social Policy*, 12, 2.

Rothwell, R. and Zegweld, W., 1982, *Innovation and the Small and Medium Sized Firm* (London).

Rugman, A. J. and Green, M. D., 1977, 'Demographic and Social Change', in Joyce (1977).

Sandwell Metropolitan Borough Council, 1979, *The Potential for Industrial Development between Wednesbury and Great Bridge: Major Problem Sites* (Sandwell).

Saunders, D., 1977, 'The Changing Planning Framework', in Joyce (1977).

Segal, M. S., 1979, 'The Limits and Means of Self-reliant Regional Economic Growth', in Maclennan, D. and Parr, J. B., (edd.), *Regional policy. Past Experience and New Directions* (Oxford).

Shore, P., 1978 (Speech to Royal Institute of Chartered Surveyors Annual Conference, Harrogate, Sept.).

Smith, B. M. D., 1972, *The Administration of Industrial Overspill: The Institutional Framework Relevant to Industrial Overspill in the West Midlands* (CURS, University of Birmingham).

—— 1977, 'Economic Problems in the Core of the Old Birmingham Industrial Area', in Joyce (1977).

—— 1978a, *Industry in Metropolitan Area Plans: Proposals and Experience in the West Midlands County Area* (CURS, University of Birmingham).

—— 1978b, 'Industry in Metropolitan Area Plans: Proposals and Experience in the West Midlands County, England', in Walker, D. F. (ed.), *Planning Industrial Development* (Chichester).

—— 1981, *The History of the British Motorcycle Industry, 1945–1975* (CURS, University of Birmingham).

—— 1982, 'Enterprise Zones in Britain: the Non-plan Myth and Reality' (Internal paper, CURS, University of Birmingham).

—— 1983a, 'A History of Birmingham and its Neighbour, the Black Country' (Internal paper, CURS, University of Birmingham).

—— 1983b, 'Population Change in the West Midlands' (Working Paper 2, ESRC Inner City Project, West Midlands Study, University of Birmingham).

—— 1984a, 'The Public/Private Sector Split in Employment in 1971 and 1978 in the West Midlands: an Exploratory Study (Working Paper 7, ESRC Inner City Project, West Midlands Study, University of Birmingham).

—— 1984b, 'The Labour Factor as an Explanation for Economic Decline in the West Midlands Region and County: Earnings in the West Midlands' (Working Paper 9, ESRC Inner City Project, West Midlands Study, University of Birmingham).

—— 1984c, 'Changes in the Numbers of Self-employed in the West Midlands Region'

(Working Paper 10, ESRC Inner City Project, West Midlands Study, University of Birmingham).

—— 1984*d*, 'Employment Change in Parts of the West Midlands Region and the ESRC Inner Cities Project Study Area 1961–1981' (Working paper 11, ESRC Inner City Project, West Midlands Study, University of Birmingham).

—— 1984*e*, 'Alternative Theories about Economic and Social Development', (Working Paper 14, ESRC Inner City Project, West Midlands Study, University of Birmingham).

—— 1985, 'Alternative Explanations for Economic Change in a Local Economy and their Applicability to the West Midlands County Economy' (Working Paper 18, ESRC Inner City Project, West Midlands Study, University of Birmingham).

Smith, B. M. D., Ruddy, S. A., and Black, L., 1974, *Industrial Relocation in Birmingham* (CURS, University of Birmingham).

Smith, B. M. D. and Smith, P. W., 1977, 'School Leaver Employment in Birmingham and the Black Country in 1974' (Report to WMCC, mimeograph, CURS, University of Birmingham).

Smith, C. T. B., Clifton, R., *et al.*, 1978, *Strikes in Britain* (DE).

Smith, N. R., 1967, *The Entrepreneur and his Firm* (University of Michigan Press).

Solihull Metropolitan Borough Council, 1983, *Unemployment and Industrial Decline in the West Midlands* (Solihull).

Spencer, K. M., 1979, 'Inner City Policy', *Local Government Studies, Annual Review '79*, 5, 2.

—— 1982, 'Comprehensive Community Programmes', in Leach and Stewart (1982).

—— 1984, 'Evaluation of Public Sector Intervention and Approaches to the Concept of Institutional Capacity' (Working Paper 13, ESRC Inner City Project, West Midlands Study, University of Birmingham).

—— 1985, 'Demographic, Social and Economic Trends: an Overview' (ILGS, University of Birmingham).

Spencer, K. M., *et al.*, 1985, 'The Challenge for Local Government Management' (Local Government Training Board discussion paper, ILGS, University of Birmingham).

Spring, M., 1983, 'Inner City Matchmakers', *Building* (25 Mar.).

Stedman, M. B. and Wood, P. A., 1965, 'Urban Renewal in Birmingham: an Interim Report', *Geography*, 50.

Stewart, J. D., 1981, 'The Dilemmas of Urban Public Finance', in Groves, R. (ed.), *Economic and Social Change in the West Midlands* (CURS, University of Birmingham).

——1982, 'Guidelines to Policy Derivation', in Leach and Stewart (1982).

Stiennes, D. N., 1982, 'Do People Follow Jobs or Do Jobs Follow People? A Causality Issue in Urban Economics', *Urban Studies*, 19.

Storey, D. J., 1982, *Entrepreneurship and the New Firm* (London).

Sutcliffe, A. and Smith, R., 1974, *History of Birmingham*. Vol. 3 (Oxford University Press).

Taylor, A., 1980, 'Industrial Strategy', (M. Phil. thesis, CURS, University of Birmingham).

—— 1983, 'Employment Change in the West Midlands' (Working Paper 3, ESRC Inner City Project, West Midlands Study, University of Birmingham).

—— 1984, 'The Changing Pattern of Unemployment in the West Midlands Region and County' (Working paper 5, ESRC Inner City Project, West Midlands Study, University of Birmingham).

Taylor, G., 1983, 'Industrial Restructuring, the State and Regional Development' (Ph.D. thesis, CURS, University of Birmingham).

Thomas, B., 1938, 'The Influx of Labour into the Midlands 1920–37', *Economica*, 5.

Thomas, K., 1976, 'The Effects of Urban Development and Renewal on Small Manufacturing Firms in Birmingham' (M. Phil. thesis, Birmingham Polytechnic).

Thompson, W. R., 1968, 'Internal and External Factors in the Development of Urban Economics', in Perloff, H. S. and Wingo, L. (edd.), *Issues in Urban Economics* (Washington, DC).

—— 1969, 'The Economic Base of Urban Problems', in Chamberlain, N. W. (ed.). *Contemporary Economic Issues* (Illinois University Press).

TI, *Annual Reports and Accounts*.

Tolliday, S., undated, 'Trade Unions and Shopfloor Organisation in the British Motor Industry 1910–39' (mimeograph, King's College, Cambridge).

Townroe, P. M. and Roberts, N. J., 1980, *Local External Economics for British Manufacturing Industry* (Farnborough).

Townsend, A. and Peck, F., 1984, 'Contrasting Experience of Recession and Spatial Restructuring', *Regional Studies*, 18, 4.

Turner, G., 1971, *The Leyland Papers* (London).

Turner, H. A., Clack, G., and Roberts, G., 1967, *Labour Relations in the Motor Industry: a Study of Industrial Unrest and an International Comparison* (London).

Tylecote, A. B., 1982, 'German Ascent and British Decline, 1870–1980: the Role of Upper Class Structure and Values', in Friedman, E. (ed.), *Ascent and Decline in the World-System* (Beverly Hills, Calif.).

Tyler, P., 1980, 'The Impact of Regional Policy on a Prosperous Region: the Experience of the West Midlands', *Oxford Economic Papers*, 32.

Tym, R. & Partners, 1982, *Monitoring Enterprise Zones, Year One Report* (D.o.E.).

—— 1983, *Monitoring Enterprise Zones, Year Two Report* (D.o.E.).

——1984, *Monitoring Enterprise Zones, Year Three Report* (D.o.E).

Tym, R. & Partners and Arthur McClelland Moores & Co., 1983 *West Midlands Investment Study*. (WMCC, Birmingham).

University of Aston, Public Sector Management Research Unit, 1985, *Five Year Review of the Birmingham Inner City Partnership* (D.o.E).

Vernon, R., 1979, 'The Product Cycle Hypothesis in a New International Environment', *Oxford Bulletin of Economics and Statistics*, 41.

Walker, G., 1947, 'The Growth of Population in Birmingham and the Black Country between the Wars', *University of Birmingham Historical Journal*, 1, 1.

Walsall Metropolitan Borough Council, 1983, 'Walsall's Economic Development Activities: Objectives, Methods and Costs' (Internal paper, Aug.).

—— 1984, 'Report of Chief Executive to Policy and Resources Committee' (5 Dec.).

—— 1985, 'Borough Economic Development and Employment Strategy: a Framework (Report of Chief Executive to Land and Property Committee, 30 July).

Ward, S. V., 1983, 'Local Authorities and Industrial Promotion, 1900–1939: Reconsidering a Lost Tradition' (Planning History Group Conference, Oxford, Sept.).

Warnes, A. M., 1980, 'A Long Term View of Employment and Decentralisation from the Larger English Cities', in Evans, A. and Eversley, D. (edd.), *The Inner City Employment and Industry* (London).

Webman, J. A., 1981, 'UDAG: Targetting Urban Economic Development', *Political Science Quarterly*, 96.

Weiner, M. J., 1981, *The English Culture and the Decline of the Industrial Spirit, 1850–1980* (Cambridge University Press).

Wensley, A. J. and Florence, P. Sargant, 1940, 'Recent Industrial Concentration especially in the Midlands', *Review of Ecomonic Studies* (June).

West Midlands Group, 1948, *Conurbation: Planning Survey of Birmingham and the Black Country* (London).

WMCC, 1975, *Time for Action. Economic and Social Trends in the West Midlands* (Birmingham).

—— 1976, *Annual Economic Review* (Birmingham).

—— 1977, *Annual Economic Review* (Birmingham).

—— 1978, *County Structure Plan. Report of Survey—Employment* (Birmingham).

—— 1983a, *County Structure Plan. Proposals for Alterations to Approved Structure Plan Policies. Technical Appendix.* (Birmingham).

—— 1983b, *The Machine Tool Industry in the West Midlands* (Birmingham).

—— 1984a, *Action in the Local Economy. Progress Report of the Economic Development Committee* (Birmingham).

—— 1984b, *The Promotion of Newer Industries in the Black Country. The Responses of the West Midlands County Council* (Birmingham).

—— 1985a, *Regional Industrial Assistance* (Birmingham).

—— 1985b, *The Birmingham to Wolverhampton Corridor Initiative* (Birmingham).

—— 1985c, *Statistics '84* (Birmingham).

WMCC, EDC, 1981, *Aid to Industry Available from the District Authorities of the West Midlands County* (Birmingham).

WMCC, EDU, 1982a, *Round Oak* (Birmingham).

—— 1982b, *New small units and refurbishments* (Birmingham).

—— 1983, *The Impact of Dudley Enterprise Zone on the West Midlands Economy* (Birmingham).

—— 1984a, *The Use of Robotics in West Midlands Industry* (Birmingham).

—— 1984b, *Economic Review No. 1* (Birmingham).

—— 1984c, *Briefing Note* (Birmingham, 9 Nov.).

WMEPC, 1967, *The West Midlands: Patterns of Growth. A first Report of the West Midlands Economic Planning Council* (Department of Economic Affairs).

—— 1971, *The West Midlands. An Economic Appraisal* (D.o.E.).

WMFCC, 1982, *The State of Housing in the West Midlands* (Birmingham).

—— 1983, *Urban Regeneration in the West Midlands* (Birmingham).

—— 1984, *Removing Dereliction from the West Midlands Region* (Birmingham).

—— 1985a, *West Midlands Strategy Review: Regenerating the Region* (Birmingham).

—— 1985b, *West Midlands Strategy Review: Background Report 10, 1985, Industrial Land, Supply and Demand* (Birmingham).

WMPAC, 1971, *West Midlands Regional Study 1971* (Birmingham).

—— 1979, *A Developing Strategy for the West Midlands to 1991* (Birmingham).

Westaway, J., 1974, 'The Spatial Hierarchy of Business Organisations and its Implications for the British Urban System', *Regional Studies*, 8.

Wilde, P. D., 1985, 'Urban Development Grants: the First Two Years' (Working Paper 19, ESRC Inner City Project, West Midlands Study, University of Birmingham).

Williams, H., *et al.*, 1980, *Industrial Renewal in the Inner City: an Assessment of Potential and Problems* (D.o.E.).

Williams, K., Williams, J., and Thomas, D., 1983, *Why are the British bad at Manufacturing?* (London).

Willmott, P., 1975, 'Action Research in the Context of Public Policy', in D.o.E., *The Use of Action Research in Developing Urban Planning Policy* (London).

Wood, P. A., 1976, *The West Midlands* (Newton Abbot).

Zeitlin, J., 1980, 'The Emergence of Shop Steward Organisation', *History Workshop Journal*, 10.

INDEX